DATE DUE			
JA 29 '92			
JY 22 80			

BR

ALSO BY CLAIRE BERMAN

WE TAKE THIS CHILD: A Candid Look at Modern Adoption

MAKING IT AS A STEPPARENT: New Roles, New Rules

"WHAT AM I DOING IN A STEPFAMILY?"

ADULT CHILDREN OF DIVORCE
SPEAK OUT

About Growing Up With— and Moving Beyond— Parental Divorce

CLAIRE BERMAN

SIMON & SCHUSTER

NEW YORK   LONDON   TORONTO

SYDNEY   TOKYO   SINGAPORE

Simon & Schuster
Simon & Schuster Building
Rockefeller Center
1230 Avenue of the Americas
New York, New York 10020

Designed by Deirdre C. Amthor

Manufactured in the United States of America

1   3   5   7   9   10   8   6   4   2

Library of Congress Cataloging in Publication Data
Berman, Claire.
Adult children of divorce speak out about growing up with—and moving
beyond—parental divorce/Claire Berman.
p. cm.
Includes bibliographical references and index.
1. Adult children of divorced parents—Mental health.   2. Divorce—
Psychological aspects.   I. Title.
RC569.5.A3B47   1991
616.85'8—dc20   90-46318
                                                             CIP

ISBN 0-671-73149-1

For Sybil

In Gratitude and Love

Contents

Acknowledgments

Those to whom I owe the greatest debt have been promised anonymity. They are the mén and women who welcomed me into their lives, present and past, in order that I might understand what it was like to have grown up as a child of divorce. They have my gratitude, affection, and respect. I hope they find that I've used their stories well.

For their help in directing me to the storytellers, I am grateful to Hilary Eth, Amy Friedman, Elaine Kramer, Marcia Miller, Naomi Miller, Irene Shapiro, Beth Teitelman, Deborah Thorne, Donald Watson, and Abby Woolf.

Teresa Adams, Judith Caligor, Barbara Marwell, Gerald Marwell, and James Meltzer offered professional advice when it was requested and friendship when it was needed. Many other scholars, researchers, and mental health professionals were generous with their time and information. Their contributions are cited throughout this work.

Judith Glassman, Matthew Lees, and Lawrence Rosen came to the rescue when my computer failed or, more accurately, when I failed to give the correct instructions to my computer. Theirs was a contribution of inestimable worth.

To Laura Yorke, a talented editor, goes appreciation for her enthusiasm, skill, and encouragement. Julian Bach, my agent, believed in the idea for this book from the start. His colleague, Anne Rittenberg, was there for me when I needed her.

Finally, I must acknowledge the support of a loving family. Eric,

ACKNOWLEDGMENTS

Mitchell, and Orin Berman were generally good about knowing when to ask how the work was going and when to change the subject. I appreciate that.

It isn't easy to live with someone who is having an affair with a book in progress. Noel Berman managed to do so with grace and good humor. That I have come to expect his support is the reason I am grateful.

Introduction

Elly Edwards has just come off the tennis court and she's slightly winded. A handsome woman, she wears her light gray hair short and close to her head, a style that suits her looks and, I quickly learn, her lifestyle. She smiles and extends a hand in welcome. Weather permitting, Elly tells me, she tries to swim and play tennis every day. It's not too hard to manage. The tennis court and pool are located on the grounds of her home that sits tucked away off a dirt road—a lovingly restored farmhouse that feels like *real country* but is, in fact, situated in a suburb of New Haven, Connecticut.

I am interested in learning about the consequences of parental divorce, over time, for the children who were involved, and Elly has graciously agreed to share her memories and to talk about the impact that the breakup of her parents' marriage has had on her life.

Elly pours herself a glass of water from a pitcher resting on a patio table made of wrought iron. I take out my notebook, place my tape recorder on the table. "Name? Age?" I ask, easing into the interview. Elly gives me her name and tells me (surely I've misheard her) that she recently celebrated her sixty-third birthday.

"Marital status? Children?" I continue down my list.

"David and I have been married thirty-eight years," she replies. "We have three children, two grandchildren, and two on the way."

_____

"Age when mother and father divorced?"

"Fifteen months. I have pictures that were taken of me in Reno with my mother."

She puts down the glass, looks directly at me, and says in a tone as intense as her gaze, "And I have to tell you that the divorce of my parents has left a hole in my heart. It is a hole that will *never* be filled."

Over the next nine months, in interviews with close to fifty men and women who, during their childhood, experienced the separation and divorce of their parents, I am to hear that very phrase, "a hole in my heart," word for word, from two other people and variations of it from perhaps a dozen more.

"The divorce is an omnipresent part of my life," declares a television news director whose parents separated when he was five. Now twenty-nine, he finds himself unable to make the commitment to marry and establish a family of his own. And from an illustrator, now fifty-five, whose parents' marriage broke up when she was eight, I hear, "There's always a cold hole in your stomach. The single most important carryover [of parental divorce] is just this feeling of lacking something, of not having something the other kids had. It's a feeling of sadness, *and it doesn't go away.*" This woman has been married and divorced—three times. Two of her marriages produced a total of two sons and two daughters, now also children of divorce. At the present time, she is single.

When I began this project, I did not know where it would take me. Over the years, as a writer drawn to issues involving families and relationships, I found myself growing more and more interested in understanding the experiences of men, women, and children who live in families that differ from the norm of a mother and father, each in their first marriage, and the children who are born into the family. *How are they making it?* I wanted to know. This curiosity carried me first to the field of adoption, to research that resulted in a book and, subsequently, to my serving for close to a dozen years as director of public education of the North American Center on Adoption, which was then a project of the Child Welfare League of America.

From families created by adoption, my curiosity extended to families formed by remarriage. *How do members of stepfamilies order their lives?* I asked in the introduction to a book I wrote on that subject. *How do they meet the challenges of adjustment? How do they merge two different lifestyles, two or more sets of rules?* The questions continued. And so did my interest in the issues.

In 1984, as president of the Stepfamily Association of America, I traveled across the country, attending many gatherings and conferences, listening to and giving speeches, and (most important of all) encountering thousands of men and women who were striving to meet the challenges entailed in creating new families following the failure of previous relationships. That it is a difficult task is attested to by the statistics—more than half of all *re*marriages are ended by divorce.

But what about the children? As I listened to present and former spouses talk about relationships in marriages new and old, *this* was the question that wouldn't go away. How do all the changes from the traditional family affect the children?

It doesn't require a social scientist to observe that the American family has been undergoing great change, but this "hypothetical life history" presented by Johns Hopkins University sociologist Andrew J. Cherlin in his book *Marriage, Divorce, Remarriage* provides a graphic representation of just how dramatic those changes can be:

> When Bill was ten, his parents separated. He lived with his mother and saw his father every Saturday. Four years later, his mother remarried, and Bill added a stepfather to his family. At eighteen, Bill left home to attend college, and after graduation he

and his girlfriend moved in together. A year and a half later, they married, and soon afterward they had a child. After several years, however, the marriage began to turn sour. Bill and his wife eventually separated, with Bill's wife retaining custody of the child. Three years later Bill married a woman who had a child from a previous marriage, and together they had another child. Bill's second marriage lasted thirty-five years, until his death.

The more I learned about divorce and remarriage, the more I pondered the consequences to the children.

For answers, I first turned to books, articles, and scholarly papers dealing with the subject of children and divorce. Only recently has there been significant research in this area, I discovered, and the vast majority of the research deals with the children *during* their childhood years. Researchers, for the most part, have not had the luxury of being able to follow the children well into their adult years, to the time when they enter marriages and become parents, even grandparents—like Elly Edwards, who to all appearances is leading a most enviable life. Except that the divorce of her parents lives painfully within her still.

Psychologists who work with adults who were the children of divorce are perhaps more immediately aware of divorce's consequences, for to them come men and women who have been unable to set down the child's burden. Still, not every child of divorce continues to be so weighed down by the past as to feel a need for therapeutic intervention.

As a journalist with some knowledge of, and a great deal of interest in, the field of divorce and remarriage, I have sought to find the answers to "What happens to the children?" by reaching out to men and women who, as children, experienced the divorce of their parents and to professionals who have interested themselves in many of these issues as helpers or researchers. (When I speak of divorce I include the period of the breakup of the intact family. As one forty-one-year-old woman, separated from her father when she was six years old, explains, "The divorce was meaningless to me. That was a technicality. To me, the divorce was when my parents split up." In many cases, the actual divorce sometimes took several years, and was by then a mere formality having little or no effect on the by-now-restructured household.)

The road that led to Elly Edwards also took me to more than forty other men and women. They were randomly selected, ranging in age from twenty-four to sixty-seven. When their parents separated, the youngest age of the people in this sampling was one year old, the oldest age at separation was sixteen. Back when the marriages broke up, the interviewees lived in areas as diverse as Hollywood and New Jersey, Boston and Santa Barbara, Copenhagen and Albuquerque, New York and Mississippi. At the time of our interviews, they were residents of California, Connecticut, Florida, Louisiana, Maryland, Massachusetts, New Jersey, and New York. All are white.

Asked to recall incidents that took place during their childhood, some spoke of being evicted from their homes and having their custodial parent forced to turn for assistance to public welfare, while others told of being picked up by chauffeurs to visit a father or mother with whom they did not reside. Today, all would be considered middle class, some more comfortably so than others.

Their stories and their insights born of experience make up the material of this book. Although I have changed their names and clearly identifying descriptions, I have retained their wisdom and their own words throughout.

The questions I asked of these men and women included: What do you recall about the divorce—why did you think it took place? How were you informed of the decision, and by whom? Do you now have a different understanding of the causes? How did your life change as a result of the divorce? Can you describe your pre- and postdivorce relationships with both parents? With grandparents, other relatives, and friends? Which actions taken by your parents at the time of divorce and after do you regard as having been helpful? What do you wish had been handled differently? What were the worst of times? The best of times?

In short, I wished to find out what "divorce and after" looked like retrospectively to the children. I was not unmindful of the fact that the pictures they painted were likely to have been tempered by time. A thirty-seven-year-old man whose parents were divorced before his third birthday speaks to this point: "Some of my recollection of the time following the divorce is shaded because people tell me how I behaved and I don't know if these were *really* my reactions or what I've constructed from the stories. But the fact is, they are real for me now." Might it not also be true that the passage of time has added to the pictures' value?

I also hoped to learn how the experience of parental divorce carries over into one's adult life. Are there certain characteristics, for example, that are common to people who have lived through this crucial childhood event? I was curious about the relationships that children of divorce entered into in adulthood. Did the divorce history affect their friendships, their decision to marry, to have children? If they were married, how important was it to them to remain in the relationship? Or did they find it easier to walk away from a marriage once they decided it wasn't working out?

When I began to look into the long-range consequences of divorce, I wondered whether, as their lives progressed, the children of divorce had found it necessary, or even possible, to make peace with their past. If so, how had this been accomplished? What importance did the adult children of divorce attach to resolving their feelings toward their parents and about the decision that so critically altered their own lives?

My list of questions grew. And as I listened to the detailed and candid accounts of the respondents, so did my understanding of divorce and its aftermath. The most striking impression one comes away with is this: For children, *the divorce of their parents never goes away.* It may be welcomed. It may be understood. It may be integrated into their lives. It may lead to new strengths. But even when it is a positive solution to a destructive family situation, divorce is a *critical experience* for its children. Although

18

there may be relief that a painful situation has been ended, there is also regret that a healthy family could not have been created.

Divorce is a destroyer of the dream of happily ever after. With some exceptions, children do not want their parents to separate. "The child of divorce learns early on that the great romance, the world of happily ever after, is false," says Amy Greene, forty-one, one of the women whom you will meet in this book. "In some ways," she adds, "divorce is harder on kids than death. At least when a parent dies, the child is given permission to mourn."

It is clear that the divorce of one's parents has lifelong reper-cussions. "We cannot view divorce as an event occurring at a single point in time, for it represents an extended transition in the lives of parents and children," cautions psychologist E. Mavis Hetherington, a leading researcher in the field. "The point at which we [researchers] tap into the course of divorce will to a large extent determine our evaluation of the results of divorce." What strikes me, however, is the vehemence that the men and women with whom I spoke brought to their discussion of paren-tal divorce regardless of the point in time when the divorce occurred or the number of years that have since intervened. "No, I have not gotten over my parents' divorce," I hear from Amy Greene, whose parents separated when she was six years old. "I will *never* get over it."

Get over it? The long-range effects of the divorce of one's parents crop up at unexpected times and often show themselves in unexpected ways, as witness this description by writer Maggie Scarf. In her book *Intimate Partners,* Scarf tells of being "deeply —seemingly irrationally—upset" about the loss of her cat, Mit-tens, a loss that occurred coincidentally with the imminent breakup of her best friends' marriage. Later on, Scarf says, her husband offered "an explanation that I'd been unable to offer myself. He reminded me of a story that I'd once told *him* . . . but then had apparently forgotten. It had to do with an incident that had occurred on the day of my own parents' separation, a sepa-ration which led to their eventual divorce.

"I was twelve years old at the time," Scarf continues, "and the furniture was being moved out of the house. But for me the most terrible part of what was happening was that our cat had gotten his neck caught in the outdoor coal grate. He had hurt himself so badly that the two men from the animal shelter, called to his rescue, had had to carry him off with them.

"Oh, yes," Scarf said to her husband, recognizing that for her that cat had been the symbol of the intact family. The loss of the cat was connected, in her own mind, with the family life that was being taken away.

Scarf goes on: "At the age of twelve one is in part an adult, but also to some large degree a child—still able to give credence to some magical ideas and notions. I suppose, looking back, that I probably maintained the belief that if our pet were to return, so would my world's stability. Or perhaps my preoccupation with the loss of the cat—so intense that the breakup of my parents' relationship seemed almost incidental—was due to my finding it easier to confront and mourn the loss of the family pet than to mourn the *intolerable* loss, which was the ending of my parents' marriage."

In interviews with adults who were the children of divorce, we hear echoes. The same experiences are repeated, the same feelings described. Often (more often than would occur by chance, it seems to me) the very same words are used. Of course the effects of divorce upon children differ from family to family and from child to child, depending on such individual characteristics as the ages of the children at the time of the marital breakup as well as on the temperaments and coping strategies of the children and of their parents. Whether the parents, now ex-spouses, are able to maintain a good relationship with one another, whether both remain actively involved in the care of the child, even the question of whether the child and custodial parent are of the same sex—all of this, and more, will have a bearing on how well or how poorly a youngster adjusts to divorce. Accepting the importance of individual differences, I nevertheless am struck by the similarities.

Although many of these similarities, these striking commonalities, tend also to be found in people raised in dysfunctional families that have remained intact, there is no question that they are perceived by the men and women themselves as consequences of having grown up divorced. These characteristics, which will later be discussed more fully, include the following:

- Many children of divorce have difficulty in trusting others.
- Many have a fear of commitment.
- Many have difficulty with intimacy.
- Many sense themselves as isolated and lonely.
- Many struggle with problems of self-esteem.
- Many see their sexuality as a matter of concern.
- Many feel a strong need to maintain control.
- Many place a great deal of emphasis on financial security.
- Many have a strong yearning for stability.
- Many are highly empathic.
- Many are fiercely independent.
- Many place a high value on being successful.

Listening to the children of divorce decades after the dissolution of their intact families, one is impressed by the freshness of their recollections, the depth of emotion that is brought to the surface in response to the interviewer's request of them to relive and reevaluate the past.

Why did they do it? Why did so many men and women make time in their busy schedules to participate in lengthy and often difficult interviews? Why did they call back later to provide added insights or to recommend another subject for this study? Why did they seem so grateful to be heard?

For one thing, people were interested in talking to a writer. *They felt that they had permission to speak about the secrets of the heart.* ("The outside me has always been super in charge and efficient" is the way the television news reporter expressed it. "The inside me always knew I was different *because* of the divorce, but *that* me has seldom been given permission to appear.") They wanted to take advantage of an opportunity to tell their stories, to recall, to bring the past up to the present, to make some sense of it all. "It's a catharsis," said one woman at the close of a lengthy interview. "You relive the divorce, bring up old memories, and you hope that with each telling you will understand it all better."

They also wished to learn what others in their situation were feeling, and to establish communication, through these pages, with other adult children of divorce.

It is clear that there are times when such peer-group support might be helpful. In recent years, for example, adults who were adopted as children have come together to discuss their feelings and special concerns many years after the fact of their adoption. Adult children of alcoholics, too, have formed groups in which they are able to confront issues that are unique to their situation. For many adult children of divorce there is a similar need—to speak with others who have been there, to free themselves from the experience, to share. They find little opportunity to do so.

The importance of sharing was brought home to me during a phone call I received from a woman who identified herself as Mallory Coburn. She was twenty-six, she said, and "the divorce of my parents, which happened when I was twelve, has dominated my life." Was it true, she asked, that I was running a support group for adult children of divorce? She'd been looking for one for some time. When I told her that I was not running a group—indeed, I knew of no such group—she asked to participate in the research for this book. We met. Mallory is an extremely attractive, accomplished young businesswoman. She has two goals, she told me. "The big goal of my life is to make the divorce *not* be a part of my life," she said. "The other goal is to help children who are currently living through their parents' divorce, to provide survival tips, to listen—nobody *listens* to the children—and to let them know they are not alone."

How could they be? The statistics on divorce in America are

startling, and the prospects for the future even bleaker. Each year, in the United States alone, over a million children experience the dissolution of their parents' marriage. Following divorce, most children find themselves living in a single-parent, mother-headed family. Despite the public perception that men are taking on greater responsibility in this area, less than 10 percent of fathers become the custodial parent.

Further, those whose business it is to study statistics and their portents find little solace in the fact that, in recent years, the crude rate of divorce has declined. "There's a sense of great relief when people think that the rate of divorce is going down," says Larry Bumpass, a demographer at the University of Wisconsin. "They are happy to believe there's a trend toward more conservative family patterns. But it's not so." Based on data from the National Survey of Families and Households, a study involving thirteen thousand respondents, Bumpass holds out the likelihood that one-half to two-thirds of first marriages will disrupt.

Because people who divorce are also likely to remarry, it is estimated that 30 percent of children will spend some time in a stepfamily before they reach the age of eighteen. And since the divorce rate for second marriages is even higher than for first marriages, it is also estimated that one out of every ten children will experience *two* divorces of the custodial parent before they reach age sixteen.

There is evidence, too, that divorced parents pass on a higher risk of divorce to their children. The meaning of all of this is dramatically brought home by Larry Bumpass and Teresa Castro in a paper on trends in family disruption. "About half of today's youth will have spent some time in a one-parent family," they write. "When combined with their own chances of marital success, only a minority will have stable two-parent families in both childhood and as an adult."

What it is like *not* to have grown up in a stable, intact, two-parent, first-marriage family is what this book is largely about. For Mallory Coburn and others, I hope it provides the sharing and support that validate and elucidate their experiences, feelings, and fantasies in growing up divorced, the realization that they were not, and are not, alone. I hope they will take from the stories the solace that they need and the strength to overcome those demons that haunt them still—as many men and women in this book have done. These are, after all, the stories of survivors. The children of divorce have much to say to, and learn from, one another.

They also have much to say, and teach, to the mothers, fathers, and the grandparents who are now raising children of divorce, and to families that are about to begin the divorce process. In looking back at divorce—at how it was managed (and mismanaged), at who was helpful and what was hurtful—these adults who were the children of divorce shed light on how this critical event in the life of a family might be handled so as to minimize the potential harm to the children.

The experiences recalled by the men and women who speak in these pages, the decisions they have made in terms of families and careers, the looks they provide us into their present lives— all of this offers a full agenda for research consideration. We need to know much more about the long-range ramifications of divorce and the short-range interventions that may help to mitigate its effects on the lives of the children.

These are healthful challenges.

"What do you consider to be *the* most unique aspect of having grown up as a child of divorce?" This is the final question I asked of each person with whom I spoke.

The regret, the solitude, the ongoingness of the experience, the hole in the heart and its several variations—all were answers that I came to hear time and again, and began to anticipate. A knowledge of life's choices, a sense of independence, the spur to succeed—these positive evaluations were also widely shared.

"It was something to realize that you *can* change the pattern of your life," said a woman whose mother entered a second, successful relationship after divorcing the woman's father. "My mother broke out of a bad marriage and her life was infinitely better. I learned that a woman can take her fate in her hands and do something about it—and that has stayed with me."

I recall, too, the woman, in her fifties, who looked back at her divorced parents as having presented her with a great drama. "Growing up," she explained, "there was this great mystery, of who my parents were and who I was, to be solved. I am still trying to figure out the characters in the story, to understand what happened to them, and why."

Listen to the echoes. A man in his early thirties speaks. He too is looking back. "In a way," he says, "there is something so natural about marriage—in a poetic, subconscious, subliminal way. But for the child of divorce, there is something about not having a central government, the parents as a unit. Instead, we grow up knowing that there are two possible roads that can be followed. There is a parent here and a parent there, a child of this marriage and a child of another marriage. It feels peculiar. It makes you wonder about life."

It surely does.

PART ONE

THE WAY IT IS NOW— LEGACIES OF DIVORCE

Chapter I

The Struggle to Love Oneself
and Trust Others

[The divorce of one's parents] is an event that plays
an integral part in shaping the psyche. It is woven
into one's values, emotional processes, sexuality,
self-esteem, sense of trust, everything. We live with
it always.

—From a letter to the editor of *The New York Times
Magazine.* The writer, twenty-nine, was two
years old when his parents divorced.

Reading the letter in the *Times,* Cassie Stevenson nods in
agreement. Coincidentally, she too is twenty-nine and a child of
divorce and, she tells me, she well understands what the author
of the letter is writing about. Although twenty-two years have
gone by since her own mother and father ended their marriage,
the pervasive effects of parental divorce remain a reality for Cassie, too.

"Last night serves as a perfect example," she says, and goes on
to explain. "At about six o'clock, my date phoned from the office
to say that something unforeseen had come up. He'd have to
work late, he said, and was unable to keep our appointment for
that night. Could he take a rain check?

"I told him 'Forget it,' and *slammed* the receiver down. I was
furious, even though it was to be little more than a casual get-

together: dinner and a movie, maybe. I mean, this was *not* a special event. Still, the thought that immediately crossed my mind when he said he'd have to cancel was: *It's happening again. Someone is running out on his promise to be there for me. Again.*

"My next impulse," Cassie recounts, "was to feel guilty. Something I had either said or done *must* have been the real cause of my date's backing out of our plans, I was certain. I began to review our previous get-togethers—what I had said, how he had reacted. I needed to know . . . in what way had I muffed things up?"

In calmer moments, as now when we speak, Cassie recognizes that her responses were inappropriate to the incident that occasioned them. But it is hard for her to be rational about certain things. "Where people who enjoyed secure childhoods are likely to feel disappointed about a change in plans," she says, "I'm more apt to be devastated. I see abandonment. I see personal failure.

"These are just some of the ways in which the divorce of my parents keeps playing itself out in my life," she says.

COMMON CHARACTERISTICS OF ADULT CHILDREN OF DIVORCE

Granted, no *one* factor can be held responsible for shaping the kind of person one becomes or the ways in which an individual tends to look at things. Each of us is the sum of many parts. We know, for example, that many elements impact upon people's lives, from the genes we inherit to the families we are born into and the communities in which we grow up.

There also are happenstances in life, unanticipated events that are capable of having a lasting impact on the way we feel about ourselves or the manner in which we tackle challenges or manage relationships. The divorce of one's parents is just such an idiosyncratic event. It leaves children with a lot of baggage. Many are weighed down by it for years afterward—some for the rest of their lives.

With the perspective afforded them by the passage of time, the adult children of divorce identify a number of their characteristic behaviors and attitudes as directly stemming from the breakup of their parents' marriage and its aftermath. Not surprisingly, we find that the characteristics they catalog are often linked.

Among these separately identified traits, for example, low self-esteem—a negative relationship between you and you—heads the list. This self-criticism then carries over into your relationships with other people: If you do not like yourself, you find it hard to trust their assertions that you are valuable. Distrusting others' promises, you hold back from making a commitment: When you think yourself undeserving of others' fidelity, you believe that their agreements with you must ultimately be broken. So the person with low self-esteem holds back, fearing that increased intimacy will result only in more pain from some later, inevitable betrayal. At some point, it follows, emotional holding-back is likely to carry over into the area of one's sexuality. . . . The effects of parental divorce are pervasive.

Although the lines separating one attribute from another are blurred, for adult children of divorce the traits themselves are instantly and powerfully recognizable. That is not surprising. They have lived with them for a long time.

LOW SELF-ESTEEM

If only I had been better . . . if I had been more lovable . . . if I had given less trouble, the child of divorce thinks, *my parents would have maintained a life together, my father (or mother) would not have moved out of our home.*

"One of the consequences of divorce is that children (especially those who were young at the time of the breakup) feel that, in some way, they're responsible—either 'I did bad things' or 'I didn't do enough to keep the marriage together,'" says psychiatrist Clifford J. Sager. Even after the child grows up and has gained a better understanding of the reasons for the divorce, there is a part of him or her that clings to the belief *If only I had been more worthy* . . .

Sager might well have been describing Danish-born John Lindstrom, who had barely passed his first birthday when his father moved out of the home, leaving the little boy to be raised by his mother and her parents. "It is painful even now to look back on myself as a child," says John, forty-three, a fair-haired, sturdily built man who stands six feet three inches tall. "The picture that comes to my mind is of a young boy who was very small, very insecure."

This self-image stayed with John well after (physically at least) it was no longer the fact. John attained his present height by the age of sixteen. A talented guitarist, he also gained professional stature early. While still in his teens in Denmark, John took jobs with one group or another that toured the country and he "made a lot of money—especially for a kid," he says. Girls flocked to the groups, but John kept his distance. "I could see all my friends who were musicians, and they were hanging out with girls right and left," he recalls, "but I did not have the confidence to be the initiator.

"Thinking so little of myself," John continues, "as I grew older I could not make a commitment to a place or person. I kept on the move—from one school to another, from one professional commitment to another, from one country to another. I also shied away from marriage, although I *have* been married twice, each time for reasons that I regarded as a practical solution to what was then going on in my life.

"My son and daughter are the first thing in my life that I have committed myself to," John goes on. "Yet I live with the fear that my kids are not going to like me, that they will not find me deserving of their love."

About fifteen years ago, John began to analyze his feelings. He says, "I realized that the reason that I lack confidence is because, after the divorce, my father remarried and didn't care enough about me to stay in touch while my mother also went on with her career and had two more husbands. This was a form of rejection by them. The message that this gave to me was: If I wasn't worth the love or attention of my mother and father, how could I feel any confidence in myself?"

Low self-esteem remains a problem for John today.

INSECURITY BLANKET

Nancy Kovach also suffers from feelings of low self-esteem that, she is convinced, were brought about as a result of her parents' divorce. "I see kids from good, functional families as having more guts and being stronger than I," she says. "They approach life with a sense of 'I can do it' because they grew up feeling secure. But when your blanket is pulled away from you at the age of six or eight, you don't have that security. The world becomes a treacherous place."

At twenty-six, Nancy steps warily into the future. Although she concedes that she's holding down a good job as an accountant in a small firm, she is quick to add, "It wouldn't come as a shock to me if they decide that they need someone with more experience." It's also possible, she tells me, that "the company could fold tomorrow." (The message that is writ large upon her psyche is this: Anything good in my life can—and probably will—come to an end.)

She is suspicious of relationships, too, and admits to having moments when she thinks: *There must be something wrong with any man who has shown the poor judgment to be interested in me.* Like many children of divorce, Nancy tends to become romantically involved with people who, she believes, are also "damaged" in one way or another.

"I NEVER FEEL GOOD ENOUGH"

With ten years on Nancy Kovach, Jennie Fuller has held similar concerns, confiding to me that she also has seen them realized. "What effects, if any, has the experience of parental divorce had on your life as an adult?" I ask her, reading from my list of queries. It is a question I ask of everyone, but Jennie's reaction to it is surprising. She becomes visibly flustered, suddenly averting my gaze. "I *hate* this question and I just knew it was going to come up," she says.

"I have a secret," she confesses, looking out the window of the hotel room where we meet. "Nobody who's met me in the last ten years knows it—not even my boyfriend, which troubles me."

The secret: "I have been married and divorced two times, and people think I've only been married once."

"The reason I keep it a secret," Jennie explains, "is because of the stigma of being a two-time loser, and because I'm ashamed of it. I'm doubly ashamed because the first person I married, when I was twenty-three, was crazy. I *mean* it. I chose him because I had a real low self-image and I thought I couldn't get anybody who was normal.

"I also thought that I could take care of him and make him well," she continues softly. "I guess that was to make up for not staying around to take care of my dad, an alcoholic, after my parents separated. From the beginning, my husband mentally abused me. He was very controlling of everything, including all our money. Because I was terrified of abandonment, I stayed with him *until* the abuse turned physical. That gave me the courage to leave the relationship."

"And your second marriage?"

"I chose wrong the next time, too," Jennie replies, adding that her second husband did not come from a healthy family. "His father abandoned him. When his mother remarried, he wasn't wanted by her either.

"We each carried too much pain to be able to give to one another. The best decision I made in that marriage was not to bring children into it."

Another decision Jennie made was to leave the marriage and enter therapy. With greater understanding of the events of her past, she has been better able to move into the present—including a return to school to obtain a degree in occupational therapy. At thirty-six, she is cautiously optimistic about what life has in store for her. She and her boyfriend ("a wonderful man") are planning marriage *and* children.

Jennie has taken a long way to answer my question—clearly an important one for her. Looking directly at me now, she says slowly, "It doesn't matter that I am constantly reminding myself about all the positive things that are going on in my life. The tragedy of it all is that, to this very moment, I never feel good enough. The negative long-term effects for me of my parents' divorce are low self-esteem and mistrust."

MISTRUSTFULNESS

The fact that children of divorce, like Jennie, experience difficulty with trusting others should not be surprising. "If the child is not afforded enough happiness in his early life," psychoanalyst Melanie Klein has explained, "his capacity for developing a hopeful attitude as well as love and trust in people will be disturbed."

When children learn that a vow can be broken (and divorce writes the end to the marital vow), they face life with uncertainty. When they do not receive the nurturing that's needed, they are likely to enter into unhealthy relationships. "If you don't grow up with trust," says psychotherapist Teresa Adams, "it results in mistrust."

In her book *Living From the Inside Out,* Adams further explains: "A universal truth for all children is the necessity to trust their caretakers for security. How a child develops trust long has been a center of psychological inquiry. Did we receive enough emotional nurturing as a child? Could we be lovingly accepted as we were or did we have to perform to earn love? Could we depend on our parents to be there for us most of the time?"

Looking back at the years following the breakup of their parents' marriage, many men and women are unable to answer these questions in the affirmative. Was there enough emotional nurturing? At critical times, they tell us, their parents were too caught up in their own grief or bickering to pay much-needed attention to the emotional requirements of the children.

Did the children have to perform to earn love? The answer we hear in many cases is "Yes." For these children of divorce, growing up, the love of their parents was not something that they were able to take for granted. As one woman explains, "I was always afraid with my father that if I was not careful I would lose him. So I *had* to be on good behavior in order to keep him, however precariously, in my life."

A thirty-four-year-old woman whose parents divorced when she was thirteen asks, "When your *parents* betray you, then who *do* you trust?" It is a rhetorical question. "For years I had the feeling that *everyone* was out to get me. It took me a long time to trust anyone."

KEEPING FEELINGS TO ONESELF

"The bottom line," says a man in his fifties, "is that, as a child of divorce, you feel yourself to be alone.... The world is not a reliable place, and you have to find a center within yourself. Then you have to protect that center. The way I did that was by not letting anyone in on what I was really thinking and feeling. It has become a lifetime habit, unfortunately, that from time to time causes difficulty between my wife and myself. She accuses me of not wanting to share my feelings with her. What she fails to understand is that I am unable to share them with anyone."

The child of divorce discovers early on that promises can be broken and that all relationships are conditional. So the young-ster endeavors to protect himself by placing a protective shell around his feelings. This characteristic can be traced right back to the divorce and its aftermath. First, the child doesn't really say how he feels, believing that if he is a good little boy Mommy and Daddy will reunite. Then the child quickly learns that he cannot speak well of Mommy to Daddy and vice versa. In fact, it is better not to mention the other parent at all. So, explains author Linda Bird Francke in her book *Growing Up Divorced,* "he keeps his feelings bottled up. . . . He doesn't dare express his anger, feeling that his [custodial parent] will turn on him or, worse yet, abandon him."

For many a child of divorce, then, reticence becomes a lifelong habit. To share true feelings, to open up, they learn, is to make oneself vulnerable to being hurt.

OPTING FOR SOLITUDE

Thoughts are not all that are kept private. Many adult children of divorce describe themselves as loners, a habit they regard as stemming from the incidents of childhood. "At the age of four-teen, my idea of bliss was going off to live in the woods and not having *anyone* around," recalls a woman whom I interview twenty years later. "That's how unhappy and mistrustful the di-vorce had made me." Clifford Sager explains, "The child feels, 'I'd rather live by myself. Nobody else cares.' "

When a youngster's world becomes a wounding place, it is not unusual for the boy or girl to seek sanctuary in a room, a nook, a private world. "With so much ugliness going on at home, I tended to remove myself emotionally," says a thirty-one-year-old man of his nine-year-old self. "I'd go to my room, study all hours, play my flute . . . do anything so that I did not have to stay with my mom, who tried to include me in her misery. Over the years, I got into the habit of being a loner. It has stayed with me."

There are times when removing oneself from the chaos and

the pain can be very helpful. Researchers Robert Weiss and Judith Wallerstein and Joan Kelly report that one way children cope with their parents' divorce is by becoming disengaged from the family. If the youngsters are then able to turn to others (see chapter nine, "Saving Graces"), they may be fortunate in finding the comfort and validation that are lacking at home.

The loner, however, is someone who is unable to utilize a Saving Grace even if one becomes available. Disappointed by previous caretakers, the loner tries to insulate himself from further disillusionment by refusing to place himself in a position where he must depend upon someone else . . . *anyone* else. Tobias Goodman serves as an example of just such a child of divorce.

"Over the years, there were a number of people who could have been there for me," says this man in his sixties who at the age of eight was heartbreakingly disappointed by his estranged father. "Two teachers in high school quickly come to mind. They took a special interest in me, but I didn't reach out to them or adopt them in any way, shape, or form—probably because of my father's failure to be there for me. Somewhere along the line, I decided never to depend on anyone, never to trust anyone. That does take a toll."

SETTING TESTS FOR FRIENDSHIP:
WHEN CONTROL AND CAUTION RULE

This wariness about trusting others plays itself out, in the lives of certain adult children of divorce, by limiting their ability to enter into and maintain meaningful and reliable friendships. "You always feel that you have to be a little bit cautious with people and not let them in too quick," explains Jennie Fuller.

At the same time, there is the wish to have good friends in one's life. Adam Norris, twenty-nine, who has lived with parental divorce for a quarter of a century, expresses his struggle as follows: "I have a real need for the positive strokes I can get from friends. I require testimonials of friendship. But"—*and this is a statement that comes up time and again when children of divorce speak of its legacy*—"I *test* everyone all of the time."

He elaborates: "There is a higher level of tension wrought by the divorce that carries over into interpersonal relationships. What other people might regard as oversights or simple errors of judgment are not easily dismissed by the child of divorce. Things are not taken lightly. Consequently, I am forever weighing what friends, business associates, and lovers say and do. If they fall short of my expectations, I drop them." Adam grows very thoughtful, then adds, "That's not *just* a matter of trust. It's also a matter of control."

Add *control* to the list of responses to crop up repeatedly in the interviews. Looking backward, many adult children describe parental divorce as something that their mother and father did *to them*. That children of divorce should react to their turbulent childhoods by wanting, as adults, to take total command of their own lives is not surprising. While *all* men and women (regardless of the marital situation of their parents) are likely to recall youthful feelings of powerlessness, those whose lives were disrupted by parental divorce complain most bitterly about the many issues that were decided without their consent or approval, issues such as: which parent they would live with; where they would make their home; how they would manage; even whether a parent remarried, an event necessitating further changes in their lives. Is it any wonder, therefore, that the child of divorce should later strive to insulate himself or herself against pain caused by others' capricious behavior? "If I drop you"—Adam Norris explains his treatment of friends—"then *I'm* the one who's in control of the relationship."

For Elly Edwards, who is more than twice Adam's age, the need for control remains as strong as it is for the young man. Elly tells me that she recognizes its deleterious effect on her relationships. Nevertheless, she comments ruefully, she may never see the day when she will be able to let down her guard.

"I am *always* judging what people say and do," she says, echoing Adam's characterization of his behavior toward others. "I won't accept anything that smacks of infidelity to friendship. And I don't share a lot of my intimate feelings. As a result, I have had some problems sustaining friendships over the years."

Such idiosyncratic behavior is hard, as well, on the people who link their lives with children of divorce. "Elly is honest . . . to a fault," comments David Edwards, her husband. "She will *not* dissemble. She won't get close to most friends and, as soon as a wart appears, she drops them completely. Because of her background, she is incapable of making the compromises that lubricate the world. That hurts me, too, because it isolates us as a couple. I miss being close to people who have been our friends."

FEAR OF COMMITMENT

Closely related to the inability to trust is a third characteristic frequently claimed by men and women who lived with parental divorce: it is their fear of commitment.

An oft-quoted manifesto on children's rights begins, "Children learn what they live." If they live with love, they learn to love. If they live with trust, they learn to trust. If they live with commitment, they do not fear to commit.

"It's not the divorce that's at fault; it's what people *do* with the divorce," we are reminded by Emily Visher, a psychologist and cofounder of the Stepfamily Association of America. It is a helpful reminder, for indeed many children of divorce do live with love, do experience trust and commitment. For still others, however, especially those who fear to commit, the history of their growing-up years is replete with vows broken and relationships forged and destroyed as their parents move in and out of romantic liaisons.

If a parent is constantly turning over partners and other close friends and steprelations with whom the youngster has formed a bond, the child will go through a loss every time. Making note of the fact that this situation is becoming more prevalent, researcher E. Mavis Hetherington surmises, "In the long run the child may become disengaged and develop a fear of commitment."

Rick Monelli talks about how real this fear remains for him even though, at age thirty-one, he is two months away from the date of his wedding. Following their divorce from one another, Rick's parents remarried: his father once, his mother four more times.

"As a result," says Rick, "I am always so afraid that things will go wrong that I have developed a habit of putting off joy. I have thought: *It will come in college. I'll have a good time there. . . . It will come after I graduate. . . . It will come when I marry. . . .* Well, I finally took the step of becoming engaged and now I'm worried about what happens if the marriage doesn't work out. I should be looking forward to the wedding, but I'm fearful. I'm very anxious about making this commitment."

STRUGGLING WITH INTIMACY—ANOTHER FACE OF COMMITMENT

A struggle with intimacy is the third side of the triangle whose other two parts are mistrust and fear of commitment. All three of these attributes are related. Yet for some people, like Elly Edwards, one or another of the three can present special problems. In contrast to the prenuptial commitment jitters that Rick Monelli is experiencing right now, Elly Edwards recalls being "quite calm" before her marriage to David, almost four decades ago.

She explains, "I determined early on that when I married it would be for life, so I did not rush into marriage in my early twenties, when most of my friends were heading for the altar. When I was twenty-five, I knew I wanted to be married and I looked around. I saw David, who had always been there for me. He was reliable and steady. He was someone I felt very comfortable with. So I made a commitment to marriage."

It is *intimacy* that was, and remains, troubling for Elly. "Making the marriage commitment doesn't mean that *emotionally* I've been trustful," she says, stressing a nice distinction. "I think that, because of my relationship with my mother who had been so hurtful to me, I have always had a problem protecting myself emotionally from real intimacy. So that while David and I have had a long marriage, and in some ways a very strong one, there have been many difficulties in terms of some of the intimacies . . . which I have also had with friends. People tend to see me as very self-contained, very unflappable, but *very* frequently I am feeling bereft, and lonely, and isolated within my own head."

"The question of intimacy is related to trust," declares Ann Kliman, director of the Situational Crisis Service of the Center for Preventive Psychiatry in White Plains, New York. (Situational crises, Kliman explains, are traumatic events that befall a person and that are outside of that individual's control. The divorce of one's parents qualifies as a situational crisis.) She continues, "You have to be able to trust to allow yourself to be intimate. (We're not talking about sexual intimacy here.) If you feel that if you dare to love and dare to be close you will become vulnerable and you will be abandoned again, you're not going to trust . . . or (the other side of the coin) you will have multiple relationships but no intimacy."

Kliman might have been speaking of Amy Greene, who told me, "I have a lot of trouble having one person be *the* most important person in my life. My ex-husband used to say, 'You know, I come about fifth in your life. I come after your mother, after your father, after your piano, after your work.' And he was right. My friends and he were sort of tied for fifth. It's very impor-tant to me to have a circle of friends *because relationships with any one person can end.*"

SABOTAGING COMMITMENT

It is not uncommon for adult children of divorce to behave in such a way that they bring about the very result they both feared and anticipated: the end of a relationship. Amy Greene did this by refusing to allow her husband to feel that he was truly important in her life. And a forty-one-year-old bachelor discloses, "I have a habit of getting involved with women and then messing things up so that they walk out on me."

Lucinda Polk, who at thirty-four has one marriage behind her, provides us with a case history of how the child of divorce can turn the fear of desertion into a self-fulfilling prophecy. "Trust has always been a problem for me," says Lucinda, whose mother was married three times, and whose father's five wives have included two who were young enough to be his daughters.

His own daughter Lucinda became a bride at the age of twenty-three. "I married Curtis because I had complete trust in him," Lucinda says. "I think I tested that trust."

As she explains it: "I was thin when I met Curtis and when I gained weight he left me." Lucinda is talking about a *lot* of weight. From the slim bride pictured in her wedding album, she has become the kind of overweight young woman about whom people tend to remark, "She has such a pretty face." And she does. Clear pale skin, green eyes, upturned nose, dimpled cheeks, and a shy smile.

With each of her two pregnancies, however, Lucinda put on pounds that weren't shed after her son and daughter were born. Curtis told her to lose weight. He told her he was ashamed of her appearance. He even appealed to Lucinda's mother, who instructed her daughter to "do what your husband wants."

Says Lucinda, "Curtis and my mother would say 'lose the weight' without understanding why the weight was there to begin with. My weight was the *one* thing Curtis couldn't control! Still, the day that he came in and said, 'I'm leaving tomorrow,' I was shocked. I couldn't believe he'd do that to the kids.

"Just like my father, Curtis was quick to take another wife," Lucinda tells me. "I found out about loyalty with friends, too," she adds. "You think that you have friends and then you discover that they still see your ex-husband and his new wife, but they drop you. When you run into them, they say, 'I know you must hate me.'

" 'It's not hate,' I tell them. 'It's just that I don't *trust* you anymore.' "

LEARNING TO TRUST

If proof is needed that a healthy relationship *can* be achieved by someone who, as a child, did not live with the model of a good marriage or enjoy the kind of affirmation that is best provided by involved, nurturing parents, one has but to meet Delia Sherman, devoted wife, proud mother, and doting grandmother. Left in infancy by her mother, Delia was kept in her father's custody but raised by a series of housekeepers because her father's business kept him on the road. Visits to the little girl by her mother were sporadic, few, and tantalizing.

After entering her dating years, Delia found herself gravitating to the wrong men. "When I graduated from college, everyone was getting married," she says, "but I kept getting into relationships which I knew could not possibly end in marriage. The men I dated were a lot like my mother in that they were more devoted to their own needs than to mine. Like her, they could give—but only on a limited, short-term basis. They were there when the going was good.

"I began to wonder why I continued to make such choices. At twenty-two, I entered therapy and promised not to commit until both the doctor and I decided that I was ready to make a healthy decision." She smiles widely, her eyes crinkling at the corners.

"Phil was my healthy decision. He and I were so committed to each other and to marriage, I can't imagine something we wouldn't have worked out. He is my best friend."

"People have to be aware that they do have the power to change their lives," says psychotherapist Teresa Adams. "Since trust of another human being is a learned process, you *can* learn new data as an adult. But here is the key variable: you must stop sabotaging yourself by choosing people who replicate your past.

"The first step is to become aware of whether the relationship you are in is healthy or unhealthy. If you surmise through *thought* and *feeling* (and you need both) that you're in a destructive relationship, chances are you're still emotionally connected to Mom and Dad and the way they *mis*treated you. If you become aware and decide that you *will* be determined to move toward health, then you articulate that to your partner by saying, 'I want to grow into a healthy relationship and I trust you want to grow with me.' I would never shut the door on a relationship without giving both spouses the chance to grow into trust.

"Trust is a major component of commitment," Adams continues. "It's been my experience that people move from mistrust to trust by, first, learning to be trustworthy themselves and then by having a loving relationship where one partner is loving enough and strong enough to continue the relationship and to be committed to the relationship. Healthy people want the people around them to love themselves. The message is: The healthier you are, the more you will be there for me if I ever need you."

CONCERNS OF A SEXUAL NATURE

Healthy people also feel good about their sexuality, which requires the ability to give and accept love without fear of hurting or of being hurt. In the interviews, men and women raise the subject of their sexuality as one of the challenging issues that emerge as a consequence of growing up as a child of divorce.

HOLDING BACK

Some say that the fear of committing has led them to hold back sexually.

"Sexual problems often are a result of a fear of intimacy, a fear of getting close and then being hurt," explains family counselor Bonnie Eacker Weil. "Many adult children of divorce try to defend against the hurt by putting up a wall between them and their partners."

In their book *Cold Feet: Why Men Don't Commit,* authors Sonya Rhodes and Marlin S. Potash, both psychotherapists, present a case history of how this fear played itself out for a couple who came to them for help with sexual problems. The therapy appeared to have succeeded, they report, until the couple, Kate and Bill, went on a vacation to Jamaica. Then: "Each night, after being together all day and feeling close and loving toward one another, Bill would fall into bed and be sound asleep before Kate had finished taking a shower. Or else he would fall asleep watching TV . . . or . . . he would suddenly want to take a walk by himself on the beach. . . .

"As a few more days went by [in this manner], Bill began to remember what we'd talked about in therapy months before: that when they were the closest, he felt the least like having sex; that when things got too good between them, he had to pull back. When he and Kate were alone here on the island, there was no escaping the double bed they shared—there was *nowhere to run.* Just the thought of it made anxiety well up inside him; he wanted to have sex with Kate, and yet he still needed to keep to himself.

"At some point he suddenly remembered how he'd felt as a child when his parents divorced; he'd never been able to trust intimate relations since then. . . . Would he allow old traumas to shape his present life and his future?"

The reader assumes that Bill and Kate will work things out

because they recognize that they are acting out old scripts and will therefore be able to alter or abandon them. Says Bonnie Eacker Weil, "Adult children of divorce have to get rid of the pain [occasioned by the divorce] before they can get to the pleasure. Love is pleasure. So is sex. That is why so many have sex problems. They won't allow themselves to enjoy a relationship."

SUBSTITUTING ACTIVITY FOR COMMITMENT

Holding back is one way to avoid commitment. Promiscuity, it turns out, is another. Some adult children of divorce engage in sex with many partners in an attempt to find love; others play the field in order to avoid a close attachment.

"Between the ages of twenty and twenty-five," recalls a man who is now in his fifties, "I got involved with many women. As soon as they began to care about me I dropped them. It was a way of not committing to anyone. At twenty-five, a young woman I was seeing made me realize that I was using her. 'Just don't hurt me,' she told me. At that moment, I understood that I *had* been hurting people by the way I treated them. And I stopped doing that."

Among those interviewed for this book, woman after woman told of having had many sexual partners and many started young. In a paper on "Effects of Father Absence on Personality Development in Adolescent Daughters," E. Mavis Hetherington reports that girls whose fathers left home before they were five will often try to make up for that first love by becoming sexually precocious in adolescence.

A forty-one-year-old woman remembers, "I became promiscuous in high school. In a curious way, I think it was because I was still being the good little girl trying to hold on to Daddy's affection. My attitude with the men I met was 'Just tell me what you want and I will do it.' "

The blurred boundaries between one and another troubling

characteristic claimed by adult children of divorce are exemplified again as this woman continues her recollections. "My self-image was so low," she says, "I didn't believe I had a right to say no. That attitude stayed with me through college (where I got involved with some of my professors), through a short-lived marriage, and through many affairs. In all, I was so intent on giving pleasure, I never stopped to think about what might please *me*."

QUESTIONING ONE'S SEXUAL IDENTITY

Other men and women draw a link between the experience of growing up as a child of divorce and the confusion they later felt about their sexual identity. Many attribute this largely to the fact that the home experience did not provide them with a model of a healthy male/female relationship. How *do* men and women interact? How do they touch? These and similar questions remained an unsolved mystery for them.

Among men raised in female-headed households, some have found themselves uncomfortable around women and uncertain about taking on the male role. "At age twenty-five," one says, "I had trouble deciding to ask a girl out. There were many reasons, including my own poor self-image and the fact that I didn't want to be hurt. Romance is such an out-of-control thing, and I like control. There was also the fact that no one had ever shown me how to act like a man. My father wasn't there for me and my stepfather was not the sort of man I wanted to model myself after."

Like other men *and* women who were interviewed, this man (now thirty-seven and engaged to be wed) regards the experience of growing up divorced as having strongly contributed to his struggles with sexual identity and some early sexual experimentation with others of the same sex. "I thought I might be interested in men—and I opened myself to that possibility a couple of times," he says. "It took me a while to understand that what I wanted from men was to find someone I could admire, someone I could hope to emulate, not someone I could fall in love with."

"There *were* homosexual feelings that came from being, in a way, the soother of my mother," says a forty-one-year-old woman in response to a question about the effect of parental divorce on one's sexuality. "I experimented some with other women."

Others among the interviewees reveal that they have gone beyond experimentation to establishing significant homosexual relationships. Describing his ten-year commitment to another man, Adam Norris says, "That was the first home I experienced. It was a friendship. Then a sexual relationship. Then a loving relationship. Then family."

Is there a connection between same-sex preference and the experience of parental divorce? Although theories abound about the nature and causes of homosexuality, not enough is known for one to make that judgment.

WHAT CAN WE LEARN FROM ALL OF THIS?

In listening to the recollections of "divorce and beyond," I am struck by the fact that some people experience long-term anxieties that they attribute to the earlier upheaval of their family while others, similarly challenged, are able to approach life relatively unhampered by the past. To what do these children of divorce—the ones who have grown up with more comfortable attitudes toward intimacy, commitment, and sexuality—attribute the healthier outlook they have been able to bring to their lives?

A respectful relationship between their divorced parents is credited by several of the men and women with having been helpful to their own self-esteem and trust—permitting them to both give and accept intimacy.

The successful remarriage of a parent was also mentioned by many men and women, especially those who lived in the home with the stepparent and developed a positive relationship with him or her, as contributing to their healthy outlook on relationships. They were enabled to participate in a loving household in lieu of a family in which anger held sway.

Perhaps the most important experience, however, was simply that of *knowing one was valued,* whatever the makeup of the postdivorce family. "Sexuality has never been a problem for me," explains a woman who attributes many of life's other frustrations to the divorce of her parents and the changes that it wrought in her life.

Why is that?

"I think it's because our original family was healthful in terms of affection and touching," she says. "There was a lot of hugging, kissing good-night, and telling each other that we loved one another. After the divorce, the same feelings continued to be expressed between my mother and us children. Whatever else happened, I'm very grateful for that."

Chapter II

The Quest for Stability

As a young adult, I was very careful in assessing the young women I met. If I thought someone was flighty, I wouldn't even phone her for a second date. I wanted a marriage that would last. My wife and I celebrated our twentieth anniversary a year ago. Over the length of our married life, there *have* been times when I've worried about the stability of the relationship. That troubled me a great deal. Stability has always been very important to me.

—Arthur Waterman, forty-seven, age five when his parents were divorced

In the interviews, the word "stability" comes up so often as to leave little doubt about its motivating role in the life decisions made by men and women who, as children, experienced its opposites: insecurity, turbulence, and change. When employed by divorce's children in connection with relationships (as Arthur Waterman uses the word), "stability" stands as a synonym for permanence and harmony. (See chapter ten, "The Past Influences the Present: Creating Home and Family," for a fuller discussion of how this characteristic is played out.) Applied to decision-making about money or career choice, it can be equated with financial security. In either situation, in seeking stability the child of divorce wishes desperately to maintain some hard-won equilibrium, wishes to feel safe.

STRENGTHENING RELATIONSHIPS: THE ROLE OF RELIGION

Among divorce's children whom I meet, more than a few tell of turning to religion for its promise of the safety and stability they want and need. In counterpoint to the chaos that these men and women experienced earlier in their lives, adhering to an organized system of beliefs and rituals offers them an order and structure that can be relied on. In many ways, organized religion provides children of divorce with another form of family—one that promises to be true to you as long as you uphold your end of the bargain and honor your commitment to it. "If you hold your faith, religion won't abandon you," says a woman whose family came apart when she herself was on the threshold of adolescence. At the age of thirty-two, she found herself returning to the faith of her childhood. "In a very real sense," she continues, "it was my way of going back home. It had the virtue of being familiar and, at the same time, comfortable. My own family, on the other hand, had not been a comfortable place in which to grow up."

What we learn from the interviews is that, in many ways, for the children of divorce the concepts of religion and family are intertwined, the former serving to support the latter.

Two years ago, at the age of twenty-six, Enid Bergstrom converted to Catholicism from the Lutheran faith in which she'd been raised. "There is no question," she tells me, "that my being a child of a bitter divorce had everything to do with that decision."

She continues, "For years I'd been carrying around with me this image of all these good Catholic families. You know the ones. They go to mass together. They sit down to Sunday dinner together. I finally decided that I wanted the promise of stability that Catholicism holds out."

Enid has also become active in Kindred Spirits, a group of single adults within her church who come together to study, to do good works, and to celebrate the holidays—much in the manner she envisions for the family she hopes to create someday when she marries. She has not yet been able to make that commitment.

For Ruth Lewisohn, the decision to join a synagogue and become religiously observant came *after* her marriage and the birth of her first child. Ruth had not been raised in a religious family. On the contrary, the thirty-six-year-old woman says, "My upbringing was decidedly left-wing." It also was decidedly disorganized. Following the hostile divorce of her parents, Ruth found herself being frequently shuttled between their two homes. "Religion was not practiced in either one," she says, adding under her breath, "Neither was civility."

What motivated Ruth to incorporate religion as an integral part of her present family's life? "Religion provides stability," she replies simply. "Once we had a child, the matter of this family's survival became a critical issue for me. There was *no way*, I knew, that I would allow divorce to happen to my child. I strongly believe that the structure that religion provides is good for families. I know that it has been good for us."

Friday evenings, no matter how busy their lives as parents and working professionals, Ruth and her husband stop everything to sit down to Sabbath dinner with their three children. Saturday mornings, the family attends services. "Among other things," Ruth says, "I appreciate the steadiness of ritual. I think it helps hold a family together."

WHAT THE STATISTICS SAY

In the interviews, more than a few adult children of divorce echo this belief that religion contributes to family cohesiveness.

Is it true, I wonder, that the family that prays together stays together? *Do* religious devotion and practice augur well for a lasting marriage?

"As best we can determine, it does not," says demographer Larry Bumpass, extrapolating from the data provided by the National Survey of Families and Households. As an example, he cites the survey's findings regarding a connection between marital stability and Catholicism. Traditionally, as Enid believes, among major religions the Catholic Church has maintained one of the strongest positions against divorce. Church teaching holds that marriage is indissoluble. Once a couple enters a valid marriage, it continues until the death of one of the partners. Yet, reports Bumpass, "we find no difference in the divorce rates between couples where both husband and wife are Catholic and couples where neither partner is Catholic."

An interesting finding that *is* emerging from the data, Bumpass points out, is that when only one partner in the marriage is Catholic and the other is not, the rate of divorce is one-third higher. One wonders if this can be interpreted to mean that shared belief (in whatever religion or in no religion at all) is an indicator of greater marital longevity than when the partners come together from different backgrounds.

"We can't leap to that conclusion," warns Bumpass, emphasizing that there are as yet no longitudinal studies on the correlation of divorce and religion that might enable making such a statement. Whether religion, *any* religion, will provide the kind of stability sought by those who have experienced parental divorce is highly subjective. What I glean from these interviews, however, is that some children of divorce, in their adult lives, find religious commitment and practice to be very helpful in their effort to achieve balance in a world gone awry.

STRIVING TO FEEL SECURE:
THE EMPHASIS ON ECONOMICS

"I wanted to marry someone who was emotionally and financially secure. More than anything else, I wanted stability," says Sheila Henderson, thirty-four, a professor of art history who has been married for ten years to a man twenty-two years her senior.

Our meeting takes place in the front parlor of the brownstone that Sheila shares with her husband, an investment banker, and their two pedigreed cats. The sofa on which we sit is of butter-soft leather. At our feet is a Chinese rug whose shadings glow subtly in a thickness of velvetlike wool. Original works of art cover the walls which are themselves covered in textured gray fabric. . . . Here, surrounded by an abundance of good things that speak of the availability of money and taste, the well-groomed young woman discloses, "I am totally screwed up about money. It's an issue I cannot get clear on."

Sheila sees a direct correlation between her feelings about money and her experiences in growing up divorced. "No matter how old or successful you get," she explains, "as a child of divorce you can never forget the bill collectors . . . the going without . . . your mother's constant complaining about your father's not sending money . . . having to go to your grandparents to ask for a handout. . . .

"Nowadays, money is an internal misconception," she declares. "In my head and my heart I *always* feel poor."

Over time, I am to hear several variations on this sentiment expressed by many other people who, like Sheila Henderson, live at a financial level that would seem to offer some sense of security —enough, at least, for them not to have to fear (as many do) that poverty lurks around the bend. It is a kind of economic paranoia. *The bill collectors are out to get me.*

Beverly Phillips echoes these sentiments: "Financial security is *very* important to me." Looking backward, she says: "Many a time I would come home from school to find our furniture piled outside because we'd been evicted. My childhood memories, following the divorce of my parents, include seeing our belongings repossessed. There were times, too, when our family didn't even have enough money for food."

A nursing supervisor, Beverly lives today with her doctor husband and their two children in an eleven-room house located in a choice suburb of Philadelphia. By her own description, she is "very comfortable financially." Like Sheila Henderson, Beverly continues to be very money-concerned—reality notwithstanding.

"I'm very responsible about it," she tells me. "I repaid my student loan *the day* it was due. A legacy of my childhood is that I will not use credit cards. I never pay interest on *anything*. If I can't afford something, I don't want it. I don't want anything taken away from me because of money."

Money tends to be an emotionally charged subject in many families. For Beverly, as for many other adult children of divorce, being financially secure stands for much more than not having one's belongings repossessed. It is another means of assuring that there will be fewer stressors in the relationship between husband and wife. It is, as they see it, part of the foundation on which a family structure can be built—a foundation strong enough to support the couple and, eventually, their children.

We rejoin Beverly: "Following my marriage, I waited eight years to have children because I wanted to be finished with school and to buy a house first," she says. "I was determined to be able to put away enough money so I could afford, as a mother, to stay at home with our children. I felt that's how a family should be run. My children would have both a mother and father who would *be* there for them. The money was something that would make that goal possible."

WHAT THE STATISTICS TELL US THIS TIME

A landmark 1980 study of divorced families in California, conducted by sociologist Lenore Weitzman, provides information that helps us better understand the genesis of feelings such as those that were expressed by Sheila Henderson, Beverly Phillips ... and many others. Among the study's findings, one sobering, oft-cited statistic stands out: one year after a divorce, Weitzman found, the standard of living of women and their children declined by 73 percent (while the standard of living of the fathers rose by an average of 42 percent). The greatest economic hardships following divorce, the study makes clear, are suffered by women and their children.

In her book, *The Divorce Revolution,* Weitzman goes on to explain: "These apparently simple statistics have far-reaching social and economic consequences. For most women and children, divorce means precipitous downward mobility—both economically and socially. The reduction in income brings residential moves and inferior housing, drastically diminished or nonexistent funds for recreation and leisure, and intense pressures due to inadequate time and money."

If this is true for divorce in the eighties, consider how much more devastating divorce was likely to have been in prior periods, decades which saw far fewer women active in the work force and able to manage the sole support of their families. So one might expect (as I did) to hear that the children of these earlier divorces place a good deal of emphasis on being, *and feeling,* financially secure.

What I had not anticipated, however, was that this emphasis would be much greater for women than for men who grew to adulthood in postdivorce households. Both sexes were asked what, if any, role the divorce of their parents played in shaping their own attitudes toward money. The men were basically noncommittal on this issue. The women leaped to respond.

There is no question that sons and daughters experienced equal hardship when the divorce of their parents left their custodial households poorer. Yet it seems to me, based on these interviews, that the quest for financial stability is a more serious long-range matter for women.

What might account for this? The difference between men and women in their reactions to the money issue may have to do with the fact that boys, growing up, accept as a given that they will have to be responsible for their own financial futures and are therefore less emotional about money in general. For men, the need to earn a living is a basic fact of life.

Girls have grown up with different expectations. Before the Women's Movement, few expected to hold down full-time jobs while raising a family. The tasks of earning a living and, further, of managing money were optional for them. And then the men they depended upon, their fathers, let them down. It is a lesson in life that makes a lasting impact. Where the sons of divorce grow up knowing that they must work, the daughters of divorce grow up vowing that they *will* work. What may once have been optional becomes mandatory: learning to stand firmly on one's own economic feet.

CHOOSING SAFE CAREERS

Hence, establishing a safe career can become especially important. For many adult children of divorce, stability is sought in the area of employment. More important to them than a large paycheck is a regular paycheck. Sally Halvorsen, twenty-six, was four years old when her parents divorced. Today she is a second-year medical student. She tells me, "I don't think I'm temperamentally suited to a medical career." She then adds, "The main reason that I'm in med school is because of my desire for financial security, because I want to be sure that I will always have a regular, dependable income."

Listen now to Lorna Kelly, whose parents divorced when she was sixteen. The last fight that she recalls between them was over the cost of her prom dress. "My nickname is Miss Frugal," says the thirty-two-year-old flight attendant, laughing at herself. "I earn a good salary and I manage money *extremely* well. I don't spend frivolously. I have a big savings account, and I keep my finances well guarded.

"I could never see myself in a situation where I would have to ask a man for money," she says. "And *if* I marry"—Lorna keeps herself well guarded, too—"I will want to see the checkbooks. My mom never knew what my dad earned, so she never knew what he could realistically be expected to contribute to our support. I won't have to write the checks in the family, but I do want to know *what* checks are being written."

Like Lorna, many women vow that they will carve out separate careers and separate identities for themselves so that they will not be as vulnerable as their mothers should they marry and their own marriages fail. Some see this mistrustfulness as a negative carryover of the divorce. Others regard it as a positive legacy, one which they proudly label "Independence."

Chapter III

The Achievement:
Turning Losses into Gains

It is not in the still calm of life . . . that great challenges are formed. . . . Great necessities call out great virtues.

—Abigail Adams, in a letter to her son John Quincy Adams

Decidedly, divorce does *not* take place "in the still calm of life." Even when it is managed with civility, when former spouses are able to point with some satisfaction to the fact that their separation was "amicable," divorce is an event that presents the children with great challenges. It creates an upheaval in their lives. In the world they are thrust into by their parents' separation, the children of divorce find that they must travel an uncharted terrain.

Having managed to traverse the territory into adulthood, some men and women look back and see mostly the obstacles that were placed in their way by the divorce. Every disappointment and personal failing, it seems to them, is directly attributable to the fact of their not having grown up in a home where there were two parents who were in harmony with one another.

Others of divorce's children—those who are the focus of this chapter—proudly maintain that they managed not only to meet the difficulties placed in their path but, further, to master them.

While regretting that they weren't able to spend their childhoods in an intact family, these men and women nevertheless take satisfaction in certain of their positive traits to have come out of the experience. To paraphrase J. P. Morgan's advice, where some adult children continue to view parental divorce as a lemon, others look back at the same experience and find that it has enabled them to make lemonade.

Among the men and women interviewed, many note with special pride these strengths and sensitivities—the virtues they have drawn from the necessity of coping.

INDEPENDENCE

Independence ranks first on many lists of characteristics that are positively viewed. A valued outcome of the divorce experience, it is, however, often achieved at a great price—in some cases at the cost of a childhood, as the following story makes clear.

TAKING ON A PARENT'S ROLE

Susan Leymond, thirty-seven, holds down a responsible position in hotel management. She describes herself to me as the "sandwich child" in her family: "There's a year and a half between me and a brother on either side." Susan was eleven when her parents' marriage came to an end and her world changed. "Everything happened so fast," she says. "Dad moved out, Mom took on a full-time job, and *I* became the mommy in the family. I was made to take on a great deal of responsibility."

She continues, "From the age of eleven, I did all the laundry, the shopping, the cooking for the family. I did what I had to do, but I didn't get any appreciation. If I did ten things right, my mother would come home and criticize me for the one thing I didn't get to. I was dutiful, but I resented it. I learned, early on, to be self-sufficient, which has stood me in good stead, but I withdrew from all the people in the family, which remains painful."

In a six-year follow-up study of children of divorce, E. Mavis Hetherington found that both sons and daughters in divorced families were allowed more responsibility, independence, and power in decision-making than were children in nondivorced families. In some cases, especially when the emotional demands or responsibilities were inappropriate, were beyond the child's capabilities, or interfered with the child's normal activities, resentment, rebellion, or behavior problems followed. Susan Leymond rebelled, for example, by leaving home at age seventeen, as soon as it was economically feasible for her.

In other situations, Hetherington noted, the greater power and independence given to the child resulted in an egalitarian, mutually supportive relationship between parent and child. Lillian Behrens fits this latter description. The thirty-one-year-old woman, who sells time for a midsize radio station, tells me, "One day, my parents and I were sitting around the kitchen table, talking about how I wanted to celebrate my upcoming thirteenth birthday. The next day, my father moved out of the house and (before my birthday arrived, I think) my mother found a job as a receptionist in a dentist's office.

"Mom relied on me a lot after that," says Lillian. "I have an older brother and two younger sisters, and it was my responsibility to keep the house running smoothly for us all. I didn't do the cleaning (Mom did that), but I did have to do the grocery shopping, prepare dinner, and be available to take care of my kid sisters from the time they got home from school.

"There were times when I resented all the responsibility," Lillian admits, "but overall I felt that Mom and I were partners in this business of survival—and I experienced a lot of pride in the fact that we *were* making it. To this day, my mother and I have retained a special relationship. We care about one another as equals. It's very satisfying."

Lillian speaks of a partnership, of becoming a kind of co-parent in the family, and, most importantly, of having her efforts recognized and appreciated. This is the critical difference between her experience and that of Susan Leymond. Although both were given a lot of responsibility for their ages and made to grow up early, Lillian alone had the encouragement and support of a parent that are vital to building a child's self-esteem (no matter what the family situation). Hence she was able to accept and enjoy her independence.

ACHIEVING SELF-SUFFICIENCY BY DEFAULT

Other children of divorce were not *assigned* responsibility, as were Susan and Lillian, but gained their independence by default. Since nobody else seemed to be paying attention to them, they explain, they were forced to manage their own care.

Where were the parents, one wonders. The stories these children of divorce relate have to do with mothers or fathers who were too caught up in their own grief over the end of the marriage to pay heed to the needs of the children. In other households, the parents' energies were consumed by continued wrangling over the divorce. New jobs and new families also served as new focuses for their attention. In a number of cases, adult children tell of having been shipped out to live with relatives or others . . . for a short time or until they reached an age where they were able to live on their own. Left largely to their own devices, these children of divorce quickly discerned that success or failure lay solely in their own efforts and abilities—and they managed to make the most of both.

Actor Gregory Peck speaks to just this point in an interview that appeared a while back in *Parade Magazine.* From the age of three, when his parents separated, Peck (born Eldred Gregory) was shuttled from one parent to another, including spending the years between ten and fourteen in a California boarding school. He describes the school: "It was run by the Sisters of Mercy, but it was really a military school. It was quite a combination—the nuns and the military . . . it was kind of a tough time. . . .

"Little by little, though," the actor relates, "I was learning to be on my own. I realized that if I didn't make things happen myself, no one else was going to."

The same perception *(I was on my own)* and response *(I will make things happen for me)* is heard time and again in the interviews conducted for this project. Listen to what Paul Norman, a state legislator, has to say: "The most unique aspect of being a child of divorce and the most important carryover is that it made me fiercely independent. I couldn't rely on other people. I never looked to other people to help me. Independence is the dominant part of my personality."

Tobias Goodman, like Paul Norman a successful lawyer, provides the echo to the legislator's experience and strong determination to succeed through his own efforts. "I learned early on that I could not depend on my father," Goodman tells me, "but I still had hopes that *someone* would come along who would make things better. When I was eleven, my mother remarried a man I could not respect. I somehow understood that she was not going to bring anyone worthwhile into my life, anyone I would be able to rely on. I knew then that *I had to run my life myself.*

"And I did," Goodman continues, "making decisions on my own about which high school and college I'd attend. I also enlisted in the army without parental consultation. Later, I even put myself through law school. I didn't take a penny from anybody because I didn't want anybody to have a piece of me. And nobody *did* have a piece of me. I owe nobody. I am my own man."

AMBITION

Listening to the children of divorce, one quickly recognizes that the trait of independence is closely linked, for many, to the drive to succeed. "I have a B.A., two master's degrees, and an LL.B.," says Paul Norman. "They're *all* a result of my drive to be successful.

"One of the main factors of independence is competition," Norman continues reflectively. "And if you carry it all the way out, it becomes narcissism—caring for no one *but* oneself. I could easily have become ruthless but for a need I had to be connected and to be liked. In high school, I received an award for being involved in more extracurricular activities than anyone else. That was an outlet. It gave me a way of belonging."

Children need affirmation. If children who are denied approval in their families can then find it in sports, academics, or leadership, the research suggests, they can be successful in spite of family disruption. Indeed, one gets the feeling that they often become successful *because* of it. Because of the need to prove their self-worth.

"I wanted to be somebody so bad that in a way the divorce . . . or the shambles of my life . . . gave me the will to succeed," says Tobias Goodman, who became a leading criminal attorney. "People talk about role models," he says. "My father was the *best* role model I could have had because I had to be everything he was not."

Goodman understands too that, in a way, he also had to prove himself to the father who (it seemed to him) didn't think enough of his son to remain in his life. For Goodman, as for others who told their stories, the drive to succeed is equated with the drive to be recognized—not by the world so much as by the rejecting parent.

AMBITION'S ROLE IN CHOOSING A CAREER

For some adult children of divorce, then, choosing a career (and striving to succeed in it) is linked to the need to prove themselves in a way that will right past wrongs. Lucy Thomason sells petroleum futures—not your typical employment for a twenty-six-year-old unmarried female, but it is a career that, she tells me, her father would understand and approve of, a career he might have chosen for a son. Lucy believes that, if she had been a son, her father would have remained an integral part of her life "even though he still might have decided to divorce my mother."

Lucy had no contact with her father during the years when she put herself through college and business school. After a title was added below her name on the embossed business cards provided by her firm, Lucy felt safe enough to get in touch with the man and arrange a meeting between them. That encounter took place. Lucy had been right in one respect: her stockbroker father clearly was pleased by her success. But she has found herself disturbed by his satisfaction. "Dad looks at me and says, 'She's so successful, I can't have done anything wrong,'" Lucy explains. "I want to grab him by the shoulders and say, 'Listen to me. You don't understand how unhappy I have been all these years.' But I don't."

Like Lucy, other children of divorce tell me that their ambitions and career choices are linked to living up to parental expectations. The basis for *their* aspirations, however, is not the desire to prove themselves to rejecting parents but, in contrast, the wish to affirm the dedication of parents who remained supportive of them. "From the time that they were divorced, my mother and father looked to me as the only good thing to have come out of their failed marriage," I hear from a twenty-eight-year-old whom I interview, explaining why he feels driven to complete a doctorate in history while also holding down a demanding job as an editor. "Growing up, I knew that every good report card I brought home was validation not so much of my worth but of theirs. In time, the need to please my parents became internalized. Now I want success not only for their own sakes, but for my own."

EMPATHY

Other men and women arrive at their career choices based on yet a different characteristic that appears to be prominent among children of divorce: *empathy*. Jennie Fuller, who is studying to be an occupational therapist, explains the trait: "The most positive part of being an adult child of divorce is that we have a capacity for compassion and understanding, a quality of emotion, that other people never experience."

The quality of being empathic is brought up again in the interviews. "Being a child of divorce has made me a very sensitive person," I hear from Mallory Coburn. "As a result, I take other people's problems seriously. And it doesn't have to be a problem that *I* think is major." She provides an example. "I don't like it, for instance, when people offer consolation only upon the death of a parent. I spent many years grieving the loss of my father, but I didn't get any sympathy because, although unavailable to me, he *was* alive and well. I had to grieve his loss alone." As a result, "I don't make snap judgments about what is a problem for someone and what is not. If people tell me they see something as a problem, I treat it as such."

The characteristic of empathy shows itself primarily in two important aspects of the lives of children of divorce: in the career choices they make and, similarly, in the quality of their friendships.

EMPATHY'S INFLUENCE ON CHOOSING A CAREER

Among the adult children of divorce interviewed for this book, there is more than a fair share of therapists, social workers, doctors, nurses, teachers, and lawyers. Midway along in the project, I began to be aware of this—and wondered why it was so, since I hadn't specifically reached out to these professions for interview subjects. I now believe that it is just this aptitude for identifying with and understanding another's situation, feelings, and motives that has led many children of divorce to choose to work in helping professions.

They tell me so themselves. "I run a group for divorced kids," I hear from a therapist who became a divorced kid herself some sixty years earlier. "It's a carryover of my having suffered so much that I want to make it better for others.

"Sometimes, I get a little unprofessional," she adds. "If I'm counseling parents *before* they divorce, I really struggle to have them see that they may be able to work their problems out *in* the relationship. Parents must care enough about their kids to struggle a bit. They have an obligation to try something other than breaking up a family where there are children."

"I think I became a psychologist in an attempt to repair," I am told by a thirty-nine-year-old man who saw his parents divorce when he was eight. "I felt that if I could get smart enough, I could help parents do things better with their kids."

A family therapist, age fifty-two, also draws a strong correlation for me between growing up divorced and his decision to make counseling his life's work, but his explanation offers a slightly different perspective. "After my parents split up," he says, "I was sent to live with my grandparents for a while, and later was shuttled between relatives from pillar to post. Growing up in many different environments and feeling insecure in each, I developed some traits that helped me later. Among them, I learned to be a good observer. I watched people and copied them because I didn't want to do something wrong, something I could be criticized for. That habit of watching others and listening to others led me to psychiatry. It has stood me in good stead."

"I understand how dangerous and treacherous life can be," says Tobias Goodman, who has often represented people regarded as society's outcasts. "There were times in my life when I had enough rage in *me* to be a murderer," he says. "Instead I have become someone who represents murderers. . . . I've spent my life saying, 'Hey, everybody is bad and good.' . . . What do I do in my job? I hold the hands of people through a bad time in their lives. And that, I guess, is what I wanted someone to do for me."

Among the children of divorce who have chosen a career in the arts, many also make a connection between their childhood experience and the work they do. "Out of what was bad, there is a desire to create something good—music, a painting, a beautiful sculpture," a thirty-six-year-old sculptor tells me.

A novelist whose parents divorced forty-seven years ago speaks of their divorce as having given her "this wonderful mystery to be solved—of how and why people behave the way they do toward one another." She says, "It is, I believe, the reason I write. I like to struggle with questions of what motivates people. I also enjoy inventing characters who do whatever *I* would have them do. That is a direct reaction to my childhood, where I felt powerless."

Later, a playwright, thirty-one, analyzes his work for me. "While I don't usually write about divorce, I do seem to be working things out in my plays," he says. "They are usually about a complex world where people seem to come together and do things to each other that in a small perspective might seem sadistic ... but I think that in a larger sense the characters are not quite in control of what they're doing.

"My plays don't tend to judge people," the playwright continues. "That's *some* of what divorce is about: complex situations that simply go on and we don't know why. And yet we must accept them."

FORGING MEANINGFUL FRIENDSHIPS

The same quality of empathy that leads many children of divorce to choose people-oriented careers encourages many also to choose people-oriented lives: to count themselves as men and women who care and, equally important, who can be trusted. As the previous chapters made clear, adult children of divorce take their friendships very seriously. (They think before they commit, and they do not make a commitment readily.)

There is another side to that coin, however. When asked to describe the positive attributes that stem from growing up divorced, quite a few of the interviewees noted, as did Nancy Kovach, "I tend to be a good friend." She explains, "The unique outcome of my childhood is my ability to be in touch with other people's feelings and to be really caring. It has helped me to be more sympathetic as a friend."

Although they are likely to exercise caution in forging close relationships (for fear of again being disappointed by those in whom they place their trust), the children of divorce speak with pride of being "a good friend," "someone who can be counted on," "trustworthy."

TRUSTWORTHINESS

In other words, divorce's children can be trusted to be true to their commitments.

"The long-range effect of growing up divorced?" Cindy Weston repeats the question I have just asked her, mulls it over in her mind before responding, "It is the strength of the commitments that I make to people." There is an adamant quality to her carefully measured words as she declares, "Unlike my parents, I *can* be trusted. I will *not* do unto others as has been done to me."

Tobias Goodman again provides the echo. "To me, loyalty is everything," he says. "And commitment. Everyone who knows me knows that my word is my bond. That's because my father was the opposite. He'd promise the moon and deliver nothing. I can be counted on."

OPTIMISM

"The single most important carryover of the divorce experience," says Goodman after further thought, "is optimism. When you take responsibility for your own life and achieve your first success *in spite of* your past, you realize that you do not have to continue to enact the script for failure that you thought was written for you by parental divorce. You begin to understand that *everything*—career, family, children, even love—is possible if you want it bad enough. And you begin to want it all, because you believe (and this understanding comes slowly) that you deserve it, that you have as much right to happiness as anybody else. I hate to sound corny, but what you find out is that life *can* be beautiful.

"The other wonderful thing," he goes on, "is that you never for a moment take that beauty for granted. You savor success, however it's defined by you. And that makes everything that comes your way, or that you cause to work out well, even more wonderful." As Goodman awaits the imminent birth of his first grandchild, it is clear that his optimism has been justified.

Adam Norris is at a very different stage in his life. At an age when he is still wrestling with both career and personal commitments, the young man nevertheless shares the older man's hopeful view of life's possibilities. "As a child of divorce, having no benchmark by which to measure myself, no standard by which to fail, I have been able to see life from a unique perspective," he says.

More and more, Adam finds himself looking back less and less. "There is a privilege of freedom that comes with divorce," says Adam, who finds himself looking optimistically toward the future and the possibilities it holds for him. "The world is truly what *I* make it," he tells me.

In the section that follows, we join the adult children of divorce in looking back at the past. "The child is father of the man," wrote the poet William Wordsworth. Having met the men and the women who grew up with divorce, I am eager now to understand the way it was for them: what it was like to have been the child.

PART TWO

THE WAY IT WAS THEN—
GROWING UP DIVORCED

Chapter IV

The End of the
Happily-Ever-After Family

Happy families are all alike; every unhappy family
is unhappy in its own right.

—Tolstoy, *Anna Karenina*

Children *expect* to grow up in intact, happy families. The idea
that husband, wife, and their offspring are supposed to live out
their days happily ever after is instilled in daughters and sons
from the time that fairy tales are first read them before bedtime.
The stories that shape our visions do not begin, "Once upon a
time there was a mama bear, a papa bear, and a baby bear by the
first marriage." Rather, they hold out the promise to children of
security and continuity.

Divorce writes the end to the promise. It tells children that
they can no longer put their faith in happily ever after.

REMEMBERING THE FAMILY THAT WAS

Looking back, the men and women who were those children
of divorce hold different memories of the intact family and its
demise. For some, like Jennie Fuller, the years before their parents separated still retain a kind of fairy-tale quality, are *still* remembered warmly as having been the best of times . . . even
though the worst of times were quick to follow.

Jennie, thirty-six, is describing her family history. She is slim, about five feet six inches, a soft-looking woman who would be noticeably pretty if she cared more about the enhancements of makeup and fashion. As she sits across from me, her upper body seems to sink in toward the back of the chair. Her hands are clenched together in the cavity of her lap. One leg is wrapped tightly about the other. She appears closed in. It is clear at the start of our interview that her childhood is not something Jennie is able to talk about with ease.

Haltingly, she begins an unsettling account, one that includes an emotionally disturbed father, joblessness, family poverty, uprooting and upheaval. Suddenly, Jennie sits up straighter. Her eyes light up and her voice brightens. "Christmas used to be *wonderful* when we all lived together as a family," she says, and goes on to share a memory that she continues to hold dear.

"We children had a ritual that Dad was part of," she says. "Each year, we'd put up the tree, and Dad would be the designer. He would stand back and direct. Everything had to be perfect. For instance, we had to make sure that the ornaments were placed according to plan, that two blues or two greens didn't wind up next to each other. And it was critical that the icicles be hung evenly." She smiles broadly. "And when we were done, everything *was* perfect. Christmas was fun before our family split up." (Once upon a time, you see, Jennie lived the myth, saw herself and her family as part of a Hallmark Christmas.)

The light leaves her eyes. "Following the divorce, Christmas was awful," she says. "It still is."

What is it like for a youngster when home life goes from being "fun" to "awful"? . . . What *do* boys and girls understand of the tensions in the home? . . . How much are they told about what is going on between their parents? . . . How much of that information do they comprehend? . . . In short, how was divorce perceived by the children—and how is it now recalled?

The answers to these questions serve several purposes—not the least of which is to help those who were the children of divorce gain a better understanding of the forces that shaped their characters and their lives, to face their demons and move on. The responses also provide insights for today's parents on how to do a "better divorce."

Among the men and women whom we meet in this book are many who were old enough when the marriage of their parents disintegrated to bear full witness. Others, over the years, have had their select recollections fleshed out by family myths and history. Still others were so young when the actual separation and divorce of their parents took place that they have no memory of living in their original intact family. Yet they, too, strive to create a picture of the once-upon-a-time marital household in order to make some sense out of the major mystery of their childhood: why the central characters in their family narrative could not go on to live together happily ever after.

Although the details of parental divorce vary from account to account, readers who have grown up as children of divorce are bound to see bits and pieces of their own experiences reflected in these fragments of someone else's shattered mirror of the past. Tolstoy's wisdom notwithstanding, the lesson one learns from listening to adult children of divorce recall their past is that, in many striking ways, unhappy families are *not* so very different from one another. Certain patterns stand out.

WHEN PARENTS KEEP SECRETS

The year when Christmas changed for her, Jennie was thirteen, the middle child between a brother, fourteen, and a sister, eleven. "At this age [adolescence], children are capable of understanding the gray areas of life and the ambivalence that surrounds so many of the reasons for contemporary divorce," writes Linda Bird Francke in *Growing Up Divorced.*

Thirteen ought to be an age of understanding, yet Jennie recalls that she was completely unprepared for the family's disruption. "The fact that my mother and father were having problems was kept a secret from us," she explains. "There were some signs of difficulty. For instance, it was clear that my mother was depressed, and that her relationship with my father had changed. They used to be affectionate, but now they seemed more isolated from one another. Still, they *never* fought in front of us. When I was told about the divorce, I cried my insides out. I felt my life was shattered."

In a paper on "Effects of Divorce on Parents and Children" written by E. Mavis Hetherington, Martha Cox and Roger Cox, the authors use the term "encapsulated conflict" to describe a situation where parents engage in frequent quarreling when alone but do not battle in front of the children. The researchers found no apparent negative outcomes of encapsulated conflict for the children whom they studied two years following the divorce of their parents.

But Ann Kliman of the Center for Preventive Psychiatry presents another view.

In her book, *Crisis,* Kliman introduces the reader to the Cramer family, who came to her for counseling when the parents were going through a divorce. Asked to briefly describe their marital situation, Marion and Milton Cramer ran down an exhaustive list of complaints about one another, proudly concluding that, their differences notwithstanding, they had *never* argued in front of the children.

Elliot Cramer, the couple's eleven-year-old son, presented a troubling symptom. Once an honor student, he was now doing poorly in school—even failing math, the subject he used to enjoy most. Observed Kliman, "As with so many children exposed to long periods of family secrets and denials of observable reality, Elliot had transposed his parents' injunctions not to ask questions, not to 'know' what was going on, into an injunction not to learn."

As his parents became better able to talk to Elliot about their feelings and their plans, Elliot's math improved remarkably. By opening up the subject, the parents gave their son permission to express his own feelings and his fears. They were able to respond appropriately.

Parents who never fight in front of their children hide the reality of their relationship in the belief that "what they don't know won't hurt them." It is a mistaken belief. Even in intact families, secret fighting deprives the youngsters of a model of how to have a healthy argument and then make up. In dysfunctional families, it seeks to establish a sense of security—which the children ultimately, often shockingly, discover is false. Ann Kliman further observes, "In an attempt to protect our children (and ourselves) from pain, discomfort and confusion, we deprive them of the opportunity to ingest small, tolerable doses of sadness and anxiety, doses which could strengthen them for possibly larger, more unexpected and uncontrollable assaults to come."

Looking back, Jennie believes that the way her parents handled the situation was "terrible." She says, "If my parents had prepared us, or if my mom had at least asked, 'How do you feel about this?' ... if someone had acknowledged in some way that they knew we kids were going to be affected, it would have been better. I now understand that the loss of control was key: the feeling that these horrible things are going to happen to you, and yet you can do nothing about them. Letting the children know wouldn't have changed the situation—my parents still would have got divorced —but it might have helped me cope better with the situation."

WHEN PARENTS ENGAGE IN OPEN WARFARE

In contrast to families where secrecy held sway, other children of divorce look back at growing up in predivorce households in which, it seems to them, *no* emotion or accusation was kept under wraps as "too personal" or "not for children's ears." Everything was out in the open—loud and all too clear.

Adam Norris has a vivid recollection of one such violent incident. As he reconstructs the scene, the pain felt by the four-year-old boy who witnessed the episode is experienced anew by the twenty-nine-year-old man who now describes it for me.

"It took place at night," Adam says. "I remember being awakened by the sound of my parents shouting. I can see my bedroom. It was yellow. I remember getting out of my bed and sneaking into the living room, a large room in pale green. My father had taken to sleeping in the living room, and I'd grown used to finding him there. I remember hiding behind a wall projection leading into the room, so that my parents wouldn't see me. But I saw *them*.

"My mother was standing behind a sofa, and my father was across the room from her behind a large chair. It was as if the two pieces of furniture were their barricades. And they were *screaming* at one another. And my father was shaking his finger at my mother. And there was such hatred and such pain. I remember crying out, 'Stop! Please stop!'

"That is the *only* memory I have of my mother and father as a couple," Adam says, adding, "Whenever I center on what the divorce was about or try to understand who I am, I start by going back to this one incident. The next thing I recall is living in an apartment. From that time on, 'the family' was my mother and I."

Where Adam remembers one terrifying argument, for many other children of divorce the "intact household" is recalled as an ongoing battleground. A fifty-one-year-old who is a respected state legislator, a man of presence and considerable power, would surely surprise the constituents of his midwestern state if they knew that he lives daily with the memory of a childhood in which "I would hide under the covers and pull at my toenails to take my mind off the fighting that was going on downstairs. It was, literally, nightmarish. There was a period in elementary school when I had picked at my feet so badly that I was no longer able to walk. But nobody, least of all my mother and father, sought to find out why I had done this damage to myself. They were too involved in their own warfare to notice, or even care, that I had become its casualty."

Where the legislator picked at his own body, a thirty-one-year-old musician confides that his response to parental violence was to pick on other children. He became a bully. "I remember my mother and father fighting all the time in a mean, humiliating way," he says. "There were many separations and reconciliations —until, when I was seven years old, they separated for good. Living in a turbulent family, I became an acting-out child. For a long time, I terrorized other children. Later I dropped out of high school and enlisted in the army. It was the best decision I could have made. That's when I began to pull myself together."

The boyhood behavior recounted by the musician has its echo in a case history presented by child psychiatrist Richard A. Gardner in *The Parents Book About Divorce*. In his book, Gardner introduces the reader to Bruce, a seven-year-old whose parents became embroiled in a violent divorce conflict. "The father 'saw red' every time his wife's name was mentioned; and Bruce's mother found fault with just about everything the father said or did. The most petty incidents became the foci of violent arguments during which [the couple] cursed at one another using the most base profanity, often threw things at one another, and on occasion even came to blows."

Within a month of the onset of the parental conflict, Gardner reports, there began a steady deterioration in Bruce's behavior. His schoolwork suffered; he bullied other children, teased and provoked them. "In Bruce's case," says Gardner, "it was clear that the anger he felt toward his parents was being displaced onto classmates, teachers, his principal. . . . His parents were serving as models for angry acting-out. . . .

"Bruce was a relatively healthy boy prior to the onset of his parents' battling." Says the psychoanalyst, "I believe that if they had been able to divorce in a more civilized fashion, Bruce would not have developed the problems that not only disrupted his education at that time but may have changed for the worse the whole course of his life."

WHEN PARENTS ARE DYSFUNCTIONAL

When a parent behaves violently . . . when a family keeps secrets, there is sometimes a lot more going on in the home than a growing disaffection between husband and wife. Fragile families are often those experiencing a multitude of problems. Hence, it is not uncommon for children of dysfunctional parents to wear more than one label into adulthood. As if being a child of divorce were not enough, several among the interviewees look back at childhoods in which they also had to cope with the adverse effects of such parental addictions as alcoholism, sexual profligacy, habitual gambling, and (to a lesser extent given the ages of those interviewed) a dependency on drugs.

Whatever the obsession, we hear from the children who lived for a time in these families, the addicted parent's energies too often were directed to satisfying the compulsion instead of to meeting the needs of the home and those who dwelt therein. As for the nonaddicted partner, he or she frequently became correspondingly caught up in the chaos created by the addiction—and thus was also unavailable to the children.

After years of being swept under the rug, the long-range problems of growing up with an addicted parent have finally begun to receive the kind of attention they deserve. The past decade has seen the appearance of a growing literature and support network for adult children of alcoholics. More recently, this kind of outreach has been expanded to include adult children who grew up with parents driven by other compulsive behaviors and who, because of their life experience, feel themselves to be different.

We have yet to learn how children with a dysfunctional parent react when divorce is sought as a solution to a situation that has become untenable. In the interviews conducted for this project, however, several men and women do in fact address these issues. Many hark back to childhoods so turbulent that, they recall, the announcement of parental divorce was greeted by them with enthusiasm. *At last* there would be an end to living with promises unkept, to yelling, to hitting, to embarrassment about today and uncertainty about tomorrow.

When I ask the men and women who have told me these stories to recall their reaction to the change in status from an intact family, they do not hesitate. Each man, each woman uses the same word: *relief.*

But listen to what they have to say, for you will hear something else as well. . . . Listen to Beverly Phillips.

Like others who spoke with me, Beverly Phillips is both an adult child of divorce and an adult child of alcoholism. At thirty-seven, she is a woman who still causes heads to turn when she enters a room. Five feet seven inches tall, she tends to wear fitted clothes in shades of soft green to set off her slim figure and hazel eyes and to complement a fullness of red hair—a heritage from her Irish ancestors. Beverly has been married to Greg Phillips for nineteen years. She is a registered nurse. He is a doctor. They have a son, fourteen, and a daughter, eleven. Beverly's parents separated when *she* was eleven. Her mother and father have not seen each other since.

"The divorce didn't just happen, the separations happened," Beverly tells me. "My memory of our family was that my mother and father fought . . . *all* the time . . . violently. Periodically, they would throw each other out. The end result was that he threw her out one night after a particularly bad fight—a fight in which I'd tried to call the police and he pulled the phone right out of the wall—and she never went back. She slept in the car for two weeks so that she could be near us until she got enough money together for a new apartment, and we moved there. It was all very frightening. And it was very isolating. I didn't have a lot of friends because we moved around so much; my father (when we all lived together) was in and out of work, and we either were one step ahead of the landlord or I would come home from school to find our furniture on the street.

"My younger brother was my father's pet, and took the separation very hard," Beverly explains. "It caused him a lot of pain, whereas I seemed to have different strengths. I could manage it." She pauses, then goes on: "What *I* felt was definitely relief... relief.... I mean, it was *so much better* that it was over, that the separation was..."

Beverly's voice trails off. She reaches for a tissue, dabs at the corners of her eyes. When she is able to go on, she says: "I missed my father tremendously. He was a child. He was one of the kids. He told us stories, fantasies. I was going to be a fairy princess.... He was going to buy a trailer and fill it with dolls, and people from all over the world would come and ask to see them.... He was going to take me in a rowboat to France and buy me a big grand piano in Paris.... And I *believed* this. When I was twenty, I traveled to Europe. I was on a train in Paris, and I wouldn't get off the train, and I didn't know why. And then I realized. It had to do with the memory of the promised grand piano."

Relief, yes. But in Beverly's story, one hears expressed another sentiment that, I found, is often paired with this reaction: one hears *regret*. There is no question that for Beverly (as for others who lived with alcoholic or drug-addicted parents), her parents' divorce was the right decision. At the same time, one can also regret (as Beverly does) the circumstances that made this "right decision" necessary.

Regret lingers. There is an interesting postscript to Beverly's story of her parents' separation. The actual divorce, she tells me, did not take place until after she was twenty-two and married. "My father had not been heard from and my mother decided that she wanted to be legally divorced. It became necessary for me to appear in court to verify that we'd had no contact with our father. The judge asked me, 'Do you think there's any chance for a reconciliation?' Mind you, my father had been gone for eleven years! I said 'No' because I knew I had to, but my heart was pounding. I guess, in my heart, there was still a glimmer of hope. My mother didn't realize that testifying was hard for me, which it was—even though my fantasy of a reunion between my parents was ridiculous and impossible."

Listen now to the echo. A sixty-two-year-old attorney tells of a night—he was six years old—when his mother roused him, dressed him, and (her finger on her lips) motioned him to follow her out of the darkened house. Upstairs slept the father whose obsessive gambling had been the cause of frequent and terrible marital battles.

How did this first-grader feel when he reached his grandparents' home, where (as it turned out) he was to live with his mother for the remainder of his growing-up years? "I felt relief," he unhesitatingly responds to my question. "It was a relief just to know that for me there was going to be no more turmoil. Kids need stability." There is a catch in his voice. In the very next sentence, the words he utters are these: "I never wanted them to get divorced but only to be able to live well together."

From the children of alcoholics, from the sons and daughters of compulsive gamblers, from the men and women who are able to speak *now* about a parent's extramarital relationships, one hears the adult's appraisal that, all things considered, it *was* better for the marriage to have ended. ("The fighting stopped.") One also hears, however, a wish that help had been sought and obtained by the addicted parent, that the dependency which led to the fighting could have been cured, and that the family could have been preserved. Even in the face of harsh reality, the fantasy of growing up in a happily-ever-after family dies hard.

FINDING OUT ABOUT THE BREAKUP

That helps explain why, for many adult children of divorce, *learning the news* that their parents planned to separate or divorce is recalled with great intensity long after the actual telling took place. "How can you *ever* forget the moment when you discover that life as you have always known it will never be the same again?" I am asked by a woman of fifty-six. The question is rhetorical. "I have an absolutely total recollection (of both where I was and how I felt at the time) connected with hearing three announcements during my life: the news that President Kennedy had been shot; the first time that the man who became my husband told me that he loved me; and (when I was eight) my parents' carefully worded declaration that my father would be moving to a different address and that, yes, he and I still would be able to see one another—but thenceforth on alternate weekends."

Men and women speak feelingly about "the telling." In the interviews, I ask the same question of all: *When and how did you learn that your parents were going to separate or divorce?* Again, many of the answers fall into definable groupings.

WHEN CHILDREN ARE ILL INFORMED

In some families, especially back when divorce was less widespread than it is today, *no* statement was made to the children; no explanation of the changed family status was ever forthcoming. In others in which the parents also basically favored secrecy, divorce *was* mentioned, but it was treated in much the same manner as some parents use to skirt any open discussion about "the facts of life." Once the obligation of providing basic information had been discharged, the topic became taboo. The children understood that divorce was shameful and not to be discussed.

The adults who were those children look back and explain what happened and why they continued to be disturbed by the unknown well beyond childhood.

"My parents *never* gave me any information about their divorce," says Delia Sherman, sixty-two, who understands that at age two (when her mother left the family to study art in Paris) she was too young to have received much explanation. But what about later? "They never even used the word," she says. "In the day and age when they split up, divorce was a social embarrassment, never to be discussed unless necessary and *then* only in whispers."

The little girl lived with her father and was cared for by a succession of housekeepers. "I remember, when I was about four or five, being taken by my housekeeper to an Our Gang movie in which someone said something about being divorced. That moment was the first time when I realized that 'divorced' is what *I* was. I started crying, had to be taken from the movie house, and I didn't stop sobbing for hours."

Even after that episode, Delia could elicit no information from her father about why her parents split up. When Delia was in the third grade, her mother returned to America and began periodic visits with the little girl. But she, too, refused to shed light on the mystery. Delia now understands, she says, that her parents' ideas on life were incompatible. "My mother was a bohemian, a woman way ahead of her time who chose career over family," she explains. "My father was a businessman who wanted his wife to be a good hostess. The marriage *couldn't* work.

"It might have helped if somebody had taken the time as I was growing up (or even after) to explain that to me," says Delia. "Because they didn't, I went through a lot of pain and spent a lot of time in therapy trying to piece some of the story together. I still have lots of questions about what happened. Regrettably, the only two people who could answer them are no longer living."

WHEN CHILDREN ARE USED AS ACCOMPLICES

In sharp contrast to children's being forced to learn the facts of their parents' divorce through innuendo and intuition, a second oft-used tactic (also recalled as "distressing" by several of the interviewed men and women) was for one or the other parent to involve their children *too much* in what was going on, often leading the child to feel (as one man described it) "like an accomplice to the crime."

Where men and women who were offered too little information about the breakup of their parents' marriage speak of feeling frustrated by their unanswered questions, those who saw themselves as coconspirators talk of feeling "guilty."

"I knew about the divorce long before my father knew I knew," says Mandy Ruiz, twenty-six, whose parents separated when she was twelve. "For some time before the actual split, my mother had enlisted me as her confidante, telling me all about my dad's extramarital affairs. Then she told me that she was going to divorce my father—but I wasn't supposed to tell him what she was planning. So I lived with the knowledge even as my dad and I sat across the breakfast table from one another, and I said nothing.

"The day my parents sat my sister and me down for 'the telling' was simply the official notification for me. My mother had warned me earlier that I had to act surprised. Dad told us he would be leaving. The key thing, he said, was that in the long run it would be better for us all. My sister, three years younger than I, cried. I felt guilty because I had known what was going to happen and she didn't. I also felt guilty because, having known that divorce was contemplated, I did nothing to stop it."

"I remember the way I learned that there would be a divorce as if it were yesterday," I hear from Russ Delbello, fifty-one, looking back at the event that, in fact, took place thirty-nine years earlier. "My mother told us children [the speaker and his three sisters]. My mother told us a lot. My mother told us, I think, more than we needed to know.

"I remember the day when the actual separation took place," Delbello goes on. "It was early in the morning. My mom woke us. She had everything packed. She told us that we were going with her to our grandparents' home in another state. She said we were leaving for good. My sisters and I began to cry. None of us wanted it to happen. We left immediately. Dad came home that night and found us gone. I was twelve years old, the only son. I felt I should have stayed."

In fact, we learn from the adult children of divorce, one does not have to have been given foreknowledge of the separation to feel co-opted by one parent against the other. Deeds (*how* the separation took place) have the power to be as guilt-producing as words (the confidential disclosure to a child that parental separation is in the offing), as the following reminiscence by a forty-one-year-old woman makes clear.

"I was six years old, and I remember being picked up at school by our housekeeper and brought to the home of my maternal grandmother," she recounts. "A lot of our furniture was there. Our piano was there. The piano was a big thing to move. The piano was my mother's. That could have been a clue that something was going on, that this was more than a visit to my grandmother. My mother was there, but said nothing. We stayed the night.

"The following day, there was a phone call from my father. He sounded hysterical. He told me he had come home late the evening before and found the house empty, and that he'd been very frightened and upset. He had gone looking for us. He arranged to pick me up later that day. When we met, he told me that he and my mother wouldn't be living together anymore. *That's* how I found out that my parents were getting divorced. I remember being very upset that my father was so hurt, and I remember feeling guilty that I wasn't able to inform him. After all, I had seen the piano. I felt that someway, somehow, I was at fault. I should have warned him.

"It would have been better," says this woman, who explains that she has spent decades in mentally rewriting the past, "if both my mother and father had talked to me about what was going on in the family and why they had reached a decision to separate. It would have been better if they'd been able to reassure me that I would be taken care of and that both of them would remain in my life. It would have been better if I could have continued to stay in our house, and if nobody had to steal out of it. I don't imagine that my father's leaving us would ever have been easy, but the way things were handled I felt as if *I* had been the one to leave *him*. Almost anything would have been better, I think, than the way the separation was managed—to be more accurate, the way it was *mis*managed. That only added pain to what became a lifelong wound."

HOW *SHOULD* CHILDREN BE TOLD?

When and how *should* children be told that their parents are planning to divorce?

Listening to men and women recall the ways in which they learned of the end of their intact family, one begins to understand that, in fact, no time is a good time to receive such unwelcome news and there is no "good way" for parents to convey it. There is research suggesting that some times may be better than others, while professionals who work with divorcing families offer recommendations on ways for parents to orchestrate the telling (undeniably a difficult task for them) in order to lessen the pain for the children.

WHEN TO TELL THE CHILDREN

The research, however, is confusing and sometimes contradictory. There is evidence, for example, indicating that divorce is very hard on preschool-age children (ages three to five), who are likely to respond to their parents' separation with fears of abandonment, sadness, and self-blame. Other studies suggest that the worst time to divorce may be when children are between three and eight, when they have some understanding of what's going on but little power to effect the marital reconciliation they so strongly desire. And there are those who believe that nine to fifteen may be the most difficult stage for a youngster to experience the loyalty conflicts created by divorce. Still other studies find that teenagers may be *more* understanding of the reasons for the divorce and more involved, at this stage of their development, in getting on with their own lives than in dwelling on the problems between their parents. Nowadays, attention is also being focused on young people who are of college age when their parents divorce and the unsettling effect that the breakup has on them.

Thirty-nine years ago, when the twelve-year-old boy and his mother and sisters stole out of the family home, there were few (if any) guidelines. Today, there is a sizable literature on creative divorce, including advice on preparing the children.

In *The Parents Book About Divorce,* psychiatrist Richard A. Gardner speaks to the issue of the age at which a child should be told. "If the child is old enough to recognize the existence of a parent, he is old enough to be told—at whatever level of communication that may have to be utilized—that that parent will no longer be living in the home," he declares.

The *timing* of the announcement is another matter requiring some consideration. The message we receive from adult children of divorce is very clear: surprise announcements and unscheduled departures add unnecessary stress to a situation that is, in most cases, already far too painful. "There are some parents who tell the children at the last possible moment, ostensibly to shorten the children's agony as much as possible," says Richard Gardner. "My experience has been that in such cases it is more likely the parental agony that is of concern. Any advantages there may have been to 'getting it over with quickly' are more than counterbalanced by the disadvantages of [the children's] having been deprived of the opportunity to work out their reactions in advance."

HOW TO TELL THE CHILDREN

Who should do the telling? Psychologist Judith Wallerstein, whose ten-year study of fifty-two divorcing couples (including 131 children) has been reported in a landmark book, *Second Chances,* suggests that, "If possible, both parents should tell the children together. By representing unity, they convey the sense that a rational, mature decision has been made. If such unity is impossible, one parent should break the news."

Wallerstein speaks to the importance of the parents expressing sadness (and allowing the child to feel sad), of being clear that the marriage has ended (so that children understand that they cannot rescue or restore the marriage), of helping children understand what lies ahead. "Children also need to be told repeatedly that the divorce does not weaken the bond between parent and child, even though they will now live apart," she writes. "Geographic distance does not translate into emotional distance or less love." Then, in a line so often employed that it has achieved the status of cliché, she continues, "Parents may divorce each other but they do not divorce their children."

I confess myself guilty of the same platitude. In a book I wrote for children about living in a stepfamily, I sought to explain divorce, reassuring my young readers, "Your parents didn't divorce you!" Then I began to listen to how reality sounds to the children of divorce, and I understood that, no matter what words are used, the children of divorce *hear* "divorce" in its finality. Later experience may teach them that the family has not been destroyed, only altered.

It is important, therefore, for parents to look upon the telling as a process. Like information about sex, information about changes in the family structure should be provided according to the child's ability to understand it at the time. The child should also be assured that added explanations (not accusations) will be provided in response to further queries.

A therapist who works with many families of divorce explains, "The preparation-for-divorce books, the how-to-break-up-better books may give parents direction, but they may also give them a false sense of security. Many parents believe that if they follow the books' advice, if they sit down together and tell their children 'Your father and I no longer love each other, but we are not divorcing you,' they have done their duty, and that, therefore, divorce is not still a devastating experience for children. Well, it is. Children need to have permission to come back, to ask again, to try to make some sense of it all."

Chapter V

Divorced Childhoods:
From Good to Worse

I remember being in court. I must have been four
or five years old. I remember the judge asking me,
"Who do you love more, your mommy or your
daddy?" I couldn't answer. I burst into tears. Then
the judge asked, "Who do you want to live with?"

I remember being terrified, absolutely terrified,
and saying, "I want to live with Mommy and see
Daddy every day."

—Laura Bennett, age fifty-five

Children want normalcy. When their intact family cannot be
preserved, they want a family that comes as close to normal as
possible. As young Laura's response to the judge makes clear,
they want ongoing, dependable relationships with both parents.
They also want continuing association with relatives and friends
of the family on both their mother's and their father's sides. If
they are of school age, many prefer to remain in the same school
that they've been attending, to be permitted to maintain as much
of their routine as possible. Like all of us, children find reassurance in familiar surroundings.

Divorce introduces the unfamiliar into a child's world. How
well a boy or girl adapts to the changes wrought by divorce
depends, in large part, on how the parents manage to relate both

to one another and to the children they have in common, during the divorce and in the years that follow.

Studies of children's adjustment to marital breakup stress the importance of a healthy postdivorce environment—one where, among other factors, there is "high involvement by the noncustodial parent," "a low level of discord between the parents," and "cooperative parenting with consistency of discipline." It is good, in other words, for the two parents to remain involved in the child's life, to maintain at least workable relations with one another, and to cooperate in making decisions that affect their children. Many divorced parents will tell you that they have met these goals. Among the grown children, however, few express satisfaction with the way the divorce was managed. Seeing the event through their eyes provides one with a more realistic look at the way parental divorce plays itself out in the lives of its children.

A HEALTHY MODEL OF DIVORCE

An acquaintance tells me about Lisa Werner. "If you want to find out what a good divorce looks like, she's someone you really ought to meet," the young woman says. "Lisa's mother and father separated when she was very young, but neither has remarried and they've gone on to enjoy a great relationship. They're always together for anything having to do with the children—birthdays, graduations, and holidays. Everybody gets along. It's great!"

I do want to learn about successful divorce from the viewpoint of the adult child and so I make a phone call that brings me, one Tuesday afternoon, to a dorm room at a prestigious law school in New York. The young woman who opens the door for me is slim, about five feet four inches, fresh-faced, with hazel eyes and light brown hair that is caught back loosely in a large bow. A bartender probably would ask to see her identification card before serving her a beer. At twenty-four, Lisa stands at the threshold of professional and personal success. In her second year at the school, she also is engaged to be married (in less than six weeks from the time that we meet) to Caleb, whom she has known for five years and who recently graduated from the same school. Lisa credits much of her success to her parents. "Even though they were unable to stay married to one another," she explains, "there was never any question about their always being there for us children."

Lisa Werner's history offers a good illustration of what it is like to grow up in a healthy postdivorce environment. At the same time, it lends support to the theory that all marital breakups, even those that are well managed, have long-term consequences for the children involved. It gives us insights into how even a "good divorce" can be made better.

ON THE PLUS SIDE: RESPECTFUL AND CONTINUING RELATIONSHIPS

Lisa's mother and father separated when she was three and her sister four. The divorce became final a year later. "I remember my parents having a fight—I don't know what it was about, but it's the only fight I ever recall between them," she says. "The next thing I remember is my father sitting on the bed and telling my sister and me that he'd see us each Wednesday night and every weekend. I remember crying."

No ugly scenes preceded or followed the telling. No accusations were made by either parent against the other to justify the decision to separate; hence, no allegations needed to be countered and the two girls were never required to take sides. To this day, "incompatibility" is the only reason either parent will offer to explain the reason for the rift between them. Says Lisa, "My mom's explanation has always been that she discovered that my father was not the man for her." However, "from day one, she made it very clear that she would never remarry. That made me wonder, *Why? Was Dad so bad?* Yet neither parent *has* remarried. And they enjoy a cordial relationship."

What was good about the way the divorce was managed? After their parents separated, Lisa and her sister lived on in their home with their mother while their father took an apartment nearby. These proved to be wise decisions. Research indicates that children adjust more easily to the changed family situation when they live, day to day, with the same-sex parent: daughters with their mothers, sons with their fathers. Studies also have found that successful adjustment to parental divorce is more likely to come about when children experience a "low environmental change occasioned by the divorce." Lisa's experience with parental divorce underscores our assumption that children are better served by stability, when the changes in their lives following parental separation are kept to a minimum.

Lisa and her sister also benefited greatly from the regular presence in their lives of the noncustodial parent. True to the promise he made that night in their bedroom, Lisa's dad saw his daughters every Wednesday ("Never Tuesday or Thursday," Lisa notes) and each weekend until Lisa turned twelve and her sister thirteen, when visitation became more flexible in order to accommodate the teenagers' busier schedules. "Our parents established a structure that was continuous, to be there for us—and generally it worked," Lisa says.

ROOM FOR IMPROVEMENT: COMMUNICATION BETWEEN THE TWO HOMES

The problems that Lisa identifies in the carefully designed agreement reached by her mother and father seem to be endemic to families of divorce: parenting functions are divided but not equal. "Each parent took a share in raising us, but they assumed different roles," she explains. "Since we spent *every* weekend with our father, the fun things were only done with him, whereas our mom had to oversee our lives day to day. As a result, we came to see Dad as a savior and Mom as the disciplinarian. That often made things difficult between us and our mother."

Better communication among all family members might have helped. Says Lisa, "While my mother and father never made negative statements *about* one another (for which I am grateful), I didn't realize that they spoke *to* each other when we were young, so I thought that everything Dad knew about me came to him from my telling. Later, I found out that they spoke to each other regularly. I wish I had known that they communicated with one another about us. I would have felt that my father knew me as a whole person, not just as a weekend person. I would have been better able to picture him as part of my everyday life and turn to him for a different, more normal father-daughter involvement."

The traditional practice of awarding custody to one parent (usually the mother) and visitation rights to the other (typically the father) has been challenged, during the past decade, by advocates of joint custody who argue that both parents have equal rights to their children. Although joint custody has several variations, the practice generally assumes that children spend equal time with each parent. The matter of equity aside, joint custody assures that there will be greater involvement by both parents in the everyday lives of the children. It *requires* that ex-spouses communicate with one another, even if all they discuss are the logistics of managing the children's schedules: what time the parent-teacher conference is set for; when the dental checkup is due.

Whether joint custody is a way to do a better divorce, however, still cannot be determined. The practice has its advocates and its detractors. Because it is a relatively new innovation and is not widely practiced, it is not yet possible to make an assessment of whether it will, in the long run, be better for children of divorce than if they are raised in one primary home and have access to the household of the noncustodial parent.

DINNER-TABLE FANTASIES PREVAIL

Whatever living arrangement is decided upon (even in a highly supportive postdivorce environment such as Lisa Werner enjoyed), children of divorce grow up understanding that the lives they lead are different from that of the family next door. Therefore, they often create fantasies of that intact family, one in which there are a mother and father and children who do indeed live happily together, sharing their daily lives in an atmosphere of love and understanding. More often than not, the scene they hold in their mind's eye takes place with the family seated around a dinner table.

For many children of divorce, I came to understand, the tableau of a family at dinner stands as a metaphor for the intact family. Lisa, the daughter of parents who managed a good divorce, is no exception. The dinner table that she grew up envying was in the home of a girl who had been her best friend in third and fourth grades. "My friend had parents who were traditional," Lisa recalls. "Every Friday night, they had roast beef and invited me to share their meal and fellowship. I felt they pitied me . . . because I didn't have this real solid happy family where you all get together at dinnertime and talk about things that bother you. My friend would ask, 'Do you think your parents will get together again?' and I would say 'Yes,' even though I knew they wouldn't. I felt that she didn't understand, and I had to make the image right for her.

"*I* felt sorry for me, too," Lisa adds, "because I didn't experience the kind of family ritual my friend had on Friday nights, and also because there was no easy conversation around our dinner table—not in the home that my sister and I shared with our mother and not when we spent time at our father's place. I *now* understand that that may have been due to my parents' personalities and the reality that they couldn't relate to children, that our mealtimes would not have been gatherings for social exchange even if we had continued to live together as a family. Growing up, however, I attributed the situation, the silent mealtimes, to the fact that my parents were divorced, that we *weren't* a family. And that caused me pain."

THE LEGACY OF A GOOD DIVORCE
IS NOT WITHOUT PROBLEMS

The legacy of the good divorce has allowed Lisa to make the important personal commitment to marriage. As the wedding draws close, however, the bride-to-be finds herself experiencing feelings of foreboding along with anticipation.

She tells of a recurring dream. "I am dressed in my wedding gown and walking down the aisle. I am growing scared, sweaty. Everything is going black before my eyes. I faint. The ceremony cannot go on." She comes back to reality, looks directly at me, and continues: "I really *am* afraid that when I walk down the aisle and stand under the wedding canopy I will faint. So I guess there is a fear within me. It is the fear of entering a marriage that will not work out.

"Do you know what I *really* hope for when I look into my future?" Lisa laughs at herself, at the presumptuousness of what she is about to say. "I want it *all:* the dinner table . . . a house nestled safely in the woods . . . a structured family life . . . financial security . . . peace."

WHEN THE BREAKUP LEADS TO PEACE,
IT'S A "GOOD DIVORCE"

Steve Barton, a thirty-nine-year-old detective whose parents separated when he was eleven, tells of another kind of good divorce—one that began with his parents' separation. "My mother was so much happier after she and my father went their separate ways," he says. "She went back to school, earned a graduate degree in history, got a job teaching at a community college, and really loved her work. For years, she had been a tense and unfulfilled woman. I don't know if she could have followed her dream within the marriage, but I do know that, after the divorce, she was a pleasure to be around.

"My father's second marriage was to the kind of woman he'd always wanted—someone who liked to go camping with him and who was happy to devote herself to his welfare," Steve continues. "When I visited their house, I liked seeing my father so relaxed. Once my parents no longer lived together, they were able to become friends, and that felt so much better than the constant arguing that had marked their marriage. I was happy because, finally, the antagonism between my parents was over."

STRESSFUL CHANGES IN THE POSTDIVORCE ENVIRONMENT

While good divorces such as those described by Lisa Werner and Steve Barton are not rare, they nevertheless stand out as exceptions against the larger panorama of family disintegration. More often than not, the picture of the postdivorce environment that is drawn for us depicts stressful conditions following the breakup of the intact family. In this and the following chapters, attention is paid largely to the resultant troubling situations. In recalling the postdivorce environment in which they grew up, the men and women provide vivid illustrations of what factors make divorce harder on children and why. Attention must be paid to what they have to say.

THE IMPACT OF NEGATIVE STATEMENTS

The worst thing about the divorce is that my parents continued to say such evil things about one another, I hear over and again in the interviews. Others who learn of this project—those who have *not* lived through the divorce of their parents—tell me, "But isn't it better for incompatible couples to divorce than to bring up their children in a home marked by conflict." This statement (for they do not pose it as a question) presupposes that hostilities between husband and wife come to an end with the end of their marriage. Unfortunately, in many families the opposite is the case: turbulence *increases* following separation; conflict between the couple grows even sharper; negative statements multiply. And, as the comments that follow make apparent, the children are poorly served.

"Until the final days of their lives, my parents were *always* bad-mouthing one another," relates a forty-one-year-old woman who has lived with divorce since the age of six. "My father tried not to, but my mother would not let up.... And then there were the times they would turn to me accusingly and say, 'You're just like your father' or 'You're just like your mother.' I am, after all, a combination of my mother and my father. Yet I grew up with an awareness that my mother *hated* some part of my father, and my father *hated* some part of my mother. So, I wondered, how do they deal with the parts of me that they each have identified as the other's? What parts of me do they find repugnant?" (Is it any wonder that this woman grew up with a poor self-image?)

A twenty-nine-year-old man whose parents have been divorced for nineteen years expresses this regret: "I wish there had not been so many negative statements about my father when I was left in the custody of my mother. I wish my mother had allowed me to like my father without guilt."

The problem of parents' speaking ill of one another is exacerbated when children not only are eavesdroppers to the ongoing warfare between their mother and father but also are made to take sides. A thirty-one-year-old man talks about himself as a seven-year-old, the age he was when his parents were separated. "They expected me to be old enough to understand that they were telling the truth," he says, "and they told me things in a way that assumed I had to agree with them. My mother would say, 'Even though he's your father, can't you see him for the way he really is. . . .' And my father would tell me, 'Of course she's your mother, but you've got to see the truth about her.' If I didn't agree with either of them, I was naive. Worse yet, I was seen as a traitor."

The recollection finds its echo in the interview with a forty-seven-year-old landscape architect. "From the time I was five and my parents separated," this man says, "my father criticized my mother a lot, which I resented. It was very, very bad when he said bad things about my mother and her family. It put me in a position of seeming to be in alliance with him against her. And I didn't want to take sides."

For a better understanding of the value of parents' not bad-mouthing one another, listen now to the positive assessment provided by a sixty-four-year-old philosophy professor, a man of great presence, who credits his parents—in what he overall regards as a bad divorce—with having done *something* right. And that "something" is this: "The best thing my parents did was not to speak ill of one another. When my mother spoke to me of my father, she always made it clear that she had loved him once and that I had all of his good qualities and none of his bad. And she ascribed the problems that made her leave him to his difficult childhood, not to his essential nature. I'm grateful to her for that."

Ann Kliman of the Center for Preventive Psychiatry speaks of the need to keep children "safe in loving both parents." It is a lovely thought. More significantly, the children of divorce teach us, it is an important goal for parents who hope to minimize the harm that divorce can create for their children.

TOO GOOD TO BE TRUE

Some words of caution are appropriate here. While it is the sense of the adults interviewed that divorcing parents must be strongly encouraged to refrain from speaking ill of one another, several also make the point that there can be negative consequences for children if a parent carries this advice too far.

"My father never, ever, till the day he died said an unkind word about my mother," I am told by a woman in her sixties who was two years old when her mother forsook home and family. "That was not so good. Whenever I asked about my mother, I was presented with this wonderful person who (not incidentally) walked out on us. Clearly, if there was nothing wrong with her, there must have been something the matter with *us*. I grew up burdened by this terrible sense of guilt, wondering what did *I* do wrong! My mother was described to me as an enchantress. I wish I had been allowed to see her as a human being."

In his book *Divorcing*, matrimonial attorney Melvin Belli admonishes parents: "Don't ever vilify or criticize your spouse in front of the children. . . . Even though they may seem to side with you, they will resent someone talking negatively about their father or their mother." True. They will. But there is a great deal of difference between the general advice to divorced parents not to speak ill of one another and its sometimes exaggerated application: to say *no* evil. At the very least, the children of divorce teach us, when youngsters grow up hearing nothing but words of mutual admiration from their parents they are bound to ponder, as did one woman interviewed, "If my mother and father continued to like each other so much, why did they ever get divorced? And what did I do wrong to keep them from reconciling so that we could all be together as a family again?"

THE BURDEN OF MESSAGE BEARING

Message bearing is the second most frequently cited evil on the grievance lists kept by children of divorce. It's bad enough for parents to continue to express negative statements about one another, they say. It's even worse when a child is co-opted by a parent into delivering those messages from one home to another. "Message bearing has been the bane of my existence," says Mallory Coburn, twenty-six. She rolls her eyes in horror as she replays a childhood's worth of messages for me, deepening her voice to imitate her father, alternating it with a high soprano to represent her mother: "Tell your father his check didn't get here" . . . "Tell your mother she doesn't deserve any more money" . . . "Tell your father if he doesn't pay me I'm never going to let him see you kids again" . . . "Tell your mother I don't care." Mallory sighs. "Oh God," she says in her own voice, which now rises in anger at the memory. "To this day they do it, *to this very day*. I get so mad at them. How *dare* they. What am I," she asks me, asks herself, asks of the mother and father who are not physically present, "a telephone wire?"

Children who are used as message bearers are placed in the midst of the marital conflict. At the least, this is inappropriate. At the most, it can be quite harmful in serving to alienate the child (the bearer of unwelcome communication) from the parent who is on the receiving end. As I write this, I am thinking of a woman who, at age thirteen, was placed by her mother in the position of having to carry on all financial negotiations with her father. It was the teenager who made the phone calls and wrote the letters saying that braces were needed or, as was more often the case, that the check was either too late or too little. "I would say things like, 'Dad, you sent two hundred dollars. That's not enough,'" this woman recalls. "But there was one day when I wrote him, at Mother's instruction, 'All we have to eat is bologna and Kool-Aid.' We *were* poor, but I knew that wasn't true. We always managed.

After my father received that letter, I later learned, he started drinking seriously. He no longer wrote to me or took my calls. I loved my father. I hated not being with him. That letter made our separation final."

THE CONSEQUENCES OF PARENTIFICATION

Youngsters who bear messages, children who are given the task (either explicitly or implicitly) of negotiating for the needs of the family, are said to be "parentified"—forced to take on adult responsibilities by mothers and fathers who are so self-absorbed by what is happening to them that they are unable to execute their parental duties. What children need at the time of family dissolution is permission to remain children, even to regress for a while. They need nurturing and reassurance *from* their mothers and fathers. Instead, it is not unusual for children of divorce to find themselves having to *be* the reassurers, the comforters of wounded and hurting parents.

"Often, following divorce, children assume a greater role in important decision-making and assume greater responsibility for organizing and carrying out household tasks, including supervision of younger siblings," E. Mavis Hetherington of the University of Virginia has written. "While this pattern may result in more responsible, mature and independent children, the parent-child relationship often becomes inappropriately intense as parents turn to the children for companionship, emotional support, and nurturance after the dissolution of the marriage."

"I lost my father to the divorce and my mother to her grief" is how one woman describes the situation in which she found herself at the age of eleven. The oldest girl in the family, she took over many of the responsibilities involved in caring for three younger siblings. "Before long I started giving my mother advice about the kids, telling her what they should and should not be allowed to do," she says. "That didn't sit very well with my brother and sisters, and I ended up having nobody in my corner. There was no one *I* could turn to for help."

At the age of seventeen, the parentified child/woman escaped the family situation by marrying a forty-two-year-old widower with two children. In a real sense, she was repeating the cycle— gaining self-esteem in the only way she knew, by taking over a family in distress and devoting her efforts to making it run smoothly. It proved to be a short-term solution. Neither her husband nor her stepchildren were accepting of her no-nonsense manner and authoritarian style. Nor were they able to meet her emotional needs.

Children are also parentified when parents take them into their confidence, telling them things they should not know. Says Ann Kliman, "Making the child a confidante is wrong *unless* the problems in the marriage, the reasons for the breakup, are already within the knowledge of the child. (Yes, if the issue is something like alcoholism or abuse; no, if the reason was the sexual dysfunction of a parent.)"

Disclosure covers other issues. Health concerns, finances, a parent's dating experiences—sometimes it seems as if nothing is too personal for a parent to reveal to a child. "You are my oldest and best friend," one woman remembers her mother telling her repeatedly. She adds, "I was nine years old when I became the repository of all the family secrets." It is tempting for a left-behind parent to turn to a son or daughter for solace. The parent is lonely, the child accessible. While some youngsters accept this responsibility, even welcoming the opportunities for increased closeness with a parent, others resent being robbed of their childhood.

Aaron Carter is one of the resenters. "My mother told me all about my father and his infidelities," says Carter, who was made privy to this information even before his parents separated— when he was five years old—and for years thereafter. "Once she remarried, she developed the habit of telling me all about her dissatisfactions with the man who became her second husband.

Mind you, this was my stepfather she was talking about, someone I was supposed to respect. Over the years, my mother told me *too* much. It made me very uncomfortable. Finally, before my *thirtieth* birthday, I got up the courage to ask her to turn to her husband with her problems. I asked her to stop being married to me."

HARD MOVES: THE EFFECTS OF RELOCATION

"The worst thing about the divorce?" Jennie Fuller repeats the question she has just been asked, then answers it: "Without a doubt it was the move that took me away from my father and my friends."

Any comprehensive look at what it was like to grow up with a poorly managed divorce has to focus not only on parental *actions* (speaking ill of one another, having children deliver negative messages, assigning them roles inappropriate to their age and place in the family) but also on a change in *conditions* that made the breakup of the family even more difficult to take. As Lisa Werner's experience of a good divorce makes clear, in general boys and girls are better able to cope with changes that take place within the family if their external world—their home, their neighborhood—remains essentially unchanged. They have a harder time adjusting to the breakup of their parents' marriage when the upheaval in the home is attended by their being up-rooted from familiar surroundings.

The decision to move is seldom capricious. As has been pointed out (in chapter two), divorce changes the standard of living for the families involved. So it is not surprising that many adult children of divorce recall having had to move from a home to an apartment, from a white collar district to a working class neighborhood in the same community after their parents were separated. Even these local moves were unsettling, for they underscored the altered status of the family.

More distant transfers were likely to have more devastating effects on the children who made them. Certainly this proved to be the case for Jennie Fuller, who was thirteen and living with her parents, older brother, and younger sister in Boston, Massachusetts, when her mother informed the children that they were leaving for a two-week visit to kinfolk in Alabama.

In the tiny southern town where their relatives lived, the children learned the news that their parents had separated. Their father would remain in Boston, their mother said, while they would continue to live here with her and their grandparents.

"In the moment of telling," says Jennie, thirty-six, "I felt as if all my happiness had gone away. I had been really happy in Boston. We had a nice life there. We lived in a good neighborhood. We children went to a good Catholic school. I had a best friend, Callie, and the two of us were totally devoted to each other in that very special way of young girls.

"When our mother told my sister, brother, and me that she and my father were separated, we felt that she was the most terrible person. How *could* she make this decision."

Jennie's devastation is understandable. Everything, it seems, was working against her. We know, for example, that a change which places distance between children and their non-caretaking parent makes it next to impossible for them to maintain the regular interactions that aid children in coping with marital dissolution. Separating children from close friends at this time removes them from another important source of support. We also know that customs are likely to differ from one community to another (as was certainly true of the different worlds of Boston and Alabama!), requiring even greater adaptability of youngsters still struggling to accept the reality that they no longer belong to an intact family. *All* of these difficulties were involved in Jennie's story.

"I was my father's favorite child, which everyone acknowledges, and here I had been taken away from him," Jennie explains. "For the first year or so after the move to Alabama, Daddy and I wrote letters to each other and talked long distance. Each time I would speak to him I could just physically feel how much I missed him. I was the one who had the worst reaction of all the children because my dad and my best friend were my strength, and now both of them were gone. I felt completely isolated."

As our earlier look at divorce's legacy made clear, "isolation" comes up frequently in conversations with adult children of divorce when they speak of parental estrangement and its aftermath. With or without geographical separation, children are likely to experience some distancing from one parent while the custodial parent (typically but not exclusively the mother) is so drawn into her own grief or so involved by the need to meet the practical demands of her new status as single parent that she is not available to the child. Consequently, for a time the child is (or perceives herself to be) alone. Many draw further into themselves, as Jennie did.

In her case, the loneliness was exacerbated by the move from Boston to rural Alabama. "It was culture shock," she says. "I had come from a good education to a small school in a poor community where there were students who couldn't even read. My feeling was that I had been *banished* to Alabama."

Reacting to the changes, Jennie went into a depression. "All I did for the first few months after we left home was cry, listen to Beatles albums (it seemed as if their album *Help!* had been written for me), write to my friend Callie, and pour my heart out in my diary," she says. "I still have that diary. The entries I made will give you a good idea of the way I felt at the time. 'I'm a stupid person,' I wrote. 'I'm terrible.' 'I'm an idiot and nobody likes me.' 'I've done something terrible and God is punishing me.' I became superintrospective, wondering about such things as whether God exists. 'If he does exist,' I thought, 'how can he be so mean?' "

SOME LIGHT IN THE DARKNESS

The divorce experiences recalled by adult children are seldom all good or all bad. Just as the model of a good divorce included certain negative elements, so do the stories of stressful divorces contain a number of positive attributes. As an example: while Jennie Fuller lists her loneliness as a disturbing aftermath of the divorce, she also credits the years of solitude and introspection with leading her to develop a spiritual side to her nature—a quality that she values highly.

"You cannot live through so much misery and not come out in life without *something* positive to show for it," she says as an afterthought, adding a second postscript. "Another benefit of the time I spent alone was my growth as an intellectual. To fill the time, I read and thought *a lot.*

"While I don't recall having any interaction with my classmates or with other young people in the neighborhood," she goes on, "I do remember getting a lot of affirmation from my teachers. They liked me. I was a good student, I caused no trouble, and I worked hard. Most of the kids in that little school didn't go on to college. I got a full scholarship to one of the best universities in the nation, and worked several jobs all four years of college in order to make it through. But I did it—and with honors." Where home was an island of self-doubt, school was an institution in which one's worth could be measured, validated through good grades.

Yet another light in the darkness of her parents' divorce, says Jennie (adding that she was slow to perceive it), is a new-found ability to acknowledge with pride that, indeed, she *is* her mother's daughter. "For years I had regarded my mom as either a traitor or a quitter," she says. "If I didn't respect her, how could I value myself as her daughter? Then I grew up and began to see life in our intact family as it really was. My father was an alcoholic. My mother's leaving him was, in fact, an act of bravery and love. She had left home, as she put it, 'with three suitcases and three children,' taking us to live near her kinfolk where she was confident that we'd be accepted and cared for. She did the best for us. And though I did *my* best to deny it, there was love in that home.

"My mother was a strong woman," Jennie says. "I come of good stock."

Among the population of adult children of divorce there are some who will read Jennie's story with envy, with a wish that *they* could have had it so good. These people are the nomads, the children who were not even given the benefit of a stable *second* home, as Jennie was. I think here of Elly Edwards, the woman who came off the tennis court to speak with me, whose parents divorced when she was fifteen months old. "I lived all over the place," Elly tells me matter-of-factly. "I lived with relatives, *many* relatives. I lived with friends. I lived with a camp counselor. During the depression years a lot of people took in children for money. It wasn't considered bad. I lived in eleven foster homes that I can count. When I was twelve, I lived with my father in a hotel for a while, but he thought it was not a life for a child, living in a hotel, eating out. I lived with my mother for two to three years during her second marriage, but that didn't work out. Over the years, I moved around so much that I attended twenty-two grade schools."

Elly Edwards's story is a far cry from the model of a good divorce. Still, she is able to point to something positive in the largely negative account of her unsettled existence. "My father was the reason I survived," she says. "Although we were unable to make a home together, it was clear that he adored me. Wherever I lived, I knew that I always had him, and that I was loved."

The chapter that follows takes a closer look at what happens to children when, for a variety of reasons, they are denied the continuity of a physical or emotional relationship with one or both of their parents. For these sons and daughters of divorce—as we learn from their stories—the road to adulthood was worse than bumpy. It was often mined.

Chapter VI

Life Without Father: Parental Distancing

It must feel fantastic, I think, to have grown up with a father. When I see my friends' fathers walk them down the aisle, it kills me.

—Nancy Kovach, age twenty-six, who was five years old when divorce changed her family and her life

For a significant number of adult children of divorce (like Nancy), their parents' decision to separate marked more than the end of residing in an intact family. At the very least, separation led to altered relationships, especially with the noncustodial parent. That is to be expected. Since 90 percent of youngsters continue to live with their mothers after their parents have separated, most find themselves having decreased access to their fathers, with negative consequences for both. As was pointed out by Lisa Werner (in describing her parents' amicable divorce), it is difficult if not impossible to carry on a normal, everyday relationship with a parent one sees mainly during weekends and holidays.

What happens once parent and child live physically apart, studies indicate, is that they tend to move apart from one another emotionally as well. Among adult children of divorce who were interviewed, several look back at separations that had far more painful consequences than strained communication. For them, divorce marked the end (or the beginning of the end) of their relationship with a parent—who was typically (but not exclusively) the father.

PATERNAL ABSENCE: WHEN FATHERS FADE AWAY

This is the story that Nancy Kovach tells. Nancy remembers leaving home with her mother, sister, and brother. She remembers carefully carrying her hamster in his cage to the place where the family would now live: with her mother's parents. She remembers that her father remained behind, and she remembers thinking, *But we'll still be able to see him.*

Here's what else Nancy remembers: "I have a vivid picture of myself at age six. In it, I am in the living room of my grandparents' house. I am dressed to go out in a pink velvet hat and coat. Although I am warm, I refuse to give in to my grandmother's urging to take the coat off. Instead, I sit at the window, my face pressed to the glass for I don't know how long, waiting for my father. He never shows up.

"When I was in the sixth grade"—Nancy calls up another incident from her past—"out of the blue one day my father phoned and asked me what I would like for my upcoming birthday. I told him, 'A bunk bed.' It never arrived, and neither did he.

"As we children grew older," she continues, "we understood that our father had problems with a lot of things: alcohol, drugs, gambling, telling the truth. Still, it was hard when long periods would go by without receiving a visit, phone call, or even a postcard from him. From the time I was six until I turned seventeen, I may have heard from my father two or three times in all. It would have been nice if he'd dropped me a line once in a while just to say 'Hello' and 'Wish you were here.' It might have made a difference during those years to know that he still thought about me."

• • •

Frank F. Furstenberg, Jr., a sociologist at the University of Pennsylvania who has long been engaged in research on the relationships between parents and children following divorce and remarriage, has studied paternal distancing. In two projects—one a longitudinal study in Central Pennsylvania of nearly two hundred recently divorced individuals in transition from divorce to remarriage, and the other, from the National Survey of Children, involving a nationally representative sample of nearly twenty-two hundred children between the ages of seven and eleven and one of each child's parents—Furstenberg looked at (among other things) patterns of contact and co-parenting after marital disruption. His findings about father absence are disquieting.

In the Central Pennsylvania study, he reports in a paper on "Child Care After Divorce and Remarriage," within four years of the dissolution of their marriages a substantial number of parents stated that little or no contact took place between the nonresidential parent and child.

"Accounts varied somewhat according to the gender of the [reporting] parent and whether he or she had custody of the child," Furstenberg writes, "but less than one-fifth of the respondents indicated that contact [between the child and the noncustodial parent] occurred as often as a few times a week, most said they saw [the children] once or twice a month or occasionally during the year, and about one-fifth replied that contact was even less frequent. . . . A distinct decline in interaction took place within the two-year interval of study, indicating that parents tend to drift apart from their children not long after separation occurs."

A low level of contact between the noncustodial parent and the child is the most striking result to emerge from the second project, which employs data from the National Survey of Children. This study found that close to half (43.7%) of all children in the survey who were living with a biological parent had not seen the other parent during the preceding twelve months. Of those who did have contact with a parent living outside the home, only a minority (34.7%) saw him or her regularly—that is, an average of once a week or more throughout the year. Only a small portion of the sample (27.1%) talked to their parent on the phone as often as once a week, ever spent a week or more at a time in the home of their outside parent (26.6%), slept over at his or her house on at least a monthly basis (27.3%), had a place in the outside parent's home to store their things (27.3%), and considered that household to be like a home of their own (28.6%).

"In very general terms," writes Furstenberg, "close to half of the sample *rarely or never* have contact with their parents [emphasis mine], another third have contact irregularly or infrequently, and about one-fifth have what might be called regular relations."

EVEN *"REGULAR RELATIONS"* AREN'T ENOUGH

"The fascinating thing about this," Furstenberg tells me when we meet, "is that despite the fact that so many fathers drop out, one would really expect that in those cases where the fathers hang in there, see the kids, stay in their lives, there would be a noticeable difference in the outcome for those children [as several other studies have indicated]. But I'm not finding that. And I'm not sure why. It may be that the kids see what they're *not* getting rather than what they're getting—that is, they see their father once a week and it's a continual reminder that they're not living together.

"That's just one example of how complex any seemingly simple observation can be."

"Regular relations" are not simple. They take many forms. "We never knew where my father lived," I hear from a young woman who saw her father regularly following her parents' divorce. "Although he visited us once a week, we were never allowed to visit or phone him. Looking back, I believe that knowing where my father was would have made the separation a lot easier. It would have been like a security blanket... knowing where he was, knowing that we had access, knowing that we could contact him if we needed to."

In the examples I come upon, in the life stories recounted by men and women who have lived for decades with the aftermath of divorce, it is generally recognized and acknowledged that continued contact with the noncustodial parent had been important, albeit still inadequate to the needs and desires of the children.

That the separation need not be total to be troubling is evidenced in an interview with Sally Field which appeared in *Redbook* magazine. Asked about the effects of her parents' divorce when she was four and of her mother's subsequent remarriage, the actress replied, "When I think about my father and stepfather, something in me turns very immature—I turn into an eight-year-old girl looking for her dad. My relationship with my father is extremely complicated. I'd go to see him every weekend, and it was really tough. It's difficult to be the child in a divorce—you feel responsible. I felt responsible for making everybody happy —certainly my father. We never really *knew* each other, even though I visited him all the time and was around him a lot growing up.

"My father once heard me say all this on a Barbara Walters show, and he got extremely offended. I find it extraordinary that he was offended, because all I was saying was that it hurt me not to have been close to him—not to have been able to reveal myself to him—and that I was lonely."

In my meeting with Sheila Henderson, the art history professor, I hear the echo of two essential statements reported in the Field interview. Listen to what Sheila Henderson recalls. "The one smart thing my father did after my parents separated, when I was

---

thirteen, was to move near us and always keep in touch." (*Regular relations,* I jot down in the margin of my notebook.)

"After their separation," she goes on to reveal, "I never confided *anything* to my parents. My mother was a basket case. All she could talk about was how much she had sacrificed for my father and how she had been wronged. I saw my father frequently, but he didn't really know me. I felt that he didn't care to. During my adolescence, I had terrible problems with depression, drugs, and being sexually precocious, but I never told them what was happening to me. I felt so alone."

My father didn't really know me. . . . I felt so alone. In looking back at their childhoods, these two daughters of divorce make the point that events and emotions in one's life cannot be addressed by appointment, but require parental attention when and as they arise. Denied the opportunity for such timely sharing, children sense that they are alone.

FEELINGS OF LONELINESS ARE INTENSIFIED

This sense of loneliness is heightened for children of divorce who find themselves not only separated but cut off from a parent. In the following incident described by a thirty-seven-year-old woman, who was six years old when her parents separated, the feelings engendered by abandonment are poignantly recalled.

"I was living with my mother and had visitation with my father, whom I loved dearly," she says. "But that first summer after the separation I was not allowed to see my father—because of some legal maneuvering, I later found out. My mother was all caught up with lawyers and papers and whatnot. I understand now that she must have been overwhelmed, but what I believed then was that she didn't care. I hated my mother during that period. I hated my father, too, although I also loved him intensely. I refused to accept that he could allow anyone or anything to come between our seeing each other.

"I was in very bad shape that summer," the woman continues. "I remember having a lot of bad falls and accidents. I'm sure it was because I wanted someone to pay attention to me, to respond to *my* needs. When the accidents didn't do the trick, I withdrew to my inner world where I didn't need others, where no one could touch me."

Isolation is a defense for many of divorce's children. Loneliness is the result.

LOOKING BACK IN ANGER

Anger, a frequent response to many of the ills that children associate with divorce and its aftermath, looms especially large when paternal alienation is the issue. Asked to look back at his life as a child of divorce, a Boston-based, thirty-three-year-old editor tells me that he is *still* angry. He gives the cause of his anger as follows: "My dad's a very successful doctor, and he lives *very* well. On a grand scale, you might say. Soon after he divorced my mother, Dad remarried a southern belle and moved to Mississippi where her family lives. I have visited him there less than a dozen times in twice as many years. He has a big house, with white pillars, where he lives with his wife and their two daughters, my half sisters. They are very pretty girls whom I have always found it hard to relate to because they are so much younger than I. Dad drives the biggest cars and belongs to the best clubs. Yet he has never extended himself in my behalf.

"I did not ask much of my dad over the years, and I received even less," the editor goes on. "When I was fourteen, I remember, I asked him to pay for my braces, and he absolutely refused." There is anger in the editor's voice as he sees, in his mind's eye, his teenage self, a young boy with imperfect teeth whose needs were once again denied by his father. "Even more infuriating was the fact that my father would not contribute one red cent toward my college tuition and living expenses. Mom couldn't manage it on her own, so I waited tables and worked in the library all four years. I didn't mind the work, and I *finally* finished paying off my loans. What *did* hurt so much was that my dad was not there for me."

ECONOMIC ABANDONMENT TAKES ITS TOLL

In the interviews, the failure of fathers to meet their financial obligations is offered as further evidence of deteriorating relationships. For the children of divorce, it is another kind of abandonment. The oft-heard complaint that fathers decrease financial support of their children following divorce—or fail entirely to contribute to the children's upkeep—is supported by research. As previously noted, a study of divorced families conducted by sociologist Lenore Weitzman found that, one year following divorce, the standard of living of divorced women and their children declined by 73 percent while the standard of living of the fathers *rose* by an average of 42 percent.

Research also shows that most fathers not only are able to pay child support but can afford to contribute even *more* than the court has ordered. Yet less than half of all fathers comply fully with court orders for child support. And many (even those who are well-to-do) withdraw their financial support entirely once the children reach the age of eighteen—coincidentally, an age when their sons and daughters enter college and require even more help with their monetary needs.

"Children's taken-for-granted expectations about the future are often altered by [parental] divorce," writes Lenore Weitzman in her book, *The Divorce Revolution.* "For example, one mother reported that the most upsetting thing about the divorce was her son's loss of the college education he'd been promised. His father, who had always pressed him to follow in his footsteps at Dartmouth, told him that a private college was now out of the question: he would have to stay home and take advantage of the low tuition at the state college. While this father could still 'afford' to send his son to Dartmouth, his priorities had changed."

Money is something tangible. Listening to adult children of divorce complain about their fathers' withholding of money, it is easy to understand why they are angry. What is evident, too, is that the money issue is *also* a symbol of a different lack. Nancy Kovach's story (which we pick up again) makes this clear.

"The year I turned seventeen," Nancy remembers, "a lawyer's letter arrived saying that my father wanted to meet with my sister, brother, and me. I saw red. So now *he* wanted to see *us*. Okay, I told the lawyer, I'd grant my father's request—but only on condition that he pay for college. He owed me a lot more than that, I figured. The following day, a check for my first semester's tuition came in the mail. My sister and brother laid down different financial conditions, which he also met. The next week we got together at a restaurant. There were three others seated at the table with our father. He introduced them as his wife and five-year-old twin sons.

"From that day on, my father began to give us material things, but he still did not give of himself. That was fine with me, I told myself. During my sophomore year at college, I was hospitalized with pneumonia. My father knew about it, but didn't get in touch with me . . . and that did hurt."

The following year, Nancy's father suffered a heart attack. As soon as she heard the news, she flew to be with him in the hospital. "All along I had thought that I was only interested in reconciling with my father for the financial support," she says. "Seeing him that time, I understood that what I really wanted was his caring. I wanted a hug. I wanted a man who would ask me, 'How was your day?' *I wanted a father.*"

Some months later, Nancy's father died. "There is so much sorrowing to make up for," says the daughter. "I feel that I lost my father twice—once to the divorce and the second time to death." Regret has replaced anger in Nancy's life. "Had my father lived and *if* I ever marry," she says, "I don't think he would have been there for me. I don't believe he would ever have become the kind of father to proudly walk his daughter down the aisle."

DAUGHTERS' STRUGGLES WITH MEN AND RELATIONSHIPS

"If I ever marry..." At twenty-six, Nancy finds herself still struggling to build successful relationships with others: women as well as men. The problem of learning to trust that is often a consequence of having grown up divorced can be particularly troubling for women whose fathers did not maintain a vital presence in their lives.

"I think that what happens in terms of the later development of children of divorce," explains E. Mavis Hetherington, "is that there's a certain wariness about human relationships and, when it comes to marriage, about whether they're going to have a good relationship. One of the ways in which you learn to feel comfortable with members of the opposite sex is by being around a father who is nurturant, who is supportive. Then two things happen. One is that it is a comfortable learning situation, so you learn skills in relating to men. And the other is that you feel *secure* in relating to men because you have had a secure relationship with your father."

Girls who are separated from their fathers reach out for love, but often in ways that do not satisfy their need for secure and affirming relationships. Those raised in one-parent households, especially during their early adolescent and teenage years, are likely to be given more responsibility than either boys in divorced families or girls and boys raised in traditional families. As a result, they grow up faster.

One aspect of this early maturing is that, as a group, they tend to become sexually active earlier and go on to have many sexual partners. Alan Booth, professor of sociology at the University of

Nebraska at Lincoln, looked into the question of whether parental divorce affects the courtship behavior of students. Booth's chief finding: The children of divorce are much more likely to have experienced sexual relations and are much more sexually active than are students from intact families or those whose mother or father had died.

In part, I believe, this is because the children of divorce are more conscious of their "single" parents as being sexually active and are more sexually aware as a result. In part, too, they turn to sex for closeness and affirmation. In her book *Second Chances,* Judith Wallerstein reports, "Indeed, many of the youngsters in [our] study use sex to shut out anxiety and to ward off a sense of emptiness and depression, and they started early. Over a quarter of the girls became sexually active in junior high school and have continued the sexual activity ever since."

That seems also to have been true for several women whom I interviewed—an interesting finding considering that many of them grew to adulthood *before* the advent of the sexual revolution. A fair number reported having had sexual relations as early as age thirteen or fourteen. Often their first encounter was with someone who shared the pain of parental separation. "There was a boy in my school whose parents also were going through a divorce," says a woman who gave up her virginity at age thirteen to this boy who was two years older. "We both needed to feel close to someone. Later, there were others. I felt that I had no parents to guide me."

"For a long time I allowed myself to be used by men," I am told by a woman, thirty-nine, who adds that she has been in a happy marriage for the past eleven years. A strikingly beautiful woman, dark haired with dark, wide-set eyes and olive skin, she says, "From the time I was fourteen, a lot of men came on to me. I thought that if I became sexually close to them, they would love me. I had a tendency to allow too much intimacy because of my need of it and lack of it. I also didn't think I had a right to say no."

But this child of divorce said no in other ways. She explains, "I really felt as though my father had abandoned us when he moved out, leaving the children to the care of a mother who was upset and miserable, so I guess I believed that in any relationship with a man I would be abandoned in some way. I managed to make that happen by screwing up all my relationships. The way I looked at it then was, 'Here's one more person I am trying to get close to, and he is destroying me, in some way, emotionally.' It took a long time for me to realize what I was doing and to change it."

Nancy Kovach is just beginning to have that realization, just beginning to address the problems she has encountered with men and relationships. "My gut reaction to men is that I totally distrust them," she says. "That has not kept me from having sex. But that is all it is. When a man I'm involved with begins to show that he really cares, I make a joke of it. I never let myself get close to a guy both emotionally and physically at the same time."

Because she has been unable to establish a meaningful relationship with a man, Nancy explains, "there was a time when I questioned my sexuality. I even tried a lesbian relationship, but it was for all the wrong reasons. It was not biologic. I thought I would be safer. I have decided that I am more sexually responsive to men. I still don't know, however, whether I will ever be able to trust one enough to get married."

WHEN SONS ARE SEPARATED
FROM THEIR FATHERS

For a long time in history, it was the father who had absolute authority over children in the family. Mother-headed households were the exception, not the rule, until the shift from an agrarian to an industrial society. As fathers began to spend the greater part of the day away from their families, child-rearing came to be regarded almost exclusively as "woman's work." Since then, courts have recognized this function by routinely awarding custody of children, sons *and* daughters, to the female parent.

An interesting finding of research on divorce is that sons *do* stand a good chance of having their fathers stay in touch with them—better, at least, than daughters. (Research also indicates that parents are somewhat less likely to divorce when there's a son in the family.)

Why this occurs can only be guessed at. "I think that our culture still puts a high investment in sons," suggests psychologist E. Mavis Hetherington. "I also think that it's easier for a father to organize some sort of activity on visitation day that his son would enjoy because father and son share a lot of masculine interests. (Even if you look at nondivorced families, this is so," she adds.)

Unfortunately, being the male offspring is not insurance enough that father will remain in one's life following parental divorce. It is unfortunate because paternal abandonment takes an even heavier toll on divorce's sons than on its daughters.

"When boys are raised without a loving, available man in their lives," writes psychiatrist Neil Kalter in his insightful book, *Growing Up With Divorce,* "they are vulnerable to a host of problems including performing below their abilities in school, being inhibited in social and competitive situations with other boys, and/or having difficulties controlling aggressive impulses."

Boys who live with their custodial mother face other stresses as well. Kalter goes on, "They are in a position of having to accept their mother as the primary parent, responsible for assigning chores, setting appropriate behavioral limits, and disciplining. Boys often have problems accepting these controls from their mother, especially in adolescence. . . . The combination of having a less solid sense of his masculinity due to the absence of his father, and being in a position of having to submit to his mother's authority, can lead the adolescent boy to have to prove (to himself and his peers) that he is not a 'wimp' or 'sissy.' "

SOME REACT TO FATHER ABSENCE BY BECOMING "BAD KIDS"

Where adolescent daughters (as we have seen) are likely to seek sexual partners for comfort or to turn inward as a way of dealing with feelings of rejection, loss, and loneliness brought on by family dissolution, many sons react to divorce by disengaging themselves from the custodial household. For these boys, aggressiveness becomes an outlet: "the gang" takes the place of the family.

"The street was everything to me," says Tobias Goodman, sixty-two, conjuring up a time and place in what he now regards as having been another life. Goodman stands over six feet. He is an angular man, sharply featured, with high cheekbones that serve to draw attention to his hazel eyes. What is most noticeable about Tobias Goodman's eyes is not their color, however, but the intensity of their gaze. When they are directed at you, you are at once engaged. "I had friends in the street," says Tobias. "Day in and day out, I virtually lived in the street until it was time to sleep. I felt that there was no one waiting for me at home."

The home Goodman refers to was a semidetached, wood-frame single-family dwelling owned by his maternal grandparents in the Bronx, New York. From the age of six, when his parents separated for the third and final time, until adulthood, the boy lived here with his grandparents and, for several years, his mother. He did not see his father's family. As so often happens when a child loses contact with a parent, ties to the grandparents and other relatives of the noncustodial parent were not maintained.

"I don't think my mother ever spent a day alone with me," Tobias says. "My mother was into her own grief and running around with men in search of someone who would become her next husband. Her mother (my grandmother) was a pious woman who didn't believe in divorce. My grandmother had a great deal of love and charity for the whole world, but she had no love for me. She said I reminded her of my father. My grandfather was a decent man, but to all intents and purposes I was on my own.

"I terrorized other kids," says Tobias Goodman of the child he once was, "because I knew there was no one there to back me up. Other kids had fathers and big brothers to stand up for them. If I couldn't control the street, then who would defend me? I also wanted to be the center of attention, to be noticed, to be loved. And that continued until I went into the army at age eighteen."

People who found themselves dealing with the bully that Tobias had become were unaware of the heartbreaking disappointments experienced by the vulnerable young boy he worked so hard to conceal. In the childhood that Tobias Goodman recalls for me, that defenseless little boy reappears. And the man is able to shed tears that the child did not permit himself.

He brings forward a long-sequestered memory of an incident that has had a profound impact on his life. Haltingly, he re-creates the scene for me. "After the move to my grandparents' house, my father came to see me approximately once a year. When I was eight years old, plans were made for us to meet at a neighborhood cafeteria. I was so eager that, on the appointed day, I showed up about a half hour early. And for the next nine or ten hours I sat at a table in that cafeteria . . . waiting. Finally, someone reached me with the message that my mother had just received a telegram from my father saying that he could not make it.

"I locked up a lot of my emotions in that cafeteria that day," Tobias Goodman says. "For years afterward, I would never let myself get into a position where I could be so vulnerable. Whatever the situation, whoever I was dealing with, I made sure that *I* would be the one in control."

Fortunately, the youngster did not turn away from school. (Research shows higher rates of school dropouts among children of divorce, especially among girls who live with their fathers and, as

127

in Goodman's case, boys who live with their mothers. So it might not have been surprising *had* Tobias given up on school.) Like the streets, however, school provided another arena where the young boy could take command and where he felt himself validated. "The message I was sending out to the other students who had both a mother and father at home was 'Don't feel sorry for me. I'm better than you.' "

In high school, Tobias was a member of the honor society, editor of the school paper, captain of the basketball team. He also logged more hours in detention than anyone else in his class. In his senior year, his fellow students voted him Most Likely to Succeed. He says now that he would have preferred to have been voted Best-Liked Senior. ("I would rather have been liked than feared.") But in his first lifetime (before he risked marriage and fatherhood, before he became a successful lawyer, before therapy helped him deal with the effects of parental divorce and paternal disengagement), he would not have admitted that to anyone. He learned well how to keep his feelings guarded.

OTHERS RESPOND BY BECOMING "GOOD LITTLE BOYS"

There are many ways of covering up one's feelings. Where Tobias Goodman kept people at bay by becoming a bad kid, Adam Norris sought to secure his relationships with others by becoming "a good little boy." This is a common response among children who have experienced the departure of one parent and fear the loss of others who are significant to them.

Adam is a slightly built, wiry young man with blue eyes that capture your attention and a warm smile that holds it. From childhood, his way of handling the outside world has been to make himself ingratiating. "I developed an impish personality," says the twenty-nine-year-old television news director. "I needed love, so I endeared myself to others." One can well imagine Adam being elected Best-Liked Senior.

Like Tobias Goodman, however, Adam speaks of being guarded in relationships with others. His childhood, too, was not one to inspire a young boy to trust. Here is Adam looking back: "I was six years old and so many things were changing. My father moved out of the house and, at about the same time, I entered first grade and a new school. I lived in a community that didn't sanction divorce. Moment to moment, I never knew whether I would be zonked with something, so I had to be very guarded. When people asked me 'Where's your father?' I was afraid to even release the information that I didn't have one.... I remember as a child watching Alfred Hitchcock on TV and peeing in my bed almost every night. I was reacting externally to the horror that I was feeling internally.

"When I was seven years old, I remember a rare meeting with my father. He came bearing a lot of gifts, and I remember thinking at the time, *I don't want all this stuff. I just want to know you.*

"I also was being asked an important question at the time. My mother remarried about two years after the breakup of our family. The question put to me—to this seven-year-old!—was whether I was willing to give myself up for adoption. I disliked my stepfather. Yet I remember just *dying* to have a name that was the same as my family's. That is a strong recollection: practicing his surname, not wanting to be different.

"After I was adopted, the name of my father was banned from the house. I was sanctioned by my new name and I was sanctioned by the appearance of a family. In reality, the connection was only between my mother and me. Growing up, that's what I had—her dependency on me, my dependency on her."

For daughters, the establishment of a closer relationship with the mother in the restructured family is recognized as one of the better outcomes to emerge from the chaos of divorce. For the sons, however, such closeness with the mother (without the balance provided by an ongoing father/son relationship) can be detrimental to their masculine development. Several men spoke of feeling "incredible insecurity when it came to women" not just during adolescence, when some timidity would have been expected, but well into the years beyond. "I was brought up by a puritanical mother and grandmother," explains one. "I was not raised as a male to be the initiator."

The account given by Adam Norris goes even further. "I was never shown a healthy male-female relationship," he explains. "I was never shown the way a functioning marriage works. Because of the divorce, there had always been a resentment expressed against men in our house. Notwithstanding the fact that my mother soon remarried, she portrayed men in a very negative fashion, and she made me her confidant. To this day I relate better to women because they are more emotionally acute. My mother told me things, inappropriate things, about her relationship with her husband.

"I didn't like my stepfather, a high school basketball coach who was forever trying to shape me up, and I didn't see my father for eighteen years, so I have always had to forge my own identity. The most meaningful relationship I have had has been with another man.

"In a way," says Adam, "although being gay is incredibly burdensome, it also entails carving out a place for yourself where you never thought you would be. Being a child of divorce is almost the same thing. There are no role models on television. There are no niches. As a child of divorce, it's a matter of setting the stage as you go, and having to confront things as they come up. There is no role to lapse into. And the same thing is true about being gay. You really are creating your own reality. But I do like family, and I would like to have children. So I don't know what the future may bring."

WHY FATHERS FADE AWAY

A number of explanations to justify distancing are given by fathers who no longer make their home with their children.

Among them, *relocation* (either by the father or by the mother and children) is prominent. As we saw in the preceding chapter, · any move that places geographical distance between parent and child is a likely prelude to emotional distance between them as well.

In recalling the short-term effects of her parents' divorce on her life, Justine Marsh describes just such an altered relationship with her father. At the age of eight, Justine saw the width of a nation placed between herself and the handsome celebrity father whom she idolized. She replays the scene for me: "One morning, my mother, my nanny, and I left our home in Beverly Hills. We got into the family car, which was driven by our chauffeur, and began a trip that took us clear across the country to New York, where I learned that this was to be my new home. Father would continue to live in Beverly Hills. That was forty-seven years ago."

Shortly thereafter, the little girl found out that her father was in the process of acquiring a new wife, an "item" that made headlines in the Hollywood tabloids. Justine now understands why her mother picked up and moved so far away. "My father's new romance and his almost instant remarriage made all the papers and it was hard for Mother to continue living in that very insular community," she says.

But the child within her adds, "I still wish we could have remained nearby so that my dad and I would have seen each other regularly. As it was, summers were the only times when I got to be with my father, about whom I romanticized the year round. He was my Prince Charming while I was Cinderella—someone who longed for attention but was barely noticed."

Although Justine was not actually abandoned by her father, she felt that he was no longer truly there for her after the divorce, that his interests and allegiance had shifted to his stepchildren. They were the ones, after all, with whom he lived daily. Theirs were the dance recitals he attended, theirs the birthday parties he hosted.

Over time, conversation between Justine and her father became stilted: "We behaved like polite strangers." Letters from her father replaced actual visits. Sorry, he wrote to her, he was in the midst of a major project and could not tear himself away now. . . . Sorry, he was spending the summer on location in Europe. . . . What Justine understood from the letters was that more than a continent now lay between her father and herself. "The reason Father stayed away," she says with a knowledge gained in maturity, "is that we both had lost the habit of being father and daughter."

In other cases, *the extreme youth of the child* is a deterrent to a continuing relationship. When divorce takes place while the child is still an infant or toddler, well before a habitual parent-child relationship has been formed, it is often difficult for the noncustodial father to handle visitation. He finds it awkward to relate to a small child whom he gets to see only from time to time and who even may shy away from him as from a stranger. The visits are unsatisfying and so they become less frequent.

Guilt and depression are other forces that keep fathers from maintaining regular contact with their children. Often (and not unexpectedly), problem-burdened parents who have not been able to meet their responsibilities within the intact family are equally unable to meet their obligations to the children after the marriage has been disrupted. "I'm just no good," one man reports his father telling him when the two men ran into each other by chance after more than a decade of not having been in touch. "I thought that you'd be better off without me."

A hostile climate following the divorce is blamed by many fathers for diminished or discontinued contact between them and their children. It is not uncommon (although it is unwise) to allow children to be so drawn into the hostilities between their parents that they become partisan to the views of one (generally the parent with custody) and refuse to have anything to do with the other.

"My ex-wife poisoned the children against me" is a complaint made to me by a father who admits that he has neither seen nor spoken to his daughter, now seventeen, and son, sixteen, for the past six and a half years. "From the day of the separation, they have refused my phone calls, have not responded to my letters, won't have anything to do with me. I finally decided, if that's how my kids want it, that's the way it will be." He shrugs his shoulders. "I bowed out of their lives and I hope that they're satisfied."

I doubt that they are. When a father accepts a child's rejecting behavior as reason to give up on their relationship, he only affirms the negative account of himself that the youngster has been given over the years. If, instead, the father behaves as the adult that he is and stubbornly continues to pursue the relationship with his child (by sending postcards, remembering birthdays even when such communication remains unacknowledged), he leaves open the possibility of future interaction between them. There may come a time when the son or daughter (no longer a child) is prepared to hear the other side of the story and reestablish the relationship with the rejected parent. When a father takes himself totally out of the picture, the opportunity for reconciliation (for the healing of both their hurts) will be lost.

LIFE WITHOUT MOTHER

We have looked long and hard at separation from father because that is the situation which overwhelmingly predominates among children of divorce who lose contact with a parent. "Mother absence is such a statistical rarity," explains a leading researcher in the field of divorce and remarriage, "that it is difficult to do work in this area. It's hard to locate the subjects."

THE CHALLENGE: UNDERSTANDING WHAT IS "INCOMPREHENSIBLE"

I am therefore surprised when I review my notes and realize that more than a half dozen of the men and women whom I interview fit the category of Life Without Mother. What they have to say is *not* surprising. Their message is that separation from mother is as devastating as being estranged from one's father. Indeed, it can be even more traumatic than father absence, I hear from those who have lived with the experience, because of the child's feeling of being stigmatized by association. Along with the rest of society, children accept a basic assumption about mother love: that, *no matter what,* mothers are not supposed to leave their children. When mothers abandon the children or even when they simply relinquish custody to the fathers and continue to maintain contact as the visited parent, their children often find the women's actions difficult to understand and harder to explain.

"My mother was a domineering woman who divorced my father and then left me in order to pursue a career as a pianist," says a forty-three-year-old man who was raised, from the age of one, by his grandmother. "That was not usual for the time. Growing up, I remember telling people that my mother had suffered a break-down and was in a sanatorium. I considered it preferable to telling them that she had chosen to leave me. *That* would have been the greater disgrace."

"Everyone knows about maternal love . . . that a mother is sup-posed to be there for her children," says a woman who was two years old when her mother left home to resume the education that had been interrupted by marriage and motherhood. "I grew up thinking that if my mother had committed such an unnatural act I somehow had to have been at fault. What terrible crime could I have done before the age of two? I spent my childhood pondering how to atone for whatever it was, how to get my mother to come back."

· · ·

I did not expect, in the interviews, to come upon so many life stories in which mothers left their husbands and children to pursue careers. What was surprising was that these events took place forty, fifty, and sixty years ago when the phrase "women's liberation" was not part of our general vocabulary. "My mother was a woman ahead of her time," say the offspring of these women. They are being descriptive, not admiring.

Adult children of divorce who were not raised by their mothers often *do* express admiration—but it is saved for those of their fathers who remained constant throughout their childhood. Even where the actual care of the children was given over to grandparents, housekeepers, or, as in Elly Edwards's case, a series of foster families, father love was treasured. Because societal expectations are different for fathers, however, the father's devotion was never taken for granted.

Sons, nevertheless, seem to have an easier time with mother absence if they are brought up by their fathers (and not by substitute mothers such as grandmothers, aunts, or housekeepers). Some studies have shown boys in father-custody families to be more mature, social, and independent, to be less demanding, and to have higher self-esteem than daughters, while the reverse is true in mother-custody homes. However, research also indicates, sons brought up in father-custody homes are less communicative and less overtly affectionate than those raised by their mothers. This very likely has to do with the different ways in which men and women tend to express themselves.

Summarizing the results of the little research that exists in this area, E. Mavis Hetherington and Margaret Stanley Hagan write: "Custodial fathers themselves report more problems with daughters, particularly with the sex education of adolescent daughters, than do custodial mothers. It has been proposed that parents may find it easier to identify with same-sex children and that an opposite-sex child may remind the parent of the ex-spouse and thus become a target of displaced aggression or withdrawal of affection."

DADDY'S "GOOD LITTLE GIRL"

In this regard, daughters in particular report that they grew up feeling that they had to *earn* their father's approval. The phrase "good little girl" is mentioned frequently in their evocations of growing up in father-headed households, attesting to the child's perception that the connection to the father was tenuous. While this fear of desertion exists even when father is the visited parent, it becomes critical when father is the only parent actively involved in the child's life.

Delia Sherman was one such good little girl. Sixty years ago, just before Delia's second birthday, her mother walked out on her husband and young daughter and moved to Paris, where she planned to paint and study art. "My father was a businessman. He traveled a lot," says the sixty-two-year-old woman, who during her childhood was left for months on end with only a housekeeper for company. "My father adored me," Delia says. She also declares, "I made *sure* that I was all the things he wanted me to be."

She elaborates: "When my father was in town, he would bring people home and I would sit with them through long dinners. In a sense, I was his hostess. I didn't dare take the chance of not being good. For one thing, I knew that if I didn't behave I couldn't be at dinner with the grown-ups, and I desperately wanted to be with my father when he was available. If I was good, I could have more of his time and attention."

Mothers who relinquish custody are less likely than noncustodial fathers to completely terminate contact with their children. Rather, they tend to stay in touch, and often flit in and out of their children's lives, enchanting and often frustratingly elusive. In this manner, Delia's mother would periodically contact her daughter by letter and infrequent visits, although she remained abroad even when she learned that the little girl was very sick. (Listening to the men and women, I am struck by how often the subject of childhood ailments comes up. A 1990 University of California study confirms my suspicions. The study found that there *is* a greater incidence of illness among children in divorced households.)

A series of ear infections kept Delia out of school for a year. In the hope that the salutary climate might prove helpful, she was sent by her father to Florida, where she lived with a housekeeper. That same year, her father remarried. "My life started all over again," says Delia. "My stepmother made my father very happy. She did everything possible to be nice to me. I learned to be grateful to her. I never learned to love her."

Sometime during Delia's tenth year, her mother returned to live in New York. Delia's father insisted on having the little girl travel from the suburbs to visit her prodigal parent in the city. "Seeing my mother was a mixed bag," says Delia. "She was Mary Poppins. She was magical. She also was moody and insensitive. The worst of times for me was *any* time before I left to visit my mother and after I came back—and it had nothing to do with whether I'd had a good time or not. The visits underscored that I was a child of divorce in an age when divorce was *shameful.* Even more unnatural was the fact that the parent I visited and did not live with was my mother.

"When I was seventeen, my father died. He was only forty-five years old. Everyone was in shock. As for me . . . I'd fallen over the edge of the world. *Nothing* was safe anymore. I remember coming home from college to attend my father's funeral, and then traveling in to Pennsylvania Station where I was met by my mother. As she threw her arms around me, her first words were *'Now* you can come and live with me!' I remember *screaming.* It was the first time in my life that my mother wanted to do anything for me, and it was so misplaced.

"My mother lived to see my children and to be a decent grandmother to them. She was a fairy person, a charmer, and they loved her—as I knew they would. They didn't need her to be nurturant as I did. As I *do*—because, you see, I still feel damaged by her desertion. I am still a child in search of a loving mother."

WHY MOTHERS LEAVE THEIR CHILDREN

In recent years, some attention has been focused on the motives of mothers who relinquish custody of their children. Society's view traditionally has been that women who would do such a thing are either unfit or unloving—that their children have either been taken from them or abandoned by them. In too many cases nowadays, unfortunately, the problem of unfitness holds true. Alcohol and drug abuse make it impossible for many parents—both female and male—to adequately care for their children. However, these dysfunctional adults generally do not voluntarily walk away from their children. More likely, they lose access to them by default.

In other cases, the decision to relinquish custody results from the mother's acknowledgment that the children may be better off with the other parent—either because of their sex ("I felt it was better for a boy to be with his father," says a woman who made the decision to become the visited parent) or because of their strained economic conditions. As was previously noted, women as a rule are economically disadvantaged by divorce, which often requires them to move to smaller quarters in less favorable neighborhoods. Moreover, many who were stay-at-home mothers in the intact family now are obliged to enter the work force, leaving little time or energy for child care. A mother who found herself in this position tells me, "My ex-husband had a house and a new wife. I reluctantly came to the decision that our children would have better opportunities if they lived with him."

Sometimes, the children reach this determination themselves. In his book *Single Fathers,* social worker Geoffrey Greif addresses this issue. "Although a tug-of-war is not uncommon," he writes, "in many situations the father and mother, when they separate, let the children decide whom they want to live with. When the father has custody, this can often be a Hobson's choice: It appears to be a choice, but there is only one real option. For many of the children interviewed [in this study of twenty-one youngsters who live with their fathers], one choice was to stay in their own home with their father, maintain their friendships in the neighborhood, and stay at their school. The other was to move with their mother, who is often unemployed or earning much less money, to much worse surroundings and a strange neighborhood.

"In one family with two girls and two boys, the children were offered this type of choice. The oldest in the family is Tracy, who is now nineteen. She describes how she saw their options: 'We could have gone with our mother, but the place she was going wasn't very nice. She was going on welfare and the place had rats. She did not know if she was going to have a job or not. Here, we knew we could stay with our friends and have better stuff.' "

The mother's preoccupation with a new relationship may also serve to weaken the ties to her children. Greif describes another family in his study. In this situation, two daughters were given a choice of whom they wanted to live with, and then one of the choices was withdrawn. The younger daughter, age sixteen, decided she wanted to go live with her mother, who was pleased to have her. Before she could do so, however, her mother became involved in a new relationship that prohibited the move. As is true for some absentee fathers, this mother's allegiance had shifted to a new relationship.

Career involvement is a reason that is increasingly being given by mothers who agree to have the fathers serve as primary caretakers of the children. Among women who struggle to meet the dual demands of career and child care, a number of mothers find themselves unable to do right by either and conclude that they must make a choice. In their book *Who Will Take the Children?*, authors Susan Meyers and Joan Lakin (both noncustodial mothers) speak to this issue. "The matter of work was at the heart of many women's decisions [to become the noncustodial parent]," they write. "Some [of the women interviewed] were just on the brink of careers and felt they needed the time and space to get established without the twin burdens of financial pressure and full-time parental responsibility. Others were continuing time-and-energy-demanding careers that existed during their marriages. Some were in school, preparing themselves for careers to come."

The authors argue that time-honored custody decisions (which are largely weighted toward placement of children with the mother) need to be reevaluated in the light of present-day reality and understanding. The reality is the fact that, in many families, both men and women hold down jobs. The understanding has to do with recognizing that many men are capable of nurture, that some, in fact, make better "mothers" than their ex-wives.

In explaining how she and her ex-husband arrived at their own solution to the custody question, Susan Meyers shares with the reader two thought-provoking questions which were raised by child psychiatrists whom the couple visited to help them decide the issue. The psychiatrists, she says, "agreed that the important criteria in choosing the full-time parent was not sex but personality and desire: Who really wants the job and will be competent and committed? Who will really enjoy it most?"

These are good questions. Regardless of the custody decisions that are reached by couples or by the courts, however, a third consideration needs to be paramount in the plans of divorcing parents: what arrangements have been made to ensure that both of them remain accessible to the children and regularly involved with them? Once husband and wife conclude that divorce is necessary, then the determination to maintain a continuing presence in the lives of their children must follow. That lesson is strongly etched on our consciousness by adults who experienced parental distancing during childhood and beyond.

As the reminiscences highlighted in the following chapter illustrate, parental involvement alone does not guarantee a smooth adjustment to divorce. In many ways, having both parents in their lives creates new and difficult challenges for the children. But challenges can be met and conquered. Estrangement, as we've seen, presents children with a more difficult trial.

Chapter VII

Mom's House, Dad's Place: Sustaining Relationships Isn't Easy

From a very early age, I was expected to make the round trip from my mother's home to my father's house and back by myself. So there I was, this little girl with a big suitcase. People weren't used to that at the time. I would get in the cab and the driver would say, "Where are you going?" I'd say, "I'm going to see my father." Then the driver would say, "Oh. Where's your mother?" When I'd tell the driver that my parents were divorced, the next question would be, "Are you going to try to get them back together?" The cab drivers would always ask me that. And I would say, "No. It's better this way." And it probably was—for my parents.

—Amy Greene, age forty-one

After the intact family comes to an end, most children of divorce who maintain contact with both parents enter into what psychiatrist Clifford J. Sager has referred to as "a dual single-parent period." Instead of one home, two domiciles must be considered. Instead of one unit, mother-and-father, each residence is now headed by a single parent.

By and large, children do not want this arrangement. When families are still in the dual-single-parent period, before either parent has made the commitment to a new marital partner, the children's hopes for a reunited family remain alive. (Sometimes they continue to exist even *after* a parent has remarried.)

BETWEEN TWO WORLDS

"Are you going to try to get your parents back together?" The question posed by the cab driver went to the core of Amy's being. The little girl was not about to admit her true feelings to the cab driver or to anyone else who raised the matter of a possible reconciliation between her mother and her father. She was (the grown-up Amy tells me) afraid to put her deepest desires into words—as if giving life to the wish would put the hex on its coming true.

Did she hope they would be reunited? Says Amy, "Did I yearn for anything else!" She smiles as she recalls, "Growing up, I was constantly making silent bargains with God. *If I finish all my brussels sprouts, God, please let my daddy come home and live with us again. . . . If I practice the piano for a full hour, let Mommy be happy and be nice to Daddy when he calls. And then they can be together again.* But it didn't happen."

Studies affirm that the reconciliation wish is common to children throughout the elementary school years and into adolescence. Like Amy, some youngsters fantasize that parental reunion will be their reward for good behavior. Others tell me of childhoods that were plagued by colds, stomachaches, migraines, asthma attacks—every sort of medical problem that might have required both parents to consult with one another and to realize how much they were needed *together.*

One son who was eleven years old when his parents separated recalls keeping information from his mother about women who were at his father's home when he visited there. "If Mom knew there were other women, you see, there'd be no chance of her getting back together with Dad." At thirty-one he understands,

"Of course my mother knew all along that there were other women. That's what led her to leave Dad in the first place. But I refused to see the reality behind their separation, because then I would have had to accept its permanence. And that is something that I could not do."

Although dividing one's life between two households is preferable to residing in one and being denied entry to the other, children who find themselves straddling the two worlds of mother's house and father's house discover that this situation also presents them with certain specific and fairly typical problems. In finding their balance between the two homes, children of divorce often need to make many adjustments.

VISITATION

Nothing else so underscores the between-two-worlds aspect of growing up divorced as visitation. Children are not supposed to visit their parents. They're supposed to *live* with them. Visitation formalizes a relationship that is meant to be taken for granted.

Fitzhugh Dodson, author of *How to Discipline—With Love,* has referred to the children who travel between households as "shuttle kids." It is an apt description. Back and forth the youngsters go from one parent to another, from one setting to another, from one lifestyle to another, from one set of expectations to another, from one list of rules to another.

Even when the heads of both houses get along, their children are likely to experience visitation as a mixed bag of pleasure and pain. One woman explains her conflicting feelings: "Every two weeks, I would visit my father for the weekend. Between visits, I couldn't wait for the time to go by before I would see him again. It was something like a romance, like the anticipation you feel before a date with a special suitor. Still, the closer I came to leaving for my father's place, the guiltier I began to feel for 'deserting' my mother. *I* was going off to have a good time. *She* was going to be left alone. Later, when the visit drew to a close, I would feel sadness and guilt again—this time because I was de-serting my father, who seemed so lonely...."

Another child of divorce, a man, recalls the visitation paradox in this manner: "If I was making one parent happy by being with him, I was making the other miserable because I knew she didn't want me to be with him. That awareness clouded the visits. That ... and the knowledge that the time my father and I had together was temporary and would be over all too soon."

WHEN THE BAGGAGE IS LOADED ... AND TICKING

Visitation is made more difficult still when parents fail to re-solve their conflicts and continue their contest through the chil-dren, the link between the two homes. A fifty-two-year-old businessman describes the scene that would take place in his custodial home whenever he and his brother were about to spend their allotted time with their father: "Before we left, our mother would get angry and bitter and cry. When we returned, she'd be suspicious."

Far too frequently, shuttle kids carry more than a suitcase with them on their visits. They carry messages.

"Tell your father that I don't have enough money for your piano lessons."

"Tell your mother that if she'd bother to learn how to budget, she would have enough from what I give her to pay the piano teacher and then some."

"Tell your father that he is not to take you out for fast food. The last time you came back from a visit, you were sick for days."

"Tell your mother . . ."

On and on it goes.

Amy Greene recalls, "The bad times were when my mother sent along messages. 'Would you tell your father to send the goddam money!' That sort of thing. And so I'd be forced to begin the visit with my father on a negative note."

The messages can be far more subtle. For example: "Our

mother *always* sent us to our father's home in torn jeans," recalls a woman who spent her childhood traveling between two homes. "We were to be a living advertisement for the fact that the support our father sent was inadequate to our needs."

As was pointed out in the studies, mothers and children often *are* impoverished by divorce. But the message of neediness that children carry along with them on visits is not necessarily confined to families where there is actual financial need. In *Haywire,* for example, the story of her growing-up years, Brooke Hayward (daughter of actress Margaret Sullavan and producer Leland Hayward) describes a typical visit, with her sister, to their father's home, recording her father's reaction: "I wish to hell [your mother would] buy you some decent clothes. Whenever you come to see me, you're all wearing the worst-looking rags. I'm sure she sends you off like that deliberately. She knows I'll have to outfit you from top to bottom before I can set foot on the street with you."

"That was true," Brooke Hayward writes. "We always came back from our infrequent visits together with a new wardrobe. . . ."

IN EACH HOME, DIFFERENT ROLES AND RULES

"I had a *different* wardrobe in each of my parents' homes," I hear from a woman who has been describing her shuttle experience, explaining what it was like for her to have to adapt to the two worlds of her parents. And what different worlds they were!

"I led a totally schizophrenic life," this woman says. "For starters, I had a different name in each home. I was Becky with my mom, Rebecca Jane at my father's home. I also had a different look. As soon as I got to my father's house, I had to take off the clothes I was wearing and put on the clothes that were kept there and were only to be worn there. I owned a pearl necklace, for example, that could *only* be worn at my father's house."

She continues, "I was a good little girl in both houses, not willing to risk the loss of either parent, but since being 'good' meant different things to my father and mother I had to change from one kind of person to another in order to gain their approval. For my father, the doctor, I became the budding scientist. Between the ages of nine and thirteen, I would see him every Sunday. We would start the day by going to his office where I would be taught to run blood and urine analysis—from age *nine*. Then I was given a twenty-question quiz on the material he'd taught me, and if I didn't get a 90 he'd be furious. I made sure to get 100 so that my father would be proud of me.

"My mother cared about being pretty and articulate. For her I had to be feminine and well spoken. When I displeased my mother, she would call me my father's child. When my father was unhappy with me, he would call me my mother's child. I put all my energy into being what each of them wanted. Both parents loved to show me off—but only if I did exactly as they wished."

The schizophrenia does not stop with one's parents, we learn from the children of divorce, but often carries over into contact with the extended family. "At age fifteen"—Amy Greene again provides us with an example—"I was about to return from a summer at camp when I received a message that my mother was ill and unable to pick me up and that my bus would be met by my grandmother. I naturally assumed that it would be my mother's mother. Luckily, I spotted my grandmother at the bus terminal before she saw me. It was my *father's* mother, a much stricter person. Off came the lipstick in a hurry. Next, I groped in my purse for a ribbon with which to tie my hair back.

"There was this horrible feeling that I had almost been caught doing something terrible. There was also the realization of how much I would internally change myself depending on *who* I was going to be with. I had become discombobulated when the other grandmother showed up because the person who got off the bus from camp was the wrong person for her, *the wrong me.*"

WHEN PARENTS ARE HOSTILE
TO EACH OTHER

Visitation is but one challenge for the child of divorce who continues to see, and have feelings of allegiance toward, both parents. Perhaps even more difficult for a child to achieve is maintaining good relationships with both mother and father when those relationships are constantly being sabotaged by parents who, although living apart, continue to have hostile feelings toward one another. Although there are men and women who can look back appreciatively at postdivorce cooperation between their parents (one has but to recall Lisa Werner, the child of a "good divorce"), the postseparation situation that is more frequently evoked by adult children of divorce is one of growing up in two worlds that were in constant danger of colliding.

Arthur Waterman, forty-seven, whose parents separated when he was five, describes what that was like for him. "Following the divorce, my mother and father refused even to *see* each other," he recalls. "If they had to talk, they would do so only over the phone—never in person. And they could not say a civil word to one another. There was *nothing,* big or small, that they would agree upon. If my father said black, my mother said white—no matter *what* the issue. That's how bad it was."

PLAYING ONE PARENT OFF AGAINST THE OTHER

Children of divorce learn how to use this situation to their advantage. Laughing as he looks back, Waterman admits, "I frequently played one parent off against the other. If either of them asked me to do something I didn't want to do or set down a rule I didn't like, I'd get a different decision from the other parent and choose the course of action I wanted.

"There was only one time when this backfired on me, and

that's probably the reason I remember the incident so clearly," he continues. "It happened when I was in the fifth grade. I had been having trouble reading. My mother took me to an ophthalmologist who said I needed eyeglasses. I didn't want to wear glasses, so I told my father that my mother wanted me to have them, fully expecting him to say that the idea was nonsense.

"Instead, my father asked, 'Did she take you to a doctor?'

" 'Yes.'

" 'And what did the doctor say?'

" 'He said that I need glasses.'

" 'Then you'll get glasses,' my father said, ending all discussion on the matter. I remember being crushed because my father had disappointed me. He hadn't behaved true to form."

Waterman's recollections include being the repository of his parents' bitterness, of having in a sense to "own" the terrible things they continued to say about one another. Yet in reply to my question about what his parents did that was good, he responds without hesitation, "They both remained in my life. My father was a volatile person—extremely impatient, yet also warm and loving. All in all, it was good that he lived nearby. I'm glad that I had contact with both parents."

SPECIAL OCCASIONS, SPECIAL TENSIONS

Sustaining relationships with both parents, however, requires children to manage a number of family situations with a certain amount of diplomacy. Certain matters that are routinely handled in the intact family take on a different significance when parents no longer live together. Matters like: Which parent will show up for Open School Night? Which one will sign the report card? Will both parents get to see it?

But it is the special occasion that is likely to cause special anxiety, if only because of heightened expectations around a birthday, graduation, or holiday gathering. Where children in intact families look forward to family celebrations hopefully, their friends in divorced families face them apprehensively. The family is getting together—*together?* At Mom's place or Dad's? Who will attend? Which relatives might feel slighted? If a formal ceremony is connected with the event, who will be asked to participate? If seating must be prearranged, where will the different parties be situated? So much *can* go wrong—and it often does.

"After the divorce, I received two presents for my birthday, one from each of my parents, whereas when we all lived together I got one gift from the two of them," recalls a forty-four-year-old man, citing one of the small consolations of living in two worlds. "But I also had to attend two Thanksgiving dinners every year. I'd eat with my mother's family and then rush off to have dinner with my father's family because I didn't dare risk offending anybody. And I don't even *like* turkey."

Even during times when parents manage to set aside their differences and come together "for the sake of the children," tension fills the air. "The worst of times, oddly enough, were when my parents got together for my birthday," says a thirty-two-year-old woman. "Birthday parties were a disaster. I was miserable. I was so stressed. I hated my mother and father being together. Consequently, I hated all sorts of events that were passages: birthdays and, later on, graduations and my wedding."

When children live between two worlds and maintain contact with two or more households (possibly including extended kinship relationships and the family*like* connections that frequently follow a parent's remarriage), communication between the parents becomes all the more important. Planning and coordination around special situations are essential if one is to avoid incidents like the following.

It was the evening of the school play, *Grease,* and Dorene, seventeen, had a starring role. Seated in the rear of the auditorium were Dorene's mother and an escort. Well before the performance, Dorene's mother announced her intention to leave the auditorium immediately after the closing number. "I don't want my date looked over by your father and his wife," she told her daughter.

Dorene understood. "It's okay," she said. "I'll go out with Dad afterward and have him drive me home."

Peeking from behind the curtain on opening night, Dorene spotted not just her father and his wife but her half brother, their three-year-old son, in one of the front rows. *Why couldn't they have left him home—this is* my *night,* she remembers thinking.

She was right to have been concerned. Up past his bedtime, the little boy grew tired and disruptive and had to be hustled out of the assembly hall by his parents. As Dorene was to find out later, they had not just removed him from the auditorium but they'd left the school grounds and had taken him home. Dorene's father simply had assumed that his ex-wife would be available to their daughter.

After the final curtain came down (Dorene took three curtain calls), the other cast members went off to celebrate with their admiring families. Dorene stood alone. "Luckily," she relates, "the drama teacher saw me and offered to take me home."

When Dorene told me of this incident, I thought it a singular experience and included it in a magazine article I was then preparing on divorce and remarriage. The episode was faithfully reported in the published piece, except that Dorene's name and the play's title were changed at the young girl's request because, she explained, she didn't wish to hurt or embarrass her parents.

I had not yet experienced the echoes of divorce's aftermath, and was therefore taken aback when I received an irate letter from another family of divorce, a family that lived clear across the country from Dorene. How had I learned of their experience, they wanted to know. Furthermore, *what right had I to bare* their *story in public!*

The tale Dorene told, while not a unique experience (as it turned out), nevertheless illustrates a particular consequence of living with separated parents. With the increase in the number of two-career couples, even parents in nondivorced families find themselves challenged to meet the many demands of their children's schedules. In divorced families, however, where more than one household must be considered, plans are harder to coordinate and mishaps more likely to occur.

If, further, the former spouses become warring factions, letting emotion guide their behavior, their children will not be well served. Mallory Coburn shares an experience that poignantly illustrates this.

"My most vivid memory of growing up divorced, and one of my worst, has to do with my sixteenth birthday," she says. "Both of my parents wanted to give me a Sweet Sixteen party, but they would *not* do it together. They started to argue about it. It became very bitter. The next thing I knew, their lawyers were involved. They each got injunctions to keep the other from hosting the party. Came the evening of my birthday, and there I was . . . sitting on the bathroom floor, alone, with a bottle of Southern Comfort. I felt myself an orphan with living parents."

Unfortunately, dissension does not end and its effects do not diminish once the minor child comes of age. A father learns of his daughter's engagement in the society pages of a local newspaper. Seeking to end years of estrangement, he phones his daughter with congratulations. "I'd like to have lunch with you and your young man," he says. "Perhaps I can do something for him."

The daughter wavers. She would like to know her father. When her mother is told about the phone call, she says to her daughter, "You can see your father if you wish, only *know* that it will kill me." The daughter is twenty-six years old and still feeling manipulated by her parents' divorce. Much against her wishes, the bride tells her father that she will not meet with him. She is fifty-five when she tells me about this incident. Her father died, she says, without their ever having set eyes on one another again. "It is something," she says softly, "that I deeply regret."

BUYING PEACE AT A COST

Arthur Waterman, on the other hand, provides us with an example of how one *can* keep two warring parents in one's life, although at some personal cost. He describes an experience—this one also revolving around a wedding—that led him to make some important decisions. "Let me tell you about my wedding," he says, going back twenty-one years. "My father announced that he could not be at a big party with my mother present and have her friends and family staring at him and his new wife—also, that he would not leave his wife at home. My mother informed me that she could not be in the same room with my father and 'that other woman.' So here's what we did. The wedding ceremony was in the rabbi's apartment, with only my mother and father and my wife Francine's parents present. Then there were separate receptions, one *week* after the other, just so that my parents would not have to be embarrassed. I was pretty upset about that."

Waterman vowed never again to be placed in such an uncomfortable position by his parents. And it has not happened again. But his personal peace has not been achieved without some discomfort surrounding the terms. In the decisions he has made, in the way he and Francine manage the special occasions of their life together, this child of divorce is still visibly straddling the worlds of mother and father while declaring his separateness.

The effort to distinguish one's own needs from the wishes and needs of a parent is not confined to men and women who grow up as children of divorce. It is experienced at some point by all of us as we assume the task of separating from the two most powerful figures in our lives and differentiating our wants and needs from theirs. The challenge is greater in cases of divorce, however, when the "children" understand that any decision they make about leading their own lives will be viewed by the parents in their two worlds not only as personal but as partisan.

"Because my parents couldn't get along, instead of letting myself continue to be torn between them, as an adult I became more independent of both," Arthur Waterman says. "The Thanksgiving before our marriage, unwilling to participate in the ongoing contest for my loyalty, I had dinner with Francine in a restaurant. Just the two of us. To protect ourselves thereafter, we established a pattern of never sharing holidays with parents or extended family members. We kept that up even after we had children. There are both bad and good sides to that."

EASING THE JOURNEY

What lessons can today's divorcing parents learn from yesterday's children of divorce to enable them to minimize the discomfort and pain for the children who travel between two worlds— to make their journey easier? The answers fairly leap off the page.

- Fathers and mothers must attempt to set aside their differences when the youngsters' welfare is at stake. Parents are, after all, the grown-ups, and their primary concern must be to act *in the best interests of the child*.

- Although each parent may wish to have the children join him or her for Easter or Passover, Christmas, or other days of celebration, both may have to compromise on alternate visits —one year, Thanksgiving will be spent with mother's family and Christmas with father and his family; the next year the schedule can be reversed.

- As little as possible should be left to chance. Parents can help their children look forward to special moments by letting them know exactly what to expect: how the event will be celebrated and who will be present.

- If parents are unable to meet on civil ground, they should communicate around how to participate in their children's lives separately. Who will be in the stands for the Little League playoffs? Which parent will attend the piano recital?

Further, parents might do well to ask the children what *they* would prefer. It's a radical notion, but one worth trying.

Chapter VIII

When Parents Remarry: More Changes

The maid of honor wore a white pinafore. The best man and the usher were attired in matching blue blazers and checked pants. After the wedding, everybody went to the reception at the country club where the maid of honor, the best man, and the usher were seen catching frogs down by the pond.

—Account of a wedding reported in *The New York Times*

The maid of honor in question was eleven, the best man thirteen, and the usher eight. In the newspaper article, all three were described as "model attendants at their mother's second marriage." Later that year, the story continues, the children attended their father at *his* second marriage. "I'm getting the hang of it now," the thirteen-year-old is quoted as saying.

Such amusing accounts of parental remarriage serve to divert our attention from the real emotions and experiences of the children involved. There is much more to stepfamily relationships, say those who were divorce's children, than simply "getting the hang of it."

For one thing, remarriage writes the end to the fantasy described in the previous chapter, the hope that Mommy and Daddy will reconsider their differences and get back together again. While the wedding may be a time of celebration for the newlywed couple, the children are likely to experience it as a time of mourning for a dream that now cannot be realized. The reaction recalled for me by a child of divorce who is now in her forties may be far more typical—and honest—than the what-a-swell-party response of the young person cited in the *Times* piece. "My mother was remarried once and my father twice," this woman revealed. "My reaction to being told about all *three* remarriages was to burst out crying. I was sad and frightened. *How would my parents' remarriages change my life?*"

MAKING THE STEPFAMILY TRANSITION

For the children of divorce, the remarriage experience is complex and highly variable. So many factors come into play, among them: age and sex of the child; whether there are other children in the family; custodial arrangements; frequency of visitation; the quality of communication between the child's parents; the relationship between a parent in one home and the stepparent in the other; the welcome accorded the child by members of the stepparent's extended family; the presence of stepbrothers and stepsisters; the later appearance of half siblings; and—perhaps the most elusive and significant factor of all—the strengths and resources of the individual child.

For today's children, even more than for those who grew up in past decades, the likelihood is good that many will grapple with several of these issues as the dual-single-parent period comes to an end and they find themselves making the next transition: the step into stepfamily living.

In the past, most remarriages followed upon the death of a parent. (The prefix "step" derives from an Old English term meaning "bereaved" or "deprived.") The stepparent was considered a replacement parent, someone who came in to rescue a grieving family. Today, more marriages with dependent children are ended by divorce than by death, and divorced parents are more likely to remarry (and even sooner) than men and women who have been widowed.

The figures are startling. Currently, about three of every four divorced men and two of every three divorced women move on to commit to new marital partners. But the statistics provide only part of the picture of the number of children who are affected. According to most recent estimates, there are more than 2.3 million stepfamily households in this country. In 1985—the last year for which figures are available—close to seven million children in the United States were living in stepfamilies. Some demographers predict that, of all children born in the 1980s, as many as a third will spend some time living in a stepfamily before they reach the age of eighteen.

But the *actual* number of children touched by parental remarriage is even more staggering than these figures indicate, for the data fail to include the many children who make their home with their single mother and whose noncustodial father has remarried. These children are classified as belonging to single-parent households, points out Marilyn Ihinger-Tallman of Washington State University in a paper summarizing "Research on Stepfamilies." Their stepfamily connection is not reflected in the statistics.

Without question, it is strongly reflected in their lives.

AMY: A CASE HISTORY

Although no one story can serve to represent the stepfamily experience in its many variations, it is instructive for us to revisit the little girl with the big suitcase. (Elements of her story are similar to experiences that were recalled for me by several other men and women whose parents remarried.) Contrary to the expressed hopes of the cab drivers who shuttled her between the homes of her parents, Amy Greene did not manage to bring

Mommy and Daddy together again. Here, instead, is what happened.

During the period following her parents' separation but before her father remarried, Amy and her dad had grown closer to one another than when they lived together in the original family. "When I lived with both my parents," she recalls, "Dad was a typical little girl's father. He went off to work, came home in the evening, and spent very little time with me. In a curious way, we probably spent more time together after the divorce than before."

"But I had learned an important lesson about love and commitment in the meantime," she continues. "I had learned that love was conditional and that commitment could not be taken for granted. From the time my parents separated, I was always afraid that if I didn't behave well with my father I might lose him. When he remarried, when there was an actual someone I could lose him to, this feeling became strongly intensified."

A year after her parents' divorce was granted, when Amy was seven, Amy's father married Esther. Although her mother had been the one who sought their separation, her father's remarriage made her mother even more bitter toward him, heightening the tension between Amy's two homes. "From the time that their marriage broke up," says Amy, "I always had this feeling that I shouldn't talk about one parent in the presence of the other *unless* I had something bad to say. When a stepmother was added, I didn't dare say anything good about her either."

In this perception, Amy's experience was typical. Studies show that the better the relationship between ex-spouses, the easier it is for a child to accept the introduction of a stepparent. (They also indicate that a child who has *no* contact with a parent—say, a boy who has not heard from his father—will have a harder time accepting a stepparent as a "replacement." When there is adequate contact with both parents *and the co-parents get along,* youngsters are better able to accept the presence in their lives of additional caregivers. No one, you see, is being replaced.)

There were many good things that could have been said about

her stepmother, Amy now understands, although she would never have made this admission at the time. "Esther was a helpful and warm woman who showed me consideration and was so much easier to take than my mother in those days," says Amy. "Another good thing about Esther was that she never passed me off as her daughter, never made me feel she was trying to take the place of my mother." When Esther became sick, the little girl was not informed that the illness was a grave one. Within the year, Esther died. Once again, Amy became her father's best girl.

The summer Amy was ten, her father visited her at camp, bringing with him the requisite comic books and candy, which were eagerly anticipated. Less welcome was the "woman friend" he also brought. Amy had met Joan during visits to her father's home. *Why is she butting in on my afternoon with Daddy?* Amy remembers thinking. The answer was not long in coming. Over a lunch of tuna salad and potato chips, the couple announced to Amy that they planned to be married. This time, the child's reaction to gaining a stepparent was stronger. "I shouted 'Oh no!' and began to cry.

"The other thing that happened was that I think I wanted to be included in the wedding—yes, even given my negative feelings about it—and I was not invited," Amy says. "That hurt. I think that was a mistake."

So *much* seemed to hurt. The fact that Joan, who was childless, took quickly to introducing Amy as her daughter hurt. ("I felt it was a way of denying my mother's existence.") The newlyweds' move to a new apartment where Amy had to sleep on the living room couch when she visited . . . *that* hurt. ("Since there was no space that was mine, it was made clear to me that I did not belong in their home.") The stepmother's efforts to assume a parentlike role were not appreciated. ("Joan insisted on the kind of behavior and respect that was a parent's due. On the other hand, my father would tell me that I couldn't talk back to her because she wasn't my mother.") In fact, Joan could do no right. Even loving attempts were viewed with suspicion by her stepdaughter. ("Joan demanded a certain kind of recognition, including being kissed hello and goodbye." Amy says curtly, "Look, I've never been the kissy type.")

FACTORS THAT PRECLUDE CLOSENESS

AGE AND SEX

There were many things working against closeness between Amy and her stepmother, not the least of which was the fact that, at ten, Amy was on the threshold of adolescence—the most difficult time, research indicates, to gain a stepparent.

The child's age at the time of remarriage is influential. Studies have shown that very young children (under five years) and older adolescents (above eighteen) assimilate into remarriage more easily than children of other ages. The middle groups present the most problems, with the period from nine to fifteen acknowledged as a particularly tough time for young people to include a stepparent in their lives. This is a time for breaking away, not for forming new attachments. A time for rebelling against authority, not for recognizing new rule makers.

The sex of the child has also been found to be significant, with daughters experiencing more long-term difficulty than sons in adjusting to either a stepfather or a stepmother. The stepfamily (whether custodial or visited) appears to be a hard place for adolescent girls. And so it was for Amy this time around.

"My stepmother seemed to do nothing but criticize," Amy says. "And all of her complaints, although focusing on something *I* had either done or failed to do, were directed at my mother. When I once neglected to completely clear the dining room table (one of my chores at my father's home), I remember Joan *screaming* at me, 'If your mother were here, I would hang her from the nearest tree,' as if somehow it was my mother who fouled up. At thirteen, when I showed up in a black velvet dress that Joan immediately deemed 'unsuitable,' she criticized my mother for buying it and letting me look 'like a strumpet.'

"There was a constant battle over who had control of my body and how it looked," Amy says. "I remember a sharp shift in my personality between the ages of eleven and thirteen. From somebody who could be a fighter, I had become much more inward, depressed, scared of expressing my feelings."

PHYSICAL REMOTENESS ENCOURAGES EMOTIONAL DISTANCING

Amy's father and stepmother soon moved again, this time to a home where there was a guest room for Amy (and a bedroom for their new baby as well). But their new home was at some distance from where Amy lived with her mother. This, too, appears to be par for the remarriage course, where the acquisition of a new spouse is frequently accompanied by a move to a new house, one that is likely to place the noncustodial parent at even greater distance from his children, adding to the emotional distance between them as well. As we have seen, visitation is rarely altogether comfortable for children. When remarriage combines a strange new person and a strange new setting, the visiting child's uneasiness is further increased.

"When my father and I lived in the same city, all I had to do was take a cab to see him," says Amy. "There was some flexibility around my comings and goings. After he married Joan and moved away, visitation had to be more precisely scheduled. Which train would I be taking? How would I get from the station to my father's home? More often than not, I was dependent on my stepmother to pick me up and drop me off at the station. That made me uncomfortable. I kept having to say thank you to her."

The world of the stepfamily is a self-conscious environment. Members of this new extended family tend to place a good deal of emphasis on the forms of relationship: on who said what to whom, on what tone of voice was used, on hearing words of appreciation even (one might say especially) when feelings of gratitude are absent.

Listen to the echo. As a child of divorce, Justine Marsh traveled clear across the country to visit her celebrity father in Beverly Hills. "I went out there for the summers," she recalls, "and kind of resented my stepmother because she had won my father—the prize. They also quickly had three children, making *them* the real family. So who was I? There wasn't a room in that large house that was mine. Yet when it was time to go home Pop would say, 'Remember to write a thank-you note to your stepmother.' And I felt angry. She got the whole shooting match, and *I* had to thank *her!* And for what—the privilege of allowing me to visit my own father?"

Aspects of Justine's story reverberate in Rick Monelli's recollections of traveling to see his father, who had remarried a woman from Nebraska and moved to live in her hometown. "At Christmas and for two weeks during the summer," says Rick, now thirty-one, "my brother, sister, and I would be flown out to spend time with our father. It was concentrated time which we not only had to share with one another but also with his wife, whom we hardly knew even though we saw more of her during those visits than we did our father. He would go off to the office or to play golf at the country club, leaving us to 'enjoy' his backyard pool.

"During those visits, Dad would ask us how things were going, but under the circumstances it was hard to fill him in on my life. What do you say? *Here's what I've been doing for the past six months. . . . These are the results of my last history test. . . . This is a program from the concert I performed in. . . . Let me tell you about this girl in my homeroom. . . .* How do you talk to a father whose life and interests lie elsewhere?

"When other children were born to my dad and his wife, I felt that any need he might have had to be involved in our lives was now being filled by his involvement with a wife who was not my mother and with children whom I hardly knew. It was their lives that were clearly the focus of his own. In time, the summer visits were replaced by phone calls on our birthdays. When I entered college, I found other things to do at Christmas than visit my father."

Longitudinal studies of the effects of remarriage on the relationship between the child and the nonresidential parent support the impression that remarriage decreases the frequency of visitation between parent and child. In 1984, sociologists Frank Furstenberg and Graham Spanier directed a study in which interviews were conducted with 104 Central Pennsylvania parents shortly after the couples had separated and again in two and a half years. At that time, 35 percent of the parents had remarried and 13 percent were living with significant others. When neither parent remarried, the researchers found, 67 percent of the nonresidential parents continued to see their children at least several times a month. This dropped to 40 percent when one parent remarried and to 34 percent when both remarried.

The *quality* of the relationship between the child and the nonresidential parent was also looked at and found to diminish if either parent had remarried, but a greater decline in quality occurred when it was the nonresidential parent who embarked on a second marriage. The researchers speculated that geographical moves that separate parent from child and the diversion of energies from the child to new relationships could account in part for these findings.

JEALOUSY REARS ITS HEAD

Jealousy is another factor that emerges strongly in interviews with adult children of divorce as they seek to explain the reasons for their distancing from the remarried noncustodial parent. It may be their own jealousy—as was true for Justine Marsh and Rick Monelli, who yearned for the attention of their fathers and saw it bestowed instead on stepsiblings and half brothers and sisters. *I don't need you* was their childish retaliation to a remote parent, when (they later came to realize) the opposite was often true.

In many cases, however, the jealousy that most burdened the children of divorce was the resentment felt by the left-behind parent toward the former spouse, especially if the ex-spouse had remarried and (to all intents and purposes) created a new and satisfactory life. In these situations, the child was used by the embittered parent to attain her own ends: the desire to punish the former spouse by withholding the affection of the children. "My stepmother was the other woman, the one who had 'stolen' my father, and my mother never let me forget it," says a thirty-eight-year-old woman who was eleven when her parents' marriage ended. "Dad remarried one day after my parents' divorce was granted. That same day, my mother announced that if I was ever to see or even speak to my father's wife I would be stabbing her in the heart. I could not bear responsibility for causing my mother any more pain, so I refused to visit my father at his home and he declined to meet me anywhere else. It was a standoff— and we both lost."

Sometimes, possessive parents come between their children and their *own* new spouses, precluding the development of a warm attachment between them. "I could have loved my stepfather," Laura Bennett says, "but whenever he tried to intercede on behalf of my brother or me, my mother would tell him, 'These are my children. You keep out of it.' So he stopped trying and became a shadow in our lives, when we would really have welcomed the presence of this decent man."

And in still other situations where children are distanced from a nonresidential parent, it is the stepparent who is pointed to as instigator of the separation. Jealousy is at the core here, too, and here is why (in these instances) it comes to the fore. In a typical first marriage, the relationship between husband and wife is established *before* the children arrive. In the remarried family, however, the association between parent and child predates that of the newlyweds. While the new spouse may entertain a fantasy of a honeymoon romance without prior history, the child stands as living proof that there was a former love. Wishing to strengthen the present marriage, the stepparent may seek to weaken connections with the past. The child, after all, not only perpetuates that prior association but also calls for a present commitment—an allegiance that the new spouse really doesn't wish to share.

There is no question that members of families fitting the marriage-divorce-remarriage spectrum often stand on jealous ground that causes some relationships to falter and others to collapse entirely. Research underscores the precariousness of the stepchild's standing, especially when the remarried family is not the one in which the child maintains a permanent residence. In their six-year follow-up study of families of divorce, for example, E. Mavis Hetherington and her colleagues observed that new wives often entered into "a particularly hostile, competitive relationship with the ex-wife in which criticism of the children and the wife's child-rearing and the economic burden of the previous family often were used as the combative focus." They further noted, "A stepmother frequently used one of two strategies in trying to isolate her new husband from his former wife. The first was to urge the father to attempt to gain custody of his children, thus reducing the need for contact with the first wife. . . .

"The second strategy used by stepmothers, particularly when they became pregnant or had a child, was to try to shut out the entire former family by making visits difficult or by emphasizing that the father's responsibilities and future lay with his new family. Whatever the causes, involvement and visits by the father with his children diminished markedly following remarriage. This decrease was most notable with daughters. Divorced fathers not only visited sons more often and for longer periods of time following divorce, but also were more likely to sustain the contact with sons than with daughters following remarriage."

Mallory Coburn tells a harsh tale that falls in line with the study's findings. "I was twelve and my sister nine and a half when our father married for the second time. His wife went into the marriage as if there was a clean slate. For her, there was no past marriage (including the kids). The word 'stepmother' was banned from Day One. It was never to be used—not even to this day, not even in a joke. To me, there is nothing wrong with that word.

"She rarely says the word 'Dad' in front of us either," Mallory continues. "When she speaks to us about our father, his wife calls him by his first name, as in 'Why don't you ask Gordon if he wants something warm to drink.' From the point that our father remarried, his birthday cards to us no longer said 'To my daughter on her birthday.' The cards I got said 'To a nice girl on her birthday.' The word 'daughter' had been dropped.

"Four years ago, my father and his wife had a daughter—one who is officially recognized. The little girl has been told that I'm her aunt. My stepmother insists on that and my dad defers to her wishes. There are pictures all over their house, family pictures, but there are none of my sister and me."

Why, at twenty-six, does Mallory go along with this? Why does she allow herself to suffer such rejection? Indeed, there were three years, while in college, when she never even saw her father. ("I put myself through college and graduate school. I'm not sure he even knew where I was or that I was studying for a career in the foreign service.")

The primary reason Mallory gives for reentering her father's remarried family is a strongly felt need to resolve for herself the issues of her parents' divorce. She cannot accomplish that task, she believes, without working on her relationship with her father. (See chapter twelve, "Cutting Loose: The Search for Understanding.") The other reason has become equally compelling: "I don't want to give up my half sister. She's just wonderful, and I love her dearly."

ENTER THE HALF SIBLING: THE CHILD OF A PARENT'S REMARRIAGE

Question: How does the birth of a half sibling affect the lives of children of divorce? *(a)* For better; *(b)* for worse; *(c)* makes no difference. The correct answer, we learn from our interviews and from studies done on the effects of divorce, is *(d)* all of the aforementioned. One might just as well ask of children in an intact family how the birth of a sibling changed *their* lives. The likelihood is good of coming up with the same range of response.

But the sibling chapters in the life histories of children of divorce include notable differences from the accounts given by brothers and sisters in traditional families. Certainly *all* kids are likely to complain, at one time or another, about the favored treatment of a brother or sister. The child of divorce, however, has more cause to believe that this is so.

"Remarriage was a disaster for me," says Ruth, thirty-six, whose parents separated when she was two. Two years later, her mother remarried. "My stepfather felt guilty about marrying a divorcée and remained distant to me, while my mother saw me as a symbol of her past marriage (a marriage she couldn't wait to get out of) and wasn't there for me. When I was five, my half brother was born. From then on, I felt like a visitor in my own home. My mother, stepfather, and their son comprised the real family."

In talking with adult children of divorce, "real family" is a term that comes up time and again. Generally it is a poignant reference to the noncustodial remarried household, especially after "real children" have been added to it.

Looking back, Adam Norris captures the moment when he first understood that there *was* a difference. "After he divorced my mother, my biological father went on to have four children," he says. "Shortly after the first of the children was born, I visited my father's home. Looking down at the baby in her bassinet, I remember thinking that my father, his new wife, and this baby were *real* and that I was now further displaced. *They* were a family. Who was I?"

But the child—the half sibling—can also provide an important focal point for the kind of extended family we are seeing more of today. When a family tree contains branches for "his" children and "her" children, the "our" child may be the one relationship that everyone has in common. It can serve to draw the family closer together. In the custodial household, as one man expressed it, "the birth of my half brother turned our makeshift family into a real family. It made me feel closer to my stepfather."

This is a not atypical reaction. In her book *The Reconstituted Family,* sociologist Lucile Duberman reported the results of her study of eighty-eight remarried families in Ohio: "We found that of those families who had had children together, 78% rated excellent in their relationships between stepchildren and stepparents, compared to 53% of those who did not have children together. It can be inferred from this that the presence of natural children in a reconstituted family enhances the relationships between stepchildren and stepparents."

Many explanations can be offered for this. One that quickly comes to mind was given to me by a stepmother who admitted that, before she had a child born to her, she had been very hard on her husband's daughter—wanting the little girl to arrive better dressed, to speak more softly, to behave more politely, in short *to be a better reflection of her.* "Once I had my own daughter, it freed me from having to make my stepdaughter into the perfect child," this woman said. "I eased up on her." She laughed. "I also learned that there are times when any child—even your own child—is going to get on your nerves, that no child is perfect. Becoming a mother had made me a better stepmother."

WHEN CHILDREN LIVE WITH THEIR STEPPARENT

Parental remarriage also introduces children of divorce to another situation, one in which the stepparent becomes a daily presence in their lives rather than a member of the visited household formed when a noncustodial parent remarries. Since children typically live with their mothers following divorce, the live-in stepparent is usually a stepfather.

As a general rule (to which there are many exceptions, having to do with such variables as the age of the child at the time of remarriage and his relationship with the biological father), sons fare better than daughters in this situation. Several reasons have been put forward in explanation. For one thing, we know that children do better when, following parental separation, they continue to reside primarily with the parent of the same sex. For the majority of sons who continue to live in mother-headed households, then, divorce ruptures the relationship with the same-sex parent. Because the mother-son relationship after divorce is often more problematic than that between mothers and their daughters, boys may welcome the same-sex parent figure.

A key variable in the boys' acceptance of the stepfather, however, has to do with the temperament and the expectation of the man who joins the family. If the mother's new husband regards himself as a savior who is coming in to take control of the father-less family, if he moves too strongly and too soon (or if the mother abdicates her role as disciplinarian and encourages her new husband to "take over"), stepfather and stepson find themselves in for a rocky time.

Herb Geoghegan, a forty-two-year-old adult child of divorce, describes just such a relationship. "The divorce occurred when I was four or five," he says. "By the time I was six, my mother was entering into a new relationship. I was *very* protective of my mother. And I remember, one day, pulling a tantrum because my mother was going out with the man who later became her husband. I was worried. I was afraid that she might be hurt, that she might not come back. And This Man spanked me, really hard. At that moment I rejected him as another man, in a way. Because my father was never around to give me stroking, and this man who was trying to reach me was not reaching me at all. I was crying and in pain, and he didn't know how to handle it properly. He didn't know what to do to make the transition for me any easier. At the time I remember thinking, *I hate this person.* He never learned how to relate to me, and I never could accept him as my stepfather."

In forging a relationship with stepchildren, the stepparent (in particular the stepfather who resides in the home) is faced with finding a delicate balance. First, he must seek to develop a warm and appropriately affectionate relationship with the child. Second, the stepparent must establish a role as a legitimate person of authority. An interesting finding of research in this area is that when this balance is reached and stepfathers make a place in the lives of their stepchildren, the relationship between mother and child generally improves as well. Mothers whose new husbands are warm and supportive may become more effective, authoritative parents, displaying greater warmth, communication, and control. This is particularly true for parents of boys, the studies found.

Regarding relationships between boys and the stepmothers who reside in the same household, E. Mavis Hetherington notes that "there is not a sufficient body of literature as a basis for comment on what may occur."

Amy Greene's response of dismay to gaining a stepfather, on the other hand, is fairly common among daughters. "My stepfather, Stuart, is the best thing that came out of my parents' divorce," she says. "And yet I still was upset when he and my mother told me they planned to be married."

The announcement of their impending marriage shouldn't have come as a surprise to Amy, for the couple had been seeing each other for ten years when they decided to wed. Stuart had long been a fixture in Amy's life, a helpful buffer in the often stormy goings-on between mother and daughter. And Amy, by then a college freshman, was already spending the greater part of her year away from home. Still, "I felt abandoned," Amy says.

In large part, as we have seen, that is because single mothers tend to turn more closely to their daughters following divorce. When they remarry, this special bond is weakened by the new commitment. "My mom's remarriage was just as devastating for me as my parents' divorce," says Nancy Kovach, who spent the years from five to sixteen in a mother-headed household. "Our family unit (my mom and the three kids) had grown very close during the time that Mom was a single parent. We were there for each other. That all changed when our mother started dating the man who became our stepfather. Suddenly, *he* was all that mattered to her. She treated us like shit. My stepfather was a major intrusion in our family life. I felt a definite loss. I still can't stand him."

It is difficult for stepfathers to break through the barriers erected by their stepdaughters. If they try to be affectionate, it can be threatening. If instead they maintain distance, it is interpreted as uncaring. What is a well-meaning stepfather to do? Recent research by psychologist James H. Bray offers some direction. Stepdaughters are better able to welcome verbal approval from their stepfathers, Bray's research suggests, than physical affection, which can be much too threatening.

Amy Greene's disappointment in her mother's marital plans was short-lived. "I liked Stuart a lot," she says. "He had already become a very important person in my life, and a major influence. He introduced me to yoga, to art, to Freud, to restaurants. Because of him, our world started to expand. He was also good at tolerating my abuse. I mean, I gave him a rough time over the years.

"The feelings I have for my father and for Stuart are very different," she says. "There's a love I have for my father that goes much deeper in some ways than the love I have for Stuart. And yet . . . my stepfather is the best thing that ever happened to me."

BEING ADOPTED BY A STEPPARENT

When remarriage creates a stepfamily-in-residence, and especially when the noncustodial parent fails to meet his financial obligations to the child or is absent or uninvolved, the question of adoption may be considered. There are many possible reasons a stepparent may seek to formalize a relationship through legal adoption. The idea may arise as an emotional response, the desire to create a "real family" that most closely resembles the traditional family. As in a nondivorced household, family members could then share the same surname. The shame of divorce would be covered over. *No one need know.*

That, you may recall, was the primary concern for Adam Norris, who disliked his stepfather yet still welcomed his name. (See chapter six.) *"I was sanctioned by [his] name and I was sanctioned by the appearance of a family."* In the context of an age and a community in which divorce was less prevalent than it is today, the desire of a child for normalcy (or at least for its appearance) can be well understood.

There are also practical considerations that can lead to taking legal action, such as, for example, the fact that adoption assures the right of stepchildren to inherit from the stepparent. (Note, however, that in some states the law currently holds that adoption by a stepparent severs the right of inheritance from the natural parent who has relinquished parenting responsibilities.) Further, it gives stepparents the power to make decisions regarding their stepchildren in times of medical emergency, as when consent must be given for an operation and the legal parent cannot be reached. All of which explains why the incidence of adoption by a stepparent is so high—comprising 40 percent of all adoptions in recent years.

But there are detrimental aspects to adoption as well. In their book *How to Win as a Stepfamily,* Emily and John Visher, psychologist and psychiatrist who are founders of the Stepfamily Association of America, point out that adoption of minor children by stepparents is a much more complicated psychological issue than is generally recognized. "Adoption is a legal cutting of biological ties," they stress, "and as such requires very careful consideration."

As Adam Norris's history makes clear, adoption does not create relationships. For many children, however, it does symbolize abandonment. "There's a basic connection to one's roots," the Vishers state. "A child may *want* to keep his or her surname. The child may have a need to feel good about the natural parent."

The depth of that need comes across strongly in the vivid childhood scene that is re-created by Cindy Weston, forty-three, who was not yet two when her parents divorced. "My earliest memories are of living with my mother, my widowed grandmother, and my sister who was one year older than I," she says. "Somehow I understood that my father had gone off to war, and accepted the fact that the women maintained the home. I did not understand divorce."

When Cindy was two and a half, her mother remarried ("He was *not* a good man") and within a year a third girl was born into the family. "One year after that, our stepfather adopted my sister and me. The way it was described to us was that we were going to change our name. Apparently we didn't want that to happen" —Cindy pauses, reaches for a tissue—"because I remember clearly, right after we were told, my sister and I going into our room and rolling down the window shade. My sister, who had learned how to write by then, printed our surname on the shade, and then rolled it up . . . to keep the name safe. I don't know if it ever was discovered."

In their book, the Vishers state, "Some adopted stepchildren have never known their other biological parent because that parent left when the child was a few months old; later they often seek to find their other parent or change their name back to their birth name despite many years of happiness in the family in which they grew up."

Cindy does not lay claim to such happiness (she was sexually abused by her stepfather), which only increased her longing to know her father. "All the relatives must have been alerted never to bring up my father's name again because we were about to perpetuate the myth that this family was a normal family, and our father was out of our lives," she says. "I lost much more than a name when I was adopted. I lost half my heritage."

WHEN REMARRIAGE HEALS

There is another side to the remarriage story, however, and it is the healing side. If divorce creates a hole in the heart for many of its children, remarriage can be likened to a life-saving transplant. While the scars do not go away, the wounded youngster (and his or her remarrying parent) may have been given a new lease on a healthier life.

We have seen, for example, that remarriage of the noncustodial parent often has a negative effect on the frequency of contact and quality of relationship between that parent and his child. On the other hand, the very same study that reached this conclusion also led the researchers (Furstenberg and Spanier) to observe: "Remarriage occasionally produced quite the opposite effect, increasing interaction between parents and children. Tensions were sometimes reduced when intermediaries entered the scene to cool down hostilities. Also, fathers who had been ill-prepared to assume a caretaking role could play a more active part when they were aided by a spouse or partner. Thus, the effect of remarriage on patterns of parenting was not simple or uniform."

Sociologist Andrew Cherlin makes a similar observation in his book *Marriage, Divorce, Remarriage.* "We should remember," Cherlin writes, ". . . that most divorced adults will spend most of the rest of their lives not living alone or in a single parent family but in a family of remarriage. Although parents and children in a family of remarriage can have difficulty adjusting to their complex and poorly institutionalized situation, remarriage improves the financial situation of single parents, creates an additional set of kin to supplement the remaining ties to the kin of noncustodial parents, and provides another stable source of affection and emotional support. The long-term adjustment of many adults and children to divorce may depend on the support provided by remarriage."

"So much attention has been focused for so long on the stepfamily as a pathological form that we've neglected to take a good look at normal stepfamilies—at when and how they work, and the fact that so many do work out," says psychologist Patricia Papernow, author of *Becoming a Stepfamily: Patterns of Development in Remarried Families.* "The remarried family is a very complex form of family. There are many good things about it."

Not the least of the good things, Papernow emphasizes, is that children who live in two worlds are provided with more than one model of how to live in a family. In illustration, she offers the following: "I recently was moderator of a discussion where a panel of children of divorce spoke about the effects on them of a parent's remarriage. One of the young people told the audience, 'In my mother's house the way we deal with things that come up is to have intimate discussions. That's great when I need to talk. But I'm not always in the mood to talk. At my father's house, I don't feel that pressure. He and my stepmother are content to leave me to myself. I'm able to read a book undisturbed in my father's house. There are times when I really appreciate the difference that each household offers.'

"This boy was so convincing," says Pat Papernow, "that one of the children in the audience, someone who did not come from a divorced and remarried family, remarked, 'Gee, my life seems so dull compared to yours, I feel as if I'm the one who's missing out by not having an alternate family!' "

In the personal histories recounted by children of divorce, the positive side of remarriage is borne out in many ways. As Amy Greene teaches us, when "family" expands to include new relationships, the child's life also expands through exposure to new ideas, new activities.

PROVIDING A HEALTHY MODEL

By far the most important benefit of a good remarriage, however, is its salutary effect on children who are battle-scarred from years of living with parental conflict. "One of the positives of the divorce situation," says Clifford Sager, who directs the Remarried Consultation Service at New York's Jewish Board of Family and Children's Services, "is that children are given the opportunity to see a model of a better marriage than they have seen before."

This is the memory that Philip Robinson holds. At thirty-nine, Robinson is an executive with a midsize computer company. He is married and has two children, ages eight and three. "For the first thirteen years of my life, up until the day my father left our house, I do not remember seeing an affectionate look pass between my mother and father," he says. "As a matter of fact"—his voice expresses wonderment—"I can't recall ever seeing my parents kiss or hug one another. Isn't that something!

"The only memory I have is of them arguing. My mom was always putting my father down. He wasn't making enough money. Or he wasn't going to church. Or he didn't appreciate what a hard job it was to raise children (besides me, there were two younger sisters) and he didn't help out enough. If he did stop and pick up something at the grocer's, it was inevitably the wrong item: the jumbo package when my mother wanted the economy size; the pink grapefruit when what she'd asked for was the white. One day, my dad simply stopped coming home. I told my mother that I would have nothing to do with him. It was *easy* for me to be angry. After all, I'd had a good teacher."

Two years later, Philip's father moved in with a woman and, a year after that, she became his wife. Although overtures were made to the children, none of them would answer their father's calls and letters, much less agree to meet *that woman*. Finally, almost to the day of the first anniversary of his father's second marriage, Philip decided that he would see his father. "The story I told myself was that I wanted to tell him in what low esteem I held him," Philip says. "Actually, I think I was curious, and I probably had a need to reconnect with my father. But I don't think I could have admitted that to myself, and certainly not to my father."

At the door of the home where his father now lived, Philip was met by a softly pretty woman who introduced herself as Peggy, his father's wife, and told him she was glad he had come. Philip ignored her, making it clear that he was there only to see his father and had no intention of staying. "It was an awkward meeting," Philip says. "But I did go back again, and I even began to stay over at their home once in a while. Peggy had a son five years younger than I, and I would spend my time with him, showing him how to build model airplanes or just watching television.

"Even so, I could not help noticing the way my father and Peggy were around each other. It wasn't that they were exceptionally demonstrative, but they kept touching. Peggy would give my father a kiss on the cheek, just in passing. And he'd put his arm around her. I didn't know how to deal with affection. It made me uncomfortable. Ultimately, being around my father and Peggy was the best thing that could have happened to me. As time passed, I could accept Peggy's kiss hello. I even got to the point (and this was in no way easy for me) where I allowed my father to hug me.

"Seeing my father valued instead of vilified helped me come to think of myself, his son, as a person of worth, too," says Philip.

"I doubt that I would have been able to make a good marriage myself had there not been my father's remarriage to show me the way."

STRENGTHENING STEPFAMILY LIVING

For a growing population of children, the stepfamily (like divorce) is a fact of life that will not go away. It is therefore important to strengthen the families children join through remarriage, to make them safe and supportive environments. It can be done.

- What the adult children of divorce tell us time and again is that, once their parents became involved in a new relationship, mothers and fathers ceased to be there for their children in ways for which they could formerly be counted on. Nancy Kovach speaks of how the closeness of the single-parent-led family was ruptured the moment a stepfather came upon the scene; for Justine Marsh, Rick Monelli, and countless others, the visited parent became a distant relation in more ways than geographically. The relationship between parent and child further deteriorated when a new love came on the scene.

  "Remarried parents need to learn to compartmentalize," says psychologist Patricia Papernow. "They need to spend time with the new partner. They need to make time to spend with their children." To this must be added: stepparents need to step back from time to time and allow their spouses the space and freedom to be alone with their children—the way they used to be.

- And parents must permit their children to enjoy relationships with the person whom the "other parent" marries. Professionals who work with members of remarried families are zealous in stressing one major issue that they see as critical to the well-being of the children of divorce, and it is this: the grown-up members of *both* families in a child's life must strive to achieve workable relationships not only between ex-spouses but among their new partners and whatever children are involved in this new form of extended family.

"All children do better in stepfamilies if parents and stepparents can lower the conflict between the children's households," says Patricia Papernow. "This means taking care of differences out of children's earshot, sending messages meant for adults to adults (and not through the children as message bearers) and being openly supportive of children's relationships with their 'other' parents and stepparents." Such cooperation greatly reduces the loyalty conflict for all: children, their parents, and the stepparents who come into their lives.

• For a long time, people in stepfamilies have been plagued by two myths that have affected their ability to forge positive relationships. The first, the myth of the wicked stepmother, comes right out of the pages of "Cinderella" and frightens not only the child who is about to obtain a stepmother but the stepmother herself. When she finds herself having less than loving feelings toward her husband's children, the stepmother's first thought is likely to be *Oh, my God, I'm turning into a wicked stepmother.* It undermines her confidence in working toward a more tolerant acceptance of the inclusion of stepchildren in the life she shares with her husband, their father.

• The second myth, that of instant love, is in a way connected to the first. Unrealistic expectations are among the stepfamily's greatest stumbling blocks. It is *all right* for a stepparent to have less than loving feelings for a spouse's children. It is all right, as well, for children not to love their stepparents or have to feel forever grateful to them for courtesies extended. While children and their stepparents don't have to love one another, it is helpful for them to realize that they do have someone they love in common. The recognition of a shared affection need not lead to jealousy but can be used instead to bring children and their stepparents together.

Chapter IX

Saving Graces: People Who Help

My parents' divorce, when I was thirteen, was the number one topic of conversation in our small community where everyone knew everybody and *nobody* ever got divorced. For years, my mother and father were in and out of court. It was a nasty trial that was written up in the local paper, which was read by just about everyone in town. I would walk up one aisle in the supermarket and hear people talking about my family in the next. It was so embarrassing. But no one, not family or friends, would talk to *me* about what was going on. That gave me the feeling that the subject was dirty.

I believe that if I'd had help at the time, my parents' divorce would not be the problem that it remains for me even now. What would I have wanted? Someone, anyone who cared. A grandparent, a teacher, a friend. A special person who said, "If you want to talk, I am here." That would have helped me a lot.

—Leila Forrest, age twenty-nine

With the awareness of hindsight, Leila Forrest identifies a factor that has proven to be a saving grace for many a child caught up in parental divorce: the solicitous concern of people who are willing to help.

Such individuals are exceptional. When it comes to divorce, people outside of the immediate family are generally reluctant to become involved. What goes on in families, most of us are taught at mother's knee, is "personal." It's bad form to wash our own dirty linen in public, and even worse manners to pry into somebody else's private affairs.

We learn these lessons at home as well as from the acknowledged arbiters of proper behavior. Here, for example, is Amy Vanderbilt's advice about what "Our Attitude Toward Divorce and the Divorcee" should be. In *Amy Vanderbilt's New Complete Book of Etiquette,* we are instructed: "Any remarks directed toward the newly divorced should be tactful indeed. Friends should not attempt to extract information concerning the proceedings from one obviously unwilling to discuss the matter. And even when a divorced person seems to feel the necessity to discuss the case with sympathetic listeners it is their cue to make only the most noncommittal remarks in return." If one is advised to tiptoe around this issue when dealing with grown-ups, think how much more circumspect one is expected to be in raising the whole matter of divorce with its children!

What we are learning from those who were children of divorce, and also from professionals who seek to mitigate divorce's harsh effects, is that attention *must* be paid. Not to do so, in many cases, is the greater offense.

The importance of outside involvement is noted by E. Mavis Hetherington in discussing some of the positive results of divorce. Hetherington mentions a *steeling effect,* where the child becomes a stronger person for having gone through a divorce and learning to cope with adversity. "But the key thing [in whether such an enhancement takes place]," the psychologist says, "is that somewhere there has to have been a close, concerned, involved adult. It might be the mother. It might be the noncustodial parent. It might be a stepparent. It might be a grandmother. It might be a teacher. But there *has* to have been someone." *There has to have been a Saving Grace.*

Family therapist Ann Kliman also makes this point. "When parents are absent or inappropriate," she says, "children can develop a relationship with a psychological parent. You often see this happen between children and stepparents. It's a corrective experience for a child. It confirms that the child is worthy of being loved. You cannot grow up without *one* good relationship. If it's not with either parent, others can supply it."

Such special "others" are accorded special mention in the accounts that men and women give of growing up divorced. In the main, these Saving Graces are the quiet heroes: the grandparent who listens; the teacher who encourages; the neighbor who welcomes; the friend who remains constant. It is their importance to the children that comes across loud and clear.

THE GRANDPARENT CONNECTION

Grandparents are the logical protectors. But when the divorce separates children from a parent (usually the father), it also often results in a weakening of the bond between the children and the extended family of the noncustodial parent. In contrast, the child's bonds with the family of the residential parent are frequently intensified. In time, stepgrandparents are likely to appear on the scene; they may also be able to fill the void.

"With large numbers of children currently affected by divorce, grandparents constitute a potential family resource to provide support and comfort," writes medical anthropologist Colleen Leahy Johnson in her book *Ex Familia,* an exploration of the ways in which grandparents, parents, and children adjust to divorce. While Johnson recognizes the practical requirement for many grandparents to financially support the daughter and her children after a marriage has ended, she also addresses the necessity for grandparents to *be* there, even to the point of becoming surrogate parents to the grandchildren.

Grandparents are powerful figures in a youngster's world.

When they become partisan and bad-mouth either parent, they make matters worse for the child. (One thinks of Tobias Goodman whose grandmother's comment, "You remind me of your father," was used as an indictment of the boy.) In contrast, Arthur Waterman provides us with an example of how a grandmother can be a positive force in a world full of negatives.

"My maternal grandmother was an extremely intelligent, thoughtful person who could, and did, put things in perspective for me," Waterman says in a tone that informs me that this is a pleasant interlude in an interview which has evoked harsher memories. "From the time I was five and my parents divorced, she became the person I knew I could turn to for a kind of comfort."

Waterman needed comfort. During his growing-up years, he saw both parents remarry, each entering a new relationship that was as conflict-ridden as their previous marriage had been. "For the most part," he says, "I was able to remove myself from the fights in my father's home because I could pick myself up and go to the guest room or, as I grew older, I could go home when things got bad. The way I looked at the battles between my father and stepmother was that this wasn't my parents who were fighting with one another, and so their arguments didn't affect me.

"For reasons I could not then fathom, I was differently involved with my mother's situation. I vividly recall this one time, when I was about fourteen, that my mother and stepfather were having a big fight. I was very upset and I left our apartment to visit my grandmother—not to talk to her about it, but just to get away. My grandmother saw that I was distressed, and asked me what was wrong. I told her that my mother and stepfather were fighting.

"She said to me (and I should emphasize that she certainly cared about my mother and wanted her to be happy), essentially, that it wasn't *my* business to take care of my mother . . . that my mother was the adult and it was my mother's responsibility to take care of her own life. My grandmother told me that I should take charge of *my* life and grow up happy. The relief that I felt upon hearing those words was incredible. It was the first time I had heard from *anyone* that I had that right."

For Jennie Fuller it was Great Aunt Mary who made a difference. "She was one of our main supports," says the thirty-six-year-old woman, recalling the wrenching move from Boston to Alabama after her parents separated. "Great Aunt Mary lived up the hill and across the railroad tracks. My sister and I would stop by her place almost daily. We'd go sit with her and (as they say in the South) 'visit.'

"We could talk to her about things we couldn't say to our mother, and she would listen politely," Jennie recalls. "She didn't take sides. She didn't tell us we were foolish. When she thought we needed cooling off, she would pile us into her car (that was the other good thing about Great Aunt Mary—she had a car) and drive us to the nearest city for ice cream."

The positive attributes of Great Aunt Mary (and of other aunts, uncles, caring neighbors who are gratefully acknowledged in the accounts of men and women who struggled with the aftermath of parental divorce) are these: *availability* and *neutrality*. In Leila Forrest's words, these are the people who in word and deed convey to the children the liberating message, "If you want to talk, I am here."

BROTHERS AND SISTERS

Little is known about sibling relationships in divorced and re-married families, and whether they're a help or a hindrance to making a smoother adjustment to divorce and its consequences. Moreover, the few reports that *are* available present contradictory findings. Some clinical studies report enhanced sibling relation-ships while other studies find few differences between sibling relationships in divorced and nondivorced families.

One might guess that adversity would bring brothers and sisters together. Yet as a general rule this does not appear to be the case. Seeking to answer the question of whether marital transitions promote productive alliances or competition between siblings, E. Mavis Hetherington has found that "ambivalent or hostile, alienated relationships were more common in siblings in remarried families and in boys in divorced families than among siblings in nondivorced families."

Among the men and women with whom I spoke, as many seemed to denigrate their sisters and brothers as appreciate them. For more than a few, the divorce of their parents served to exacerbate the kind of rivalry that is par for the course at one time or another in most families with more than one child. This increased competition should not come as a surprise. The contest to determine whom Daddy loves best becomes far more serious when meetings with Daddy are few and far between and children find themselves having to vie for the attention of this elusive suitor. Time and again in the interviews, I am told by adult children of divorce (and this was especially true for the women), "I'm the one who was my father's favorite."

Hetherington's study did find, however, that older girls in divorced families frequently played a supportive, nurturing role in relations with younger female siblings. When this occurs, the relationship can be a saving grace for both. As Jennie Fuller recalls, "My sister and I mourned together and we commiserated over our situation. She was the one person who truly understood what I was going through. After all, she was living through it too."

Nor does one have to be female to appreciate the presence of other children in the family, Rick Monelli makes clear. "After my parents were divorced, my mother got me a Big Brother for a while. She thought it would help because we no longer had a father in our home. It didn't help me to have a Big Brother, which was an artificial relationship, but it helped me to *be* a big brother. Both my younger brother and sister looked up to me. That did a lot for my self-esteem. I was flattered."

WITH A LITTLE HELP FROM FRIENDS

Friends can be supportive during periods of stress. And many are. But friends who live in intact families, say the children of divorce, often don't know how to react and what role to assume with the friend who is going through a hard time. Furthermore, the troubled youngster is unlikely to be able to point the way for them, to let them know which questions are welcome and which are off limits.

Leila Forrest explains the dilemma: "When my mother and father were divorcing, I felt awkward around my friends—not because of the way they acted or didn't behave towards me, but because I was so sensitive. I mean, what do you say? None of them was going through a similar experience. I was also very jealous, seeing my friends with all their intact families. Then I felt guilty because I envied other people their families. So I pulled away from them and isolated myself from everyone."

Where some youngsters, like Leila Forrest, turn inward, others reach out—but to new and different cliques. In a paper on "Coping With Family Transitions," Hetherington writes: "About one third of adolescent children become disengaged from the family following divorce and remarriage. They become involved in school activities and the peer group or, if they are fortunate, they attach themselves to a responsive adult or to the family of a friend. Whether these are desirable coping mechanisms depends on the child's family situation and on the particular activities and type of associates with which the child becomes involved. If they are socially constructive activities and the child's associates are well adjusted, this move can be advantageous. Undesirable activities and an antisocial or delinquent peer group, on the other hand, usually have disastrous consequences."

In my interview with Justine Marsh, the choreographer ponders this question of friends. Like Leila Forrest, following her parents' divorce and her father's remarriage she too found herself withdrawing from classmates who lived in intact families. "Everybody else seemed to have a mother and a father who were married to each other," she says. "In the sixth grade, I became keenly aware that I didn't have a father in my house. I became embarrassed to bring my friends home."

But Justine did not withdraw. Instead, she turned to a different group of friends.

"You wouldn't call my new friends 'delinquents,'" says Justine Marsh, "but we were an oddball group—all of us waifs in some way or other. However, the people who *saved* me were these friends, my peers, in that I could talk to them and they were always there. They didn't leave me as my father had done.

"You know, I never thought about this till now," she says. "I guess that I was always afraid that if I *really* said what I thought, if I really behaved the way I wanted to be and was as hostile and horrible as I thought myself, I would be deserted. My father *had* left me. My mother would marry and in a sense leave me. This was the unconscious fear. But my friends were just as nasty as I was. They wouldn't leave me. That was their saving grace."

FINDING A MENTOR

When parents are unavailable to their children or when they fail to meet their needs, it is helpful for the children to find others who will serve as their role models. Judith Wallerstein underscores the value of seeking such substitutes. "Of the children in our study, only very few formed and made use of mentors," she says. "And yet each and every one of these children, who feel that they have less priority in the parents' eyes, deeply need adults who will bolster their self-esteem and affirm their potential."

"Why do some children of divorce survive while others don't?" In the course of the afternoon we spend together, Sheila Henderson asks this question, and then provides an answer. "I think some of us survive because we remove ourselves from the fray.

We turn to sports, to friends, elsewhere . . . and we find a mentor. I was lucky to do that."

After school each day, Sheila would babysit for the children of a woman who was her teacher. "I needed the money," she says. "But I also needed to feel connected to someone and to some-place where I was valued. My father and mother abandoned my sister and me emotionally. This teacher, who *liked* me, became my psychological parent. Her home and family became my haven."

MANY HELPING HANDS ALONG A ROUGH JOURNEY

Among children of divorce, there are some who are not only emotionally but also physically abandoned by their parents. In such cases, the involvement in their lives of other caring individuals is more than just helpful. As Paul Norman's history makes clear, it can be critical to the young person's survival. "If a lot of good people hadn't been there for me when I needed them," says the state legislator, "I have no doubt that I would have come to a bad end."

From the age of twelve, the adolescent youth lived a childhood worthy of a Dickens novel. One day his mother took the children and moved out of the home. The next day, Paul was shipped out to an aunt in Kentucky "on a farm that had no running water and a wood stove for both heating and cooking." There were five children in the family. And there was his aunt's husband, who dispelled any possible notion of charitable intentions. "We agreed to take you in on condition that you help out" were his welcoming words to the boy whose world had so recently been upended. "He worked me *hard*," Paul says, shuddering at the memory.

Eight months later, without warning or explanation, Paul was shipped to the home of his father's elderly parents in New Mexico. "Then one day my father's brother came and took me to an uncle in Nevada. I stayed there for a year. When I was a freshman in high school, my mother remarried and came to get me. Two weeks later, my father kidnapped me from her home."

In the intervening years, Paul's father had married a woman with six children and they proceeded to have a mutual child. "The baby, my half brother, is fourteen years my junior, but *he* is the son who was given my father's name," Paul says. "Now what does *that* tell you!

"I don't know why my father took me away from my mother," says Paul. "It was made very obvious to me that I wasn't wanted in his house. I'd always had after-school jobs and bought my own clothes; still, my father insisted that I turn all my money over to him. That Christmas while I was visiting my mother, my father sold the '32 Chevy I had bought with twenty-five dollars that I'd managed to save out of my earnings. I demanded the money and he threw me out. I was fifteen years old and I hadn't a place to go.

"A *lot* of people were helpful to me," Paul says. "For instance, one of my after-school jobs was driving a tractor for the father of a friend. When I was thrown out by my father, this family allowed me to live with them. (Otherwise, what would I have done?) The cost of room and board was deducted from my wages, which was only fair. They were very decent to me.

"The principal of my school was also very thoughtful," he continues. "After I left home, my father got in touch with the high school to let them know that I was no longer his responsibility. The principal called me to his office and said, 'I'm worried about you. I don't want you to drop out of school. If you need help, let me know.' I didn't go to him for anything, but it helped for me to know that I could have.

"And I had a girlfriend in my sophomore year in high school. We stayed together until after I went away to college. She was nurturing and I needed to be nurtured. I was welcome in her home.

"The tremendous loss for me in the divorce was that I had lost my family—literally my whole family," Paul says. "I was alone. Then, when I went away to college, I met a professor who needed a houseboy. We became friends. He has a warm, nurturing quality and over the years he's befriended a number of students. We've become family. It's a big family—fourteen, fifteen guys.

"I look upon that professor as my adoptive father," says Paul. "He's where I go when I go home."

PART THREE

LIFE DECISIONS

Chapter X

The Past Influences the Present: Creating Home and Family

When I was a child of eight or nine, I remember seeing a Deanna Durbin movie in which, at the end, she and her mother and her father all clasped hands. I remember her smile and her laughter as she walked off with her parents. That was the only wish that I ever experienced dramatically as a child —the wish to belong to a happy family.

—A sixty-two-year-old man whose parents separated when he was five

You know those commercials for the phone company—the ones that say, "Reach out and touch someone"? They show connection after separation. I cry at those commercials. I'm a real sucker for the illusion of family.

—A forty-one-year-old woman who was six when her parents' marriage ended

I used to listen to the radio and my favorite show was "Ozzie and Harriet." And I believed that the Nelson family was the norm, and that the family *I* headed someday would *be* the Nelson family. The idealization was a reaction to my own family. But even as a child I did not see myself as David or

Ricky, the Nelson sons. I was Ozzie. Later, when I married, I wanted children so that I could have the Ozzie and Harriet family.

—Arthur Waterman, forty-seven, age five when his parents divorced

At one time or another, all children engage in fantasies of belonging to families differing from their own. What would it be like, they wonder, to be raised by royalty or movie stars? To grow up with younger parents or with parents who are more relaxed about discipline? If an only child, what would it be like to have brothers and sisters? If raised in a large family, what would it be like to be an only child—or the oldest or youngest of the children in the family?

Not surprisingly, the youthful fantasies recalled by adult children of divorce tend to center on life in an intact, perfect, everybody-loves-one-another family. A "Father Knows Best" family. An "Ozzie and Harriet" family. A family like the one next door, where everybody sits down together to Sunday dinner.

As writer Linda Bird Francke explains in *Growing Up Divorced,* "Often the child feels cheated out of what he or she perceives to be the rights of childhood, and the feelings of deprivation and neglect grow to exaggerated proportions. Suddenly the life of every intact family in the neighborhood becomes as perfect as hers is imperfect, and fantasy supersedes reality. She alone has no mother at home to bake cookies in the afternoon, no father to come to soccer practice—*even if the parents rarely did these things before the divorce.*"

In the previous section, "The Way It Was Then," we looked at what it was like for boys and girls to grow up divorced. The chapters comprising this section focus on how the realities *and* the fantasies experienced by divorce's children have influenced the life decisions made by the men and women they became.

FULFILLING THE FANTASY: LIVES DEDICATED TO COMMITMENT

As they plot the course of their future lives, many children of divorce vow to make the fantasy of the intact family their reality. From the time they begin to go out with members of the opposite sex, they do not take relationships casually. "I would never just date," says Jared, twenty-seven, who never did. "Since the year I turned thirteen and divorce destroyed our family, my whole goal in life has been to achieve something stable, a relationship I can maintain and work on." Three years ago, Jared was married. "I place the relationship with Nicole above all else," he says.

SELECTING A PARTNER: STABILITY IS A SOUGHT-AFTER QUALITY

For children of divorce who are committed to achieving permanence, selecting a lifelong partner becomes very serious business. "When I was a young adult," Arthur Waterman declares, "it was extremely important to me that I not get into the situation that my parents had gotten into . . . that I choose the right person for me and create a lasting marriage. And so, as a young man meeting young women, I was very conscious of possible problems and the potential for things that *seemed* right going wrong. I was very wary of making the wrong decision, and always had this concern in the back of my mind: *How could I be confident that the relationship would work out well?*

"I don't think I had a checklist," he says, "but I certainly didn't have what most people in their early twenties have: the assumption that whoever you fell in love with would be fine, that the marriage would work. On the contrary, it seemed to me that you had to choose very carefully, because otherwise it *wouldn't* work. I was supercautious. I felt very strongly that if I made a commitment to a young woman who was going to be my wife, it was going to be a permanent, absolute commitment. I couldn't stand the idea of being divorced.

"My only hesitation about marrying Francine," he says of the courtship of his wife, "was that she was too mercurial, and I worried a lot about *stability*. It was two years before I could feel confident enough about us to risk marriage. But once I made my commitment (which I count as the day I asked Francine to marry me and she said yes), I felt it as permanent. It was not something that took time to get used to. It was there immediately."

The couple have been married twenty-one years and have a son, nineteen, and daughter, sixteen. Says Arthur, "The kids are great and, all things considered, I am quite satisfied with my life, although I have not become Ozzie and we have not turned out to be the Nelsons. But then," he asks rhetorically, "what family is?"

Arthur Waterman is one of several persons to use the word "stability" during the interviews when describing the qualities sought in a lifetime partner. Another oft-heard word is "steady." When Elly Edwards lists the characteristics that attracted her to David, for example, "reliable and steady" head the list. Someone who could be counted on, she says, as her parents could not.

The theme is repeated by Sheila Henderson: "I *knew* the kind of person I wanted to marry. Someone who was emotionally and financially secure. I wanted stability. That's why I always went with men who were a good deal older than I. I'm sure that I chose my husband, who is twenty-two years older, because he's everything that my father was not. My father was an impulsive person. The man I married is dependable, steady, a very serious person who takes his responsibilities seriously. I felt that I had to find that balance."

THE ADDED ATTRACTION OF A CLOSE FAMILY CONNECTION

Similarly, when Delia Sherman enumerates the sterling traits of her husband, Phil, she notes that "he was ten years older than I, came from a close family, and had strong feelings about religion and structure. All of that was very appealing."

In the interviews, several other adult children of divorce mention "belonging to a close family" as one of the attributes that attracted them to their partners. "One of my reasons for marrying my husband was that I adored his parents," I am told by a fifty-five-year-old woman whose parents divorced when she was a toddler. "He had a very solid family."

It is easy to understand the appeal. For many of these men and women, marrying into a tightly knit clan is seen as the next best thing to growing up in one. It helps to satisfy their yearning for cohesion, for togetherness. Henceforward, they *would* be part of a family gathering around a dinner table, albeit the table sat in the dining room of the home of their in-laws.

For Tobias Goodman, marrying someone raised in an intact, caring family served another important function by providing the newlyweds with a successful family model on which the life of their future family could be patterned. "One of the things that attracted me to my wife, Gloria, was that she came from a family that was everything I never had," he says. "I had no concept of family, of how it was to be, but I knew that Gloria understood how to create a family . . . and I knew I wanted one."

HAVING CHILDREN EXTENDS THE COMMITMENT

In the life plans made by many men and women who experienced parental divorce, having children of their own is high on the list of important goals. There is a strong desire to build a family—"a nesting instinct," in Elly Edwards's words. Their aim is to create a family and, unlike their own parents, to get it right!

The nesting instinct is strongly expressed by Delia Sherman: "Once I suspected that Phil was going to be important in my life, I shared my past with him, including what it was like to grow up as an only child with a housekeeper in place of a family. I told him that I wanted children, *many* children. Fortunately, he felt that way, too. So we married and moved to the suburbs in order to raise the children who we hoped would come along, and we had two sons and two daughters—all through natural childbirth." She smiles widely at the memory. "I didn't want to miss any part of the experience," she says.

A strong sense of caution also emerges in many of the accounts. For those who recall divorce as having been personally devastating, the possibility that they might cause similar harm to their own children is a major concern. "Although there was never any question that I wanted children," says Tobias Goodman, "I was also terribly afraid of having kids, of not being a good father to them. After all, look at the track record. My father had been abandoned by his father, and he in turn abandoned me. The fact that I *have* been able to be a good father is of monumental importance to me."

John Lindstrom is still struggling with that fear. "I don't know *how* to be a husband and father," says the forty-three-year-old musician, who was one month shy of his first birthday when he last lived with his own father. "I have trouble living up to what seems to be expected of me. To take a small example—I don't send Hallmark cards or gifts to my wife or children on their birthdays. I don't make a fuss about Christmas. Growing up, I found Christmas and other holiday rites somewhat hypocritical. It became in our family like trying to make up for the neglect that I experienced day in and day out. I can't put myself in the mold of husband and father that my wife expects from me. That makes her very unhappy."

People who were raised in dysfunctional families need to learn positive ways of interacting with their spouses and children. It is not something they pick up from their surroundings. As a direct reaction to his chaotic upbringing, for example, John Lindstrom has developed a terrible fear of all confrontation. "For me, you see, any fight between a husband and wife is seen as a prelude to ending the marriage and living apart from your children, so I back away from arguments when perhaps it would be better to have them out. I never learned how to fight the good fight."

Demographically, there is no evidence that couples stay together for the sake of the children. Among the men and women with whom I spoke, however, it was very clear that many regard being a parent as the ultimate commitment and would even struggle in an unhappy marriage in order to keep their family whole once there are children. Lindstrom exemplifies this attitude. "I would not remain in this marriage were it not for the children," he says. "In a sense, I can't do to them what my parents did to me."

Ruth Lewisohn has been in John Lindstrom's place. She has faced a crisis in her marriage. And she has seen it through. "Five years ago," says the thirty-six-year-old mother of three, "my husband and I went through a very bad time. We sought help, and today things are much better between us. Yet even at the lowest point in our marriage, I knew that there was *no way* I would allow it to end. I would have stayed in a very unsatisfactory relationship rather than break up this family." She adds with great fervor, "And I did not feel like a martyr when I was thinking those thoughts. The fact is, I would never do divorce to my children."

It is interesting to me to hear Tobias Goodman, who takes such pride in achieving a successful family, express a somewhat different point of view about the subject of family dissolution in a more general sense. "I think divorce is necessary to life," says the lawyer, who has represented clients in divorce proceedings. "It's one thing to be committed. It's quite another thing to be imprisoned. I am not committed to marriage at all costs. I *am* committed to good marriage at all costs. If there are children, divorce is a major step."

LEARNING TO FIGHT THE GOOD FIGHT
HELPS ENSURE COMMITMENT

Before pursuing divorce, therefore, Goodman counsels his clients to take any and all steps that might lead them to achieve a healthy family, one in which both they and their children will be secure. Mental health professionals who specialize in working with families agree with Goodman that it is not enough to have a family that simply stays together—in the way that John Lindstrom continues to reside at the same address as his wife and children. The odds are good in this situation that the Lindstrom children do not feel secure, and are waiting for a rupture that they know is inevitable. It would be better for the children if the conflict that they sense between their parents were brought out in the open and dealt with. "Conflict occurs naturally in any healthy family," says psychotherapist Teresa Adams. "The expectation [of the parents] that there be no conflict creates the most conflict of all."

Unfortunately, for those who have experienced parental divorce, there is often the need to create a "perfect" family as a counter to the dysfunctional family in which they grew up. And that translates into having a conflict-free family. When problems arise (as inevitably happens at one time or another in all marriages), the child of divorce who is hell-bent on preserving the family *at all costs* will be unwilling to confront them. Paradoxically, the parents' need to create an *illusion* of safety for their children often works against getting those problems out in the open where they can be addressed and worked on in ways that might strengthen the marriage. "I won't fight," says John Lindstrom, who prefers instead to store his accumulated grievances. One has the feeling that, someday, the burden will prove too great. Then, like his father, he will walk out of the marriage.

In contrast, marital disagreements are acceptable to Marilyn Freeman, thirty-eight, another adult child of divorce, but having her children be aware of any discord in the family is not. Like John Lindstrom and so many other children who remember bitter fighting between their parents, she is struggling to give her children the sense of a perfect family—that is, a family in which there is no conflict. To accomplish this, John Lindstrom doesn't fight. Toward this same end, Marilyn Freeman proudly tells me, "My husband and I *never* fight in front of the children."

"Keeping silent is terrible," comments a child psychologist who was herself a child of divorce. "When parents tell me that their child knows nothing about the problems going on between them, when they say, 'We only argue when she's asleep,' I tell them that kids *know*. They're not scared of the fighting. It's the stillness that frightens them."

In keeping confrontation from them, the Freemans deprive their children of an important lesson: that families do not have to be perfect to be healthy. Children need to learn that people who love one another can also feel free to disagree with one another, to argue, to have "a good fight." In *Understanding Children,* psychiatrist Richard A. Gardner writes: "If the parents are indeed successful in hiding their fighting from their children, they deprive them of the opportunity to observe effective self-assertion and anger expression and may thereby contribute to their children's development of anger inhibition problems similar to those exhibited by the parents. . . . The child who does overhear the fighting is generally getting healthier exposures than the one who doesn't."

Delia Sherman agrees. "Phil and I have always regarded any differences between us as things that we had to work through," she says. "It's *how* you fight that's important. That's what I have always told our kids." She goes further: "And I do believe that children should be part of the process. I'm adamant about that. My own parents never spoke to me about their divorce. They never gave me permission to try to understand that major event in my life. What happens between parents *is* children's business. Sure, our kids have seen us fight. But they also have seen us kiss and make up."

Delia adds, "From the beginning, however, Phil and I were so committed to marriage, I can't imagine something that we wouldn't have worked out." A good marriage takes work. Partners who are committed to marriage and children say that they are prepared to do whatever is necessary to make a marriage good.

THOSE WHO FEAR COMMITMENT

The same event can trigger different responses in different people. Just as some men and women are motivated by parental divorce to strive *toward* establishing successful families of their own, other adult children of divorce have a terrible time with making a commitment, and steer clear of marriage and family. Lorna Kelly belongs in this latter category.

I meet Lorna, a flight attendant, on an airplane. As she moves up the aisle, attending to the needs of the passengers, her gaze comes to rest on the cover of the book I am reading—it is a book about divorce and remarriage—and she stops to ask me about my interest in the subject. I tell her that I'm on my way to a conference of educators where I am scheduled to speak about the challenges of living in a stepfamily. She tells me that she is a child of divorce.

When she learns that I am involved in researching the long-term effects of divorce on its children, Lorna expresses interest in participating in the study. We arrange to get together at my hotel the following afternoon.

Lorna is an uncommonly pretty woman who wears her airline uniform well. Heads turn as she walks across the hotel lobby. One notices her blond hair first, softly curled and worn at shoulder length; then her green eyes and apple blossom complexion.

She smiles openly, revealing straight white teeth. She is thirty-two and single, Lorna tells me even before I get to ask the basic questions about name, age, and marital status. "My greatest fear right now is that I will never trust anyone enough to marry him," she says. "How can I have confidence that *any* marriage will last?"

As she begins to tell the story of her parents' marriage, the basis for her concern grows clear. "My father is an emotional, abusive man, and my mother must have left him about a thousand times and gone back to him as often," she says. "Both my parents have volatile tempers. I am the oldest of five children, and I think Mom was terribly afraid of either alternative—leaving us with our father or taking us with her when she walked out on him.

"One time, Dad grew so angry that he tried to strangle her. After Mom ran from the house, I followed and told her not to go back to him. That time she stayed away. Later, I got dragged into everything. Each parent tried to sway me. They used me to talk to the lawyers. After the divorce, Dad dropped out of our lives. Then Mom remarried, and I felt that there was no home to go to anymore.

"I took the job with an airline in order to get as far away from my family as possible," Lorna tells me. "But I haven't yet been able to achieve *emotional* distance from my past. Unless I do that, I don't think I will ever be able to bring myself around to saying yes to a proposal of marriage."

It is not for want of opportunity that Lorna remains single. She has been proposed to half a dozen times and once even came close to accepting. "That was when I was nineteen and still very vulnerable to being alone," she says. "Then one day I looked at my boyfriend and thought, *This man is going to dominate me just as my dad dominated my mother,* and I walked away from the relationship.

"I don't really trust men," Lorna continues. "I'm *very* cautious. The carryover of being a child of divorce is the guarded way I look at things." She laughs for a moment, providing some relief from the intensity with which she has been discussing her feel-

ings, and says, "I do have a checklist for what I want in a man."
Marking the points on the fingers of her left hand, she says, "One
is personality. Two, good manners. Three, a high tolerance of me
and my ways. Four, kindness. I *really* want kindness. And five,
generosity—not financial but in spirit."

She laughs again—it is her way of covering up a lot of emotion
—and says, "I'm afraid I don't have a very good history to go on.
My grandma put two in the grave. My mom divorced two. I sometimes think I shouldn't even bother to try."

FACTORS THAT WORK AGAINST MAKING A COMMITMENT

Lorna is bogged down by her family history. Identifying the
factors that lead people to shy away from commitment isn't a
simple task, as E. Mavis Hetherington and Frank Furstenberg
make clear. In a book review written for a professional journal,
they make this point: "Young people may believe it was their
parents' divorce which has made them reluctant to marry. Had
their parents remained together, they might have attributed the
same reluctance to some other circumstance—their parents' inability to get along, their intense emotional tie to their father, or
merely their strong interest in occupational success."

Indeed, the story that Lorna Kelly tells contains a number of
circumstances that could well explain why this beautiful young
woman is so wary of commitment. Not the least of these are the
abusive character of her father and the submissive response of
her mother. As Lorna made clear when she broke off her one
serious romance at age nineteen, she is wary of entering a relationship like the one that existed between her parents. There is
also the element of the speedy remarriage of her mother, which
left Lorna as a young girl twice abandoned.

Cause and effect are unclear. What is certain, however, is that
(like Lorna) many adult children of divorce do see a strong correlation between their anxiety about entering into serious rela-

tionships and their experience of growing up divorced. There is no question that, in their view, the breakup of their parents' marriage has been a major contributor to their own concerns about commitment. These men and women have not yet been able to free themselves from the emotional legacy they inherited, to separate their own lives from the lives of the families in which they grew up.

"People who come from divorced homes are always living with the fear that a relationship will end," says family therapist Bonnie Eacker Weil, citing one of the causes. "It plays a big part in the fear of committing."

Some recent studies also draw a correlation between parental divorce and the ability of the affected children to take seriously others' promises of faithfulness. In her research with young adults whose parents waited to divorce until after their sons and daughters had gone off to college, Katherine Stone Kaufmann identified *a change in attitude toward relationships and marriage* as one of the lasting effects of the experience on the children. There is a tremendous amount of skepticism and wariness affecting the young people's capacity to form intimate relationships, she found.

A second study involving a similar population came up with a like observation. "Perhaps the most uniform finding . . . was the radically altered attitudes toward love and marriage held by many following their parents' divorce," wrote Barbara S. Cain of the University of Michigan, describing the reaction of students in the study, which was conducted at the University of California at San Diego and the University of Michigan at Ann Arbor.

"Several categorically forswore marriage, vowing to spare themselves and their unborn children the pain and dislocation they had recently endured," Cain reported in *The New York Times Magazine*. "Others allowed for a long-term live-in relationship but pledged to forestall indefinitely a legally binding commitment. A disenchanted young man spoke for many: 'Since [my parents'] divorce, I'm gun-shy about love and spastic about marriage. To me, getting married is like walking over a minefield. You know it's going to explode . . . you just don't know when!' "

SABOTAGING RELATIONSHIPS: A MATTER OF CONTROL

It is not unusual for adult children of divorce who fear commitment to attach themselves to a series of unsuitable suitors in order to avert a situation that could lead to a long-term relationship. Commitment requires a person to give up some control. As has earlier been observed, this task can be especially difficult for men and women who feel aggrieved because they were given *no* say in determining the one most significant event in their lives: the divorce between their parents and the breakup of their original family. Marriage is difficult for these children of divorce not only because of the degree of commitment that it requires but also because of the inevitable dependencies that are part of a healthy union. Simply put, they do not wish to leave themselves vulnerable to the whims and decisions of anyone else—not *ever again*.

One way of effectively exercising control and staving off commitment is to sabotage any relationship *before* it gets too serious. Mallory Coburn is all too familiar with this ploy. "I get into relationships easily, but then I put a lot of burden on the men I become involved with," says the twenty-six-year-old. "I seem to need to be reassured that someone won't walk out of the relationship. (If your father didn't love you enough to stay around, why should anyone else?)

"I did have one long-term love affair," she says, "but I kept devising test after test of my boyfriend's loyalty until finally, *as I knew would happen,* he failed one of them.

"There's a lot of emotional baggage that I have to get rid of before I can commit myself to a marriage," she says. "I am still struggling to resolve the relationship between me and my father. You have to work out the issues of your old life before you start a new life." (See chapter twelve, "Cutting Loose: The Search for Understanding.")

AVOIDING RELATIONSHIPS BY CHOOSING INAPPROPRIATE PARTNERS

Others among the children of divorce keep from making a permanent commitment by selecting lovers who are in some way wrong or inappropriate for them: they may be too old, too young, of a different religion, or simply unavailable.

Bernard Singer, thirty-five, uses religion as a barrier. While he informs one and all (including the women he dates) that he will never marry outside of his faith, Judaism, his address book does not contain the name of even one Jewish woman. Thus, the women whom he phones and sees are all ineligible based on their religious affiliation. "They know from the outset that we can never get serious," he says with evident pride in his gallantry. "I always play fair."

Nancy Kovach manages to maintain her distance from appropriate partners by making sure that there's always some factor to stand in the way. "My gut reaction to men is that I totally distrust them," she says, echoing Lorna Kelly. "Any guy who shows me attention, I can't handle. It's simpler to go after someone I can't reach because of geographic distance or because he's involved with a friend. It's easier being in a triangle than to allow myself to get emotionally close to someone."

Dark-haired, dark-eyed Patsy Sturgess, thirty-one, spends her days as a social worker and her weekends performing as an exotic dancer. I am surprised when she tells me that she spends most of her Saturday nights and vacation times alone—surprised until she explains that the man in her life, the director of the agency where she works, is married. Weekends are reserved for his wife and children, he told her at the outset of their affair. Patsy will do nothing to come between him and his children, she assures him. Indeed, his devotion to them is one of the things she admires about the man, she tells me. "Staying with his wife and children is a lot more than my father did," she says. She also confides that the director is the third married man she's been involved with. "I keep falling for the wrong kind of guy," she complains, as if her choice of lovers is accidental. By gravitating toward men who cannot be available to her on a full-time basis, Patsy actively avoids commitment.

Twenty-seven-year-old Judy Benson, who has heard from her father only four times since he remarried when she was eleven, also has a history of dating men who are older and married. She does not expect her current lover, with whom she has been involved for almost two years, to leave his wife and children, she tells me. Yet in almost the same breath she says, "I want to be married and I want to have children. And I can guarantee you that *if* I married a man who was divorced and had children, I'd be a wonderful stepmother. I would actually look forward to it and welcome that responsibility."

In expressing the desire to be a stepmother, Judy Benson wishes to redress the wrongs that she believes were done to her by her own stepmother, a woman she holds responsible for having alienated her father from the children of his first marriage. By becoming a stepmother, she would be able to replay the scripts of her past. And here is her fantasy: she would demonstrate to all that the divorce story (including the introduction of a stepmother character) could be given a happy ending.

FEAR OF BEING A PARENT

Among children of divorce, there are also men and women who have been able to marry but who fear extending the commitment to include children. Brian Neville, forty-two, describes a dramatic scene from his past in which that nebulous fear assumed actual shape. "It was about seven years ago," he begins. "I'd stayed late at work and was rushing to meet my wife when I noticed a young mother and father with their child. They weren't doing anything out of the ordinary; they were just being a family. Suddenly, this terrible feeling came over me—the feeling that I could never be a father, that I did not have the ability to raise a child. It was a feeling of great depression, but it is a reality I cannot shake." Brian has not seen his father since the age of nine, three years after his parents separated. He has spoken to the man less than a dozen times in the intervening years. Acting on his concerns, Brian has not had children. There are no snapshots of toothy youngsters that he could share with the older man.

"I was always ambivalent about having kids," says Sheila Henderson, thirty-four. "There are several reasons for this. I grew up not only in the drug culture but as a feminist. I was intent on education, on having a career as paramount among my life achievements. Most of all, however, *I was terrified that history would repeat itself.* I didn't want to be the kind of parent my mother had been—a woman I saw as weepy, deserted, bitchy, and poor. I didn't want to have children who would either be deserted or torn between two families. All things considered, I've been very lucky with the way my life has turned out. I've managed to have a career and a successful marriage. I don't feel that I want to tempt fate any further."

There's no question that Rick Monelli, who is engaged to be wed, feels that in making the commitment to marry he *is* tempting fate. "The question of whether marriage is right for me is scary," says the thirty-one-year-old songwriter, whose parents separated when he was seven. "As the wedding to Kate gets closer and closer, I get more and more frightened. What if it doesn't work out? . . . But having a child and getting divorced is *really* frightening to me. Spending your life explaining, apologizing, and justifying to a child. . . ." He shudders at the image that has been culled from his past, an image that strongly affects his concern about the future.

"Yet the main reason I want to get married, as opposed to our

---

living together," he says, "is because I want to have children. I tell Kate, 'We'll try.' She doesn't like it when I express doubt. She comes from a very strong family, so the idea of marriage and children comes naturally to her. But 'we'll try' is the best that I can promise."

Although the child of divorce may bring a certain ardor to the wish for a permanent commitment, creating a successful marriage is not a one-sided endeavor. There is a good deal of wisdom in Rick's use of the plural subject—"we'll try" instead of "I'll give it my best shot"—which recognizes that even the most well-intentioned spouse cannot single-handedly make a marriage work. As the following chapter makes clear, it takes the combined efforts of both partners to create a healthy family.

Chapter XI

When History Is Repeated:
Hand-Me-Down Divorce

The topic under discussion on a nationally syndicated television talk show one afternoon is "Long-term Marriages." As we watch, the camera zooms in on a softly pretty woman with a peach complexion and gently waved gray-brown hair and her partner, a jovial-looking man with a full brown mustache. A caption superimposed upon the television portrait of the pair provides viewers with the information: "Married 38 years."

"Tell us," the interviewer asks the wife, "what makes it work? To what *one* thing do you most attribute the success of your relationship?"

"My grandparents were married forty-seven years," the woman responds. "My mother and father lived to celebrate their fifty-sixth anniversary." Her smile lights up the screen. "I come from a long line of love."

Children of divorce inherit a different kind of family history, one of marital instability, which they too are likely to repeat in their own adult lives and relationships. A consistent finding of studies has been that divorce rates are higher for children who grew up in divorced families than for children raised in intact families. There is no accord, however, on just how great this difference is. Estimates have ranged from "about 2 percent higher" to "half again as much" for children from divorced families as compared with children from nondivorced homes. The higher statistic, provided by demographer Larry Bumpass, is based on data from the National Survey of Families and Households, involving thirteen thousand respondents.

Bumpass nevertheless cautions against making the assumption that divorce is simply a hand-me-down experience. He points out that there are several possible contributors to the higher divorce rates among children of divorce, explaining, "We have found, for example, that people with lower education and lower income are more likely to divorce. This is true throughout society, and certainly fits the situation of many post-divorce households. Thus, children of divorce are perhaps doubly handicapped by their parents' marital history and by their educational and economic situation."

REPEATING THE PATTERNS

In another study that examines the impact of parents' divorce on children (albeit their research was limited to daughters), Kathryn London, Joan Kahn, and William Pratt also found that experiencing parental divorce increases the risk that a youngster will separate or divorce after she grows up and marries. But the researchers do not interpret this result as necessarily negative. On the contrary, the theory that was best supported by their data is that, having been provided with a role model of a "successful" divorce, the daughters felt freer to leave an unsatisfactory marriage.

London, Kahn, and Pratt explain: "Experiencing a parental divorce removes some of the stigma associated with divorce. It may also demonstrate that while divorce is stressful, it may be the best solution in the long run. But probably most important, it provides [the daughters with] a model of a parent being able to cope alone, at least temporarily."

In the previous chapter, we heard the voices of men and women who experienced parental divorce and who vowed that there was *no way* that they would repeat their parents' history. Here we meet adult children of divorce who took the plunge—in spite of their concern that marriage is a risky venture. Not only is divorce viewed by many of them as "possible"; some of these children of divorce see separation as an almost "inevitable" outcome of their own marriages.

"COMING FROM A LONG LINE OF DIVORCE"

For Justine Marsh, a fifty-five-year-old illustrator who has been twice married and twice divorced, this clearly has been the case. "I come from a long line of divorce," explains Justine, the only child of her father's middle marriage, providing a counterpoint to the TV panelist who explained the secret behind the success of her long-term marriage. Justine continues, "I think that, if your parents divorced, you *will* have that as an option. You might be more inclined to get married because you think, 'Well, if this doesn't work out, I'll just get divorced.'

"That is the attitude that I took with me into my first marriage," she continues. "My husband was in the military. At first I thought that was exciting. We would have an opportunity to travel. Then, when I found myself marooned in some tract house in Central America, I became homesick and wanted out. As a child of divorce, you do know that you don't have to stay in a marriage, that you *can* get out.

"He was a nice enough man and a good father," Justine says of her first husband, "but I left him, taking our children with me. The thought of raising two children by myself was not at all frightening. After all, hadn't my mother raised me, and wasn't I just perfect!"

Marsh continues, "I also believe it's easier for kids of divorce to remarry. It certainly was easier for me because there was a pattern in my family of remarrying. So I married again and had two more children. But husband number two was abusive to me and to the two children from my first marriage, so I got out of that marriage, too.

"I didn't grow up with a solid concept of a marriage that could last for ever and ever," Justine says. "If I ever imagined the way I'd be at age fifty-five, I would have thought of myself as I am now —living alone, with kids. Like my mother."

RE-CREATING OUR FAMILIES OF ORIGIN

In some ways, we all re-create our families of origin. "Haven't you ever had the sensation of looking in the mirror," asks psychiatrist Clifford Sager, "and finding yourself staring directly at the face of your parent?" Sager is not talking about features, necessarily, but about an expression, a slant of the head, something that is reminiscent of the way your parents looked, that unconsciously links you to them—if only for the space of a glance. "We may even have detested something about our parents," Sager continues, "yet we find ourselves doing and saying the same things they did and said."

We bring our past with us. Thus it is that individuals in a marriage re-create, sometimes even unknowingly, the same situation that existed in their families of origin. Amy Greene describes just such a "coincidence" in her own life. "While I was married to Craig," she says, "I began an affair. I felt so guilty that I went to talk to my mother about it. My mother confessed that earlier in her life she, too, had initiated an affair. It was her way of getting out of her marriage to my father. I understood then that that's what *I* had been doing: I had let myself become involved with another man not because I was in love with him but because I no longer wanted to be married to my husband. In initiating an affair, I was doing just what my mother had done."

Family systems practitioners make use of a therapeutic tool called a genogram—a graphic representation of family relationships past and present—to help people understand the ways in which the experiences that make up a family's history affect the patterns of behavior governing their own lives. For David Rollins, who sought professional help to strengthen his second marriage, working with the family therapist on a genogram was very important in helping him see (quite literally) how closely he had been repeating the patterns of the family in which he grew up. As his story illustrates, only then could he begin to change those patterns.

DAVID: A CASE HISTORY

A muscular, darkly handsome man of fifty-seven, David Rollins sits in his large, executive's office on the corner of a high floor of a glass-walled Manhattan skyscraper. His back to the view, he begins to speak of the divorce of his parents more than four decades earlier and the long-term impact it has had on his own life. David's articulateness is enhanced by years of working to understand himself in therapy, yet the wounded teenager who lies within the man's frame has not yet been fully exorcised. He tells his story with emotion, describing a dramatic history of infidelity and divorce being passed down from one generation to the next.

"My parents separated when I was two years old, came together, separated again, and divorced the summer I turned sixteen," says David, "but my memory goes back to when I was six or seven years of age. My father was seldom home—he was a schoolteacher and held a second job as a salesman after school. But I have a striking childhood memory. You know how, when you're a child, you go down to the pavement and you walk with one foot on the curb and one foot in the street—it's sort of a lilting walk—and you make up singsong rhymes as you walk along? Well, I remember doing that, hippity-hopping along and singing to myself, 'My fa-ther has-a girl-friend, my fa-ther has-a girl-friend.' I don't know how I knew it, but even at the age of seven I was aware that there were women other than my mother in my father's life. Although I knew that he worked two jobs, I felt that there had to be another reason for his being away from home so much. Around the time that I was twelve, his philandering came out in the open. I remember my mother telling my younger sister and me, 'Your father has another woman.' He left the house that time, but came back several months later. When I was sixteen, my father left home for good.

"He even took me to Reno with him for the divorce," recalls David. "Can you beat that! I remember my mother being very angry at me for going, but I was sixteen and I didn't want to give up a chance to drive across the country and see places I'd never been. The summer of 1948, going with him to Reno, I rationalized it as an eight-week vacation.

"Soon after we returned, however, I learned that my father had married again. He invited my sister and me to his apartment once. There was a woman there whom he introduced to us as his wife, Selma. *That's* how we learned that he was married. Soon afterwards they moved, but he would not tell us where they lived or give me his phone number. I was so starved for affection that I took what little attention I got from him and made it so important. I'd create fights with my mother to go to where my father kept his car (I had keys) and sleep there, and he would come upon me in the morning. It was a ploy. I was hoping he'd take me in, but he never did.

"Still," David says, "I continued to idolize the man—so much so that, when I grew up, for many years I walked in my father's footsteps. I got married, had two children, and started a series of meaningless affairs, mostly with younger women. One day, my wife and I were having a fight. Our son and daughter came into the room and asked what was wrong. My wife turned to the children and said, 'Your father is having an affair with another woman.' I was so angry at her for disclosing the matter to them that I packed my bag and moved to a hotel, returning home after three months because of the financial pressures of maintaining two residences.

"Would you like an example of how closely I'd been patterning myself after my father? When I had to re-create these events in therapy in order to fill in the genogram, I was astounded to realize that my son learned of my affair when *he* was twelve years old, the same age I'd been when my father's infidelities were first spoken of openly. The year I left the house to move in with the woman who has since become my wife, my son was sixteen—the same age *I* had been when my father divorced my mother and married Selma. The parallels are striking.

"But there was one major difference between how my father and I behaved," David stresses, "and I think it is critical. When my children asked me where I was going, I could have said to them, 'I have an apartment.' It might have made things easier for all of us. But I wouldn't say that because I wanted them to know where I was. In that way I was *not* like my father. So I said, 'I met somebody and I will be moving in with her.' And I gave them her name, address, and telephone number, and told them they could reach me any time of the day or night.

"In their minds," he continues, "I was abandoning them for another woman, and that precipitated a lot of hostile emotions and actions. But I stood it all—and for a long time I allowed my present wife to suffer many indignities from my children—because I felt such guilt. I was not only trying to atone for *my* sins, you see; I was trying to right the wrongs of my father as well."

Outside the windows of David Rollins's office, the sky has changed from day-bright to twilight. Inside, too, the mood is somber. Clearly, these memories—of David the son and David the father—remain painful. They are also liberating. "People *have* to find out if they're walking in their parent's shoes," says David, "if for no other reason than that having that knowledge begins to make it possible for a child of divorce to take those shoes off."

THE PLATINUM RULE

The "astounding" similarity between the events that David Rollins experienced as a child and the circumstances that his actions brought about in the lives of his own children (especially his son) comes as no surprise to Ann Kliman, director of the Situational Crisis Service of the Center for Preventive Psychiatry. It is, she says, predictable.

Kliman explains, "Perhaps the most powerful and potentially pathological thing that occurs in divorce is something I've learned to call 'the platinum rule.' It is a repetition compulsion, and it is one of the most powerful drives in human behavior. The platinum rule is: *Do unto others as has been done to you.* It is an unconscious, driving need to repeat an experience with the unconscious wish that somehow it will be better this time. But it doesn't get better.

"The repetition compulsion," says Kliman, "is often connected with an anniversary reaction, and anniversary reactions are very complex. For example, let us say that a female child was five when her parents divorced. She may go along doing really well for years and years. Then she marries. And when she has a daughter who is five, all of a sudden the marriage falls apart and she gets divorced. *You are catapulted back to the time when your parents divorced.*

"It doesn't have to be when her daughter was five," Kliman goes on. "The divorce could fall on a different anniversary. Let's say that her parents divorced after seven years. It could happen when *she* has been married for seven years. Or suppose that her mother was twenty-eight at the time of her divorce. The daughter might divorce when *she* turns twenty-eight. Any one of a whole group of dates, times, and anniversaries can be translated and then, without knowing why, you suddenly find yourself reliving what you lived as a child. It is important to recognize that there is a pattern at work in order to be able to change that pattern. Once we recognize the pattern, it no longer controls us."

WHY SECOND-GENERATION DIVORCE OCCURS: OTHER THEORIES

Bonnie Eacker Weil adds a different perspective to re-creating a parent's history. "Some people even feel guilty if they're having a better marriage than their parents," says the family therapist, "and so they sabotage their relationship. If men and women *haven't* worked out the divorce of their parents, they carry it with them into their own marriage and play out their own scripts. Not infrequently, this leads them to divorce—just as their parents did."

FATHERS, THOUGH ABSENT, CAST A LONG SHADOW

Other explanations have been given for why children of divorce develop problems in their own marriages. Nora Johnson, daughter of playwright Nunnally Johnson, for example, cites the unrealistic expectations that daughters of divorce bring to their relationships with men as the reason that some marriages may fail. In an article she wrote for *McCall's* on the carryovers of parental divorce, Nora Johnson notes: "The adoring daughters who report good relationships with their fathers over the years —and a couple more who don't—were all afflicted, as I.was, with romantic fantasies of intermittently appearing Dad that have affected their relationships with men throughout their lives. If Dad isn't around much, appears only for holidays and vacations, he's inclined to be rather a holiday item himself—and any flaws, later discovered and/or reported by Mom, are taken harder than ever. This dichotomy is difficult to square with real, live men, who are inclined to be neither black nor white but some ordinary shade of gray."

It is hard to achieve a permanent relationship with a "gray" sort of man when one is dazzled by the shining armor worn by the idealized father. It is also difficult to build a trusting relationship when one lives in fear of the reappearance of the deserting parent in the person of the chosen mate. One has but to look back at the example provided by Lucinda Polk, who gained weight in order to test her husband's loyalty, to understand this: abandonment by one's spouse can be brought about as a self-fulfilling prophecy. When the "inevitable" happens, the child of divorce thinks: *I knew it all along.*

PREMATURE TRANSITIONS AND THEIR CAUSES

Low self-esteem, a characteristic frequently claimed by children of divorce, also leads several to select partners for reasons that do not augur well for lasting relationships. Among the findings of the National Survey of Families and Households, for example, is a tendency for children of divorce to marry early—before age twenty, well before most are ready to make a commitment that will last. Several explanations for why this occurs have been offered. It is well documented, for example, that children experience emotional stress when their parents divorce. This may cause them to make premature transitions, such as dropping out of school, becoming sexually active, or becoming pregnant out of wedlock—all of which are associated with a higher-than-average risk of divorce.

Another hypothesis offered by demographer Larry Bumpass is that the young people want to get out of a home situation that remains uncomfortable or unhappy for them. When children have experienced rejection by a mother or father following parental divorce, or find that there is neither physical nor emotional room for them in the remarriage household, the desire to make another attachment leads them to commit prematurely.

UNWILLING PARTICIPANTS IN DIVORCE

Paul Norman is a child of divorce who married young. Still, he never expected to be a man who divorced young as well. Paul

Norman tells me that he never expected to divorce at all. In his junior year of college, Paul married the high school sweetheart who had stood by him when his family cast him out. "The commitment I made when I married was not an adult commitment," he says. "The commitment was that my wife would take care of me and I'd allow myself to be taken care of. She was nurturing and I needed to be nurtured. Once I began to achieve some success in my life, I didn't want the mothering anymore. Still, I was devastated when my wife left me and ran off with her golf partner. I wanted to be in the marriage. We had adopted a child. I certainly never wanted divorce."

Like Paul Norman, many children of divorce who are themselves divorced are unwilling participants in the breakup of their own marriages. When divorce comes, it is very painful. "After I got divorced, I went through a ten-year period of being a vagabond," says Paul Norman. "I was in and out of relationships. I couldn't let go of the old relationship and I couldn't make a new one. I was very depressed. I went into therapy. That helped me get hold and understand and begin to build back."

The new structure of Paul Norman's life includes a loving relationship with his second wife, to whom he has been married for sixteen years, and a much-loved son who was born to the couple eleven years ago. "I don't think there are circumstances in which we would ever break up this family," Paul says. "There have been times in our marriage when we've gone for help—and we would do it again if it was necessary. Divorce is now the farthest thing from my mind."

Vic Santini lives clear across the country from Paul Norman and is fifteen years younger, yet the two men have much in common. "My wife and I were two kids who were each running away from a bad family situation," says the thirty-six-year-old electrician about his teenage marriage to Tiffany, who, like her young husband, was seventeen at the time. "We stayed together for five years, even though Tiffany was seeing other men throughout that time. One time she even ran off with her boss. Still, I went after her, begging her to come back. She did, but later ran off again. I really tried to make a go of that marriage. When Tiffany left for good, I was in a lot of pain."

Vic was not quick to remarry. Of his marriage to his present wife, Melissa, he says, "It began as a friendship that later developed into a relationship. I was leery of marriage. I didn't want anyone to leave me again."

After three years of seeing one another, Melissa and Vic were married because Melissa wanted children. Vic was not comfortable with that decision. He remembers thinking, *What if this marriage does not work out . . . what would that do to the children?* The couple now are parents to a daughter and son, yet Vic tells me that he is still obsessed with the question and unable to trust his good fortune. "If anything happened to disrupt *this* family," he says, "I'd be shattered. I really would."

Cindy Weston did see divorce happen to her children when her first husband, a historian, walked out of their marriage and moved in with one of his graduate students. For Cindy, a child of divorce who swore never to repeat the pattern in her own life, it *was* terrible. "I didn't want the divorce," Cindy vehemently proclaims. "I think it was the biggest tragedy of my life and in my children's lives."

Cindy had been a graduate student herself, one of the bright young teaching assistants in the history department of a major university in the Midwest, when she met her husband, Thayer, then an assistant professor.

"When we married," says the forty-three-year-old who has bitter memories of the aftermath of her own parents' separation, "I felt commitment . . . if not to the man, then to the children we would have together. I *knew* that I was not going to 'do divorce' to my children. This was etched into the cement of my soul: that my children would not suffer as I had. One of the results of being a child of divorce, I thought, was that I would be a better mother; the children would be safer because of the knowledge I had.

"And I worked hard at being a good wife and mother," she continues. "I tend to do things intensely, and I was homemaking intensely. Thayer said he didn't like the person I'd become. He said it was better when I was a student, that 'the things you do now are unimportant,' and he waved his arm around to indicate that our home was all that I now did. I thought we'd agreed that, at this time in our lives, he'd earn the living and I'd take care of the home and children. I'd said once, 'After the children are grown and in school, I'll either get a job or go back and earn my graduate degree.' He responded, 'You can do anything you want with your life so long as it doesn't impact mine.' Well, heck, *I* knew that our lives were intertwined, didn't *he?*

"Still," says Cindy, "those were not issues that warranted the breakup of a family. During my second pregnancy, two weeks before the baby was born, Thayer told me he was leaving. I said, 'You *can't* just end a marriage, period. Can't we go into counseling? Can't we talk, for God's sake!'

"I think we could have, and should have, worked on saving the marriage. It did not occur to me—*this sounds so dumb*—that you *can't* make that happen by yourself, because if your spouse wants to leave he can make the divorce happen even if you never would. I learned that you don't save a marriage by yourself."

DOING DIVORCE DIFFERENTLY

However the decision to divorce is reached, for adult children of divorce the resolution to conclude their own marriage is likely to be extremely painful. This seems to be the case whether or not the marriage that is being ended includes children. "Many people have told me that divorce isn't a serious matter if there are no children," says George Bevins, who at thirty-one is childless and newly divorced from his wife of four years, "but those people haven't grown up with divorce. They don't understand that going through divorce in your own marriage leads you to see yourself as a two-time loser. It's awful to be faced with the knowledge that you haven't been able to come out from divorce's shadow."

Still, George confronted divorce differently than his parents had done. "When I finally faced the fact that I wasn't happy in my marriage, I was quite insistent that my wife and I go for counseling to see if we could be helped to make a go of things," he says. "My parents did not do that, and they had an even greater obligation to seek help. No, call that *two* greater obligations: they had my brother and me."

George continues, "I also felt strongly that if there *was* going to be a divorce, it was better to acknowledge that and get it over with before we had children. So there was a kind of timetable in my mind. And when the marriage didn't improve, we saw a lawyer and began divorce proceedings. I did not take the divorce lightly *because* there were no children. I did take the decision to have children more seriously, I know, because there was a likelihood of divorce."

There are so many variables that affect how *anyone* is likely to react to being divorced, including such important factors as the age at which one is divorced and the length of time that the marriage has endured. As family therapist Hollis Steer Brown points out, "Of course it makes a difference if the divorcing couple is twenty-five and has only been married for a short time or if they are thirty-eight and the wife has put off having children until either her career or her husband's was on steady ground. It makes a difference if the couple was recently married or if they have been in the marriage for ten or twenty years. And it does make a tremendous difference if the couple is childless or has children. If they are young and have not had children together, some years down the pike they can almost forget that first marriage. If there are children, the divorce is intensified. They can never really end the relationship with the marital partner."

WHEN CHILDREN ARE INVOLVED

Listening to those who were the children of divorce, one has little doubt that passing the experience down to their children (regardless of which partner made the decision to end the marriage) is deeply troubling. At the very least, they hope to be able to "do divorce better" with their own sons and daughters and not repeat the errors made by their parents.

For Laura Bennett, a better divorce has meant *keeping their father in her children's lives.* "My mother forced me to make a choice between my parents," she says. "Since I continued to live with her and was dependent on her for my daily survival, there really wasn't a choice: I severed all relations with my dad. My continuing sorrow is that he died before I could make amends."

How has Laura Bennett done divorce differently? "Even though I do not have good feelings toward my ex-husband, I would *never* put my kids in the middle or have them make a choice." She adamantly restates her position: "I would not do that to them. Instead, I have actively seen to it that they spend time with their father and his wife by, for example, contacting my ex-husband and asking him whether he expects the kids for Thanksgiving or Christmas. Note that I do not ask him *if* he wants them, but when. When they were young, I would go with them to the card store so they could select greeting cards for him on Father's Day or on his birthday. The children are encouraged to feel good about each parent."

Since the age of twelve, when his parents divorced, Norbert Friedmann, a thirty-nine-year-old architect, calculates that he has met with his father no more than two dozen times. In this case, the decision was his father's—and it hurt. Friedmann's feelings about paternal distancing have made him determined to *remain involved in his children's lives.* This resolve serves as the basis for a somewhat complicated joint-custody arrangement that he has worked out with his former wife regarding the residential arrangements of their three daughters, ages four through eleven. He explains, "The children alternate between their mother's house and mine, spending Monday through Wednesday with one of us and Thursday through Sunday with the other. Midway during the year there is a crossover of this arrangement, so that each of us gets to spend weekends with the children." It is a fairly rigid arrangement that has required both parents and children to give up some of the flexibility that might be preferable from time to time. Nevertheless, says the girls' father, "it has been worth some stress and strain. My children will never feel that I have abandoned them."

For David Rollins, as we learned earlier in this chapter, doing a better divorce meant *keeping the lines of contact open* between him and his children—even if making it possible for his children to reach him at all times required an admission (painful for them all) that he was leaving their mother for another woman.

For Annalee Knossos, forty-four, doing a better divorce translates into *keeping the family unit intact* in the face of a struggle to make it as a single mother that sometimes has threatened to overwhelm her. At the age of eight, when her own parents parted, Annalee and her sister were sent to live with relatives. Thereafter, there were periods when the two girls also were separated from one another, with one sister at times going back with their mother or at other times living with different foster families. Since her own divorce eleven years ago, Annalee tells me, there have been many occasions when she again found herself without a home and had to rely on relatives and friends to take her in. "But my two boys have always come with me," she says proudly. "There is just no way in the world that I would do to them what was done to me and split this family up."

. . .

Although unable to protect her children from the ordeal of divorce that she herself experienced as a child, Cindy Weston tells me that she has determinedly attempted to *minimize divorce's harmful consequences* for them. "Of course being a child of divorce affected the way in which my own divorce was managed," she says. "Knowing the extreme way in which my parents handled my situation (to the complete denial of my father's existence), my handling has been in the other direction. The most important thing to me, after the divorce, was maintaining Thayer's connection to the children. He has *always* had unlimited access to them, restricted only by common courtesy. (He can't call at the last minute and expect all of us to drop everything we're doing.)

"Ours is a busy household," she says. "I work. I did go back to school (although sooner than I had intended) to earn my doctorate. And I am married to a wonderful man who, like me, did not seek the end of his first marriage. While my ex-husband and I live a thousand miles apart, money is not a problem for either of us and I pay half the costs of visitation. Unfortunately, he does not take advantage of the situation. He sees the kids no more than five days a year."

COMMUNICATION IS KEY
TO HELPING CHILDREN COPE WITH DIVORCE

"I've tried to help my children cope with divorce, over the years, by explaining the reality they're in," says Cindy. "They feel, for example, that they are not welcomed by their father's wife. (Yes, he is now married to the very young woman he left me for.) My daughter is now seventeen, my son fourteen. I tell them that their stepmother is not familiar with teenagers and their needs.

"What do you do to help your own children of divorce? It's multifaceted. It's definitely on my mind all the time in dealing with my children. We talk. My daughter has asked me the same basic questions about my relationship with her father at every stage of her development, and she will continue to do so. I keep no secrets from the children about why their father and I are not together, but I do try to soften some things. At the same time, it's a fine line you tread because you cannot tell them that their perceptions are wrong. I have a feeling that when she's married and has a three-year-old, my daughter will turn to her husband and say, 'Could *you* leave this child? I was this age when my father left me.'

"I think it's enormously helpful, in raising children of divorce, to have been there yourself. Your empathy is with them. In almost every imaginable way, I wish the divorce of my parents had never happened. It has affected my whole life. In terms of being able to help my children, however, I'm glad I was there."

PART FOUR

LETTING GO

Chapter XII

Cutting Loose: The Search for Understanding

For many years, the divorce was a given in my life,
but it was never an understood phenomenon.

—Adam Norris, age twenty-nine

At some point in their adult lives (whether they have achieved successful marriages, are themselves divorced, or are still struggling with commitment), men and women who grew up with parental divorce find a need to confront their demons—the unresolved issues that stem from the breakup of the once-intact family—in order to be free of them.

They learn that letting go is not easy. It is often a cathartic experience, however, which requires one to bring to the fore many painful memories of childhood in order to later reevaluate them from the perspective of the adult whom the child has become. It forces the sons and daughters of divorce to see the separation *as it really was,* not through the eyes of the child and not through the myths that were created and handed down by parents, grandparents, and friends of the family. Only when divorce is understood, say those who have faced and mastered the task, can it be laid to rest.

For Adam Norris, as for others among the adult children, the search for understanding has been the major challenge in ap-

233

proaching the goal of letting go. Between the ages of five and twenty-five, Adam declares, "I took being a child of divorce as a curse and felt that I was doomed because of it." Over the years Adam had struggled with a multitude of problems which he attributed to fallout from the breakup of his parents' marriage. "People seemed to come in and out of my life, relationships ended, and I saw that as my lot. As far as I was concerned, the divorce was a black mark that I would have to live with forever.

"A couple of years ago," he continues, "I realized that I had been using the divorce as an excuse for any and every failing in my life, *and that it was time to stop.* Before I could do that, however, I needed to gain some understanding of my mother and father's relationship to each other and to find out just where *I* fit in the scheme of things. Only then could I hope to leave the injured child behind and emerge as a healthy adult."

"It's as if the divorce held you back and you never grew up," echoes a thirty-one-year-old woman who was seven when her parents decided to separate. "There are so many unresolved issues in my life, among them: What was so terrible about my parents' relationship that they couldn't manage to stay together? Why didn't their parents or other relatives try to step in and save the family? Why did I count for so little in their decision to part? What about them and what about me?" Ruminating over the past that so strongly affects her present life, the woman describes her resolution to set the record straight. "If I was ever to become unstuck from the seven-year-old child I'd been carrying around," she tells me, "I needed to gain an understanding of my family situation and how it relates to me." And so, like many other adult children who try to make some sense out of their parents' divorce, this woman sought help.

While there are no statistics to verify that adult children of divorce are disproportionately represented among the population of men and women who seek therapeutic help in addressing their fears and their feelings, I find myself agreeing with a thirty-seven-year-old actuary whom I interview, a man whose parents separated when he was nine years old. "Even in seemingly happy, healthy families there is often undercurrent," he explains. "But a child of divorce will likely address some of the failings in his own life more readily than a child who has grown up in a seemingly healthy family and has been taught to ignore the negatives or the strained interpersonal relationships. As a child of divorce, you almost have a heightened obligation to address the things that go wrong because you don't want to fail in your own life as you believe your parents did in theirs."

EMOTIONS THAT INTERFERE WITH PERSONAL GROWTH

The combinations of factors that determine how people react to parental divorce are numerous, as are the concerns that lead them to seek assistance from mental health professionals. Because the subject is too varied and too vast to be fully treated here, this chapter necessarily confines its attention to those left-over emotions of divorce that stand out as most troubling for many of the adult children who were interviewed: issues having to do with unresolved anger, fear of commitment, and feelings connected with low self-esteem. Further discussions with therapists and researchers confirm that these problems are relevant to a larger population of adult children of divorce as well.

CONFRONTING THE ANGER

In the interviews, the problem that is most frequently raised by the adult children as reason for seeking professional help is their *unresolved anger.* "Frequently, anger is a defense against depression," explains Ann Kliman of the Center for Preventive Psychiatry. "For the child, now grown, the anger comes with the recalled powerlessness of the child to do anything about the changes that were wrought by the divorce."

The anger can have different causes. For Tobias Goodman, as for others who were physically or emotionally forsaken by a mother or father once the couple split up, anger revolves around parental abandonment: not just the physical abandonment by his father but (for a long time) the emotional abandonment by his mother. If anything makes a child feel powerless, it is just this estrangement, which says to the youngster, in effect, *There is nothing you can do, no magic wish upon a star, to hold on to me.* . . .

Like Laura Bennett, other adult children of divorce become angry when they realize how they were manipulated by one parent to cut off the other . . . or, like Amy Greene, at having been used as a pawn in the ongoing contest between their parents and, subsequently, their stepparents. . . . Nancy Kovach speaks for many others when she says that she is angry at having been given too much responsibility by her mother, the custodial parent, at too early an age. "I am angry," Nancy says, "because the divorce robbed me of years that should have been happy and carefree."

At one point, I mention the intensity of the anger I'd been hearing discussed—an outrage so strong at times as to be almost palpable—to William Koch, a child and adolescent psychiatrist who founded the "Skhool for Parents" in New York. "I am not surprised," Koch says, and explains, "Children of divorce are unable to express their anger for fear that they'll lose the remaining parent. So they wait till they grow up . . . and then find that they are filled with it."

The psychiatrist might well have been describing Delia Sherman, the "good little girl" who had not yet celebrated her second birthday when her mother went off, leaving the toddler to be raised by a series of housekeepers and a fond but often absent father. In the interviews, it is Delia Sherman who first introduces me to anger as a long-term carryover of parental divorce.

One afternoon, Delia and I spend several hours together. A thoughtful woman, she has been candid and insightful in recalling for me the divorce of her parents some sixty years earlier and its role in her life. As our meeting draws to a close, I ask what I expect to be a final question: "Is there anything important that I have not touched upon—are you surprised by what I did *not* ask?"

"Yes," Delia replies without a moment's hesitation. "You haven't asked me about my anger."

And so I do.

"As a child, you see your parents as all-powerful," says Delia. "Even when they do hurtful things, you want to believe that the fault is not with them (because you want them to be perfect), but that it is with you. So it took me years to be able to be angry at my parents.

"The question is not *why* I am angry," she says, the softness leaving her voice. "I can tell you why. I am angry at my father because (I finally came to understand) he didn't *have* to hold on to a job that kept him on the road so much of the time. He could have—no, he should have—arranged for a transfer to the home office so that I could at least have had dinner with him fairly regularly, or had him around to read me a bedtime story or, later, help me with my lessons. But I am even angrier at my mother and I can pinpoint the exact moment when I allowed myself to feel these feelings. It was when I was seventeen and right after my father had died. It was at the moment when my mother inappropriately suggested that now I was free to live with her, as if it was my father who had come between us all those years instead of because *then* it suited her to have me in her life. At that moment it became clear to me that this was a narcissistic woman who cared only about herself, who had *never* cared about me. And I was furious.

"The real problem," Delia goes on, her voice quivering, "is not *why* I am angry but that I can't *stop* being angry at my mother, even though she's been dead for thirteen years, and even though my anger hurts those whom I love. Let me give you an example that I'm not too proud of. Not too long ago, my older daughter met a friend of my mother's who spent an entire afternoon telling her how great my mother was. When my daughter told me of the conversation, my response to her was, 'You think my mother was so great? She was an awful, selfish person.' I still have the drive to tell this to my daughter who loved my mother . . . to burst her bubble." Delia shrugs her shoulders helplessly. "Why do I do this?"

One possible answer to why people continue to feel angry long after they have left childhood behind is supplied by psychiatrist Clifford Sager. "Part of the anger that many children of divorce have towards their parents is because of their feeling of 'I've been cheated,' " he says, explaining: "As a child of divorce, you missed something that it would have been nice to have had in your childhood: a mother and a father who both loved you and were there. Although you can't change what happened, you *can* try to understand it in some way and try to drop the anger."

There are many good reasons for doing so, not the least of which is the potential of anger to destroy other relationships entered into by the party who feels himself to be injured. As we saw in chapter eleven, if children of divorce do not resolve their past, the feelings and experiences are likely to be repeated in the present. For example, the adult who has not worked out the angry feelings of his or her inner child may go on to transfer that unresolved anger to a spouse's shoulders, eventually destroying the bonds that, like those linking parent to child, were meant to be permanent.

Clifford Sager acknowledges that trying to understand and drop the anger is hard to do. "Therapists must not blame adult children of divorce for their anger, not make them feel that they're wrong to have anger, but support them in their feelings and then help them feel that they have to give it up for their own sakes," he says. "We do that by helping people recognize that the anger is no longer being helpful to them, and that it is important to get over the mourning of their painful past and to get on with their own lives."

Learning to let go of the anger

"It's easy to lose a good friend," the late author Truman Capote is reputed to have said. "It's harder to lose a good enemy." Ask Nancy Kovach what this means to her, and she will tell you, "Getting on top of one's anger takes work."

In her determination to become a survivor of parental divorce, the twenty-six-year-old woman has been seeing a therapist for the past three years. It is, she tells me, the hardest thing she has ever done. "Telling someone that you've been going to a shrink doesn't say anything about the pain of the experience of reliving and trying to understand the past," Nancy says. "Letting go is scary. Sometimes it's easier to repeat the patterns and retain the anger because it's comfortable. You've lived your whole life with these feelings. If you let go, what are you left with?"

I would have liked to introduce Nancy to Tobias Goodman, for he has been where she is now and he is able to provide a reassuring answer to the question she poses. "Until the age of thirty, I never told *anyone* about my anger or resentment or about what happened to me as a child," Goodman says. "Up to that point, I devoted so much energy to leaving behind the world that I *didn't* want to be a part of and to gaining entrance into another world that I wasn't even familiar with, I had no time to look at myself. When I turned thirty, I began to recognize that I should start looking.

"I'd achieved everything: wife, family, professional success," the lawyer continues. "Yet the thing that was missing in this overachiever life of mine was an emotional quality. I had bottled up emotions, fears and pain. I needed to open up this container and let my emotions out. So I entered therapy. The effort took ten years. Worst of all [*and here we hear the echo of what Nancy Kovach is experiencing*], there was terrible pain involved in dredging up experiences and feelings that I had spent so much time in burying. Many a night I lay crying in my wife's arms.

"But it was all worth it," Goodman says. "When I sit here today telling you about my life, I am really speaking of two different lives, two different people. One before therapy, the other after."

FACING FEAR OF COMMITMENT

"A desire to conquer the fear of commitment" is another concern that often leads divorce's children to seek help in therapy. As chapter ten illustrated, there are many men and women who, for a variety of reasons stemming from their experience with parental divorce, are averse to making a permanent commitment to a relationship. In the interviews, Ernie Stavros describes the effect of this fear in his life and, also, how it was conquered.

"Angela and I had been going together for four and a half years before I could agree to setting a date for our marriage," says Ernie, a thirty-three-year-old who is built like a linebacker and earns his living servicing computers. "Plans were made for a large church wedding, a hundred and eighty people were invited, and I began to grow more and more anxious. I couldn't sleep and had trouble breathing. On the day that the invitations were to be mailed out, I told Angela that I just could not go ahead with the wedding.

"There was no question about the fact that I loved Angie enough to marry her—both she and I knew that I did," Ernie says. "The problem was my family history. My father, mother, and grandparents on both sides have all been multiply married and divorced, in my father's case as many as eight times. As a result, I grew up feeling that divorce was in my blood and I was concerned about whether *any* marriage that I entered into would last. I finally faced the fact that I would have to get help before I could make a marriage commitment.

"Angie was understanding; I had been completely honest with her," Ernie continues, "but her family (a close-knit Italian clan) was up in arms. My family just shrugged their shoulders, like *so what?*"

At the suggestion of a psychiatric social worker he consulted at a local mental health center, Ernie first entered individual therapy to work on understanding the legacy of his parents and learning to separate himself from it. At a later stage, Angie joined him so that the couple could work on constructive ways of communicating their needs and feelings to one another without either of them feeling threatened with loss.

Learning to manage conflict

"A lot of things were made clear to me in therapy," says Ernie. "For one thing, I learned that I had never seen conflict resolved positively. The attitude in my family seems to have been 'Get rid of the partner; get rid of the problem.' I had to learn not only to recognize that there is a problem but, more importantly, how to handle conflict in a responsible manner. I had to learn intimacy, which meant allowing myself to trust. That is still a challenge, one that my therapist and I are working on.

"Most of all," he says, "I learned to see my father and mother as products of the environment in which they, themselves, were raised. They had also grown up in homes that were broken by divorce—so they had a couple of strikes against them going into their marriage. But I know now that I do not have to follow that pattern."

Having shed the leftover feelings connected with being a child of divorce, Ernie feels more confident about being able to move into the future unencumbered by the past. Two years after their first wedding date was canceled, he and Angie exchanged vows before a gathering of forty family members and close friends. Ernie tells me, "Everything was manageable this time around."

STRIVING TO GAIN SELF-CONFIDENCE

Low self-esteem is another burden that is carried over from the experience of parental divorce, say its children, adding that it is also one that is not easily set down. As Nancy Friday explains in her perceptive work *My Mother/My Self,* "Children think their parents are perfect, and if anything is wrong it's their fault. We have to think our parents are perfect because as children we are so totally dependent. We can't afford to hate mother, so what we do is turn our anger against ourselves. Instead of saying she is hateful, we say, 'I am hateful.' " This kind of transference is especially true for many children of divorce.

As with the problem of anger, low self-esteem shows itself in many ways. For Nancy Kovach, as we have seen, it comes up in her inability to trust the reliability of others' promises of commitment to her. *(If I was not worthy of my father's love,* she thinks, *how can I believe that I am deserving of the love of any other man?)* For a thirty-six-year-old man named Danny Brewer, whose parents divorced when he was four and who lost all contact with his father from the age of eleven, feelings of low self-worth were behind his inability to make the decision to leave a "safe" job as a salesman for a national discount record chain and try to get into arts management. "I gave myself lots of 'good' reasons for staying put," he says, "when (I learned in therapy) the real culprit was my fear of failure and the conviction that I *would not* succeed."

When we part, Danny hands me his curriculum vitae. "In case you know someone who might be interested . . ." he says, laughing. The sense of unworthiness generated by the child's perception of not having been "good enough" to hold the original family together (and, in cases like Danny's, to merit the continuing love and involvement of a parent) lingers on in the lives of many children of divorce long after, chronologically at least, they have left the child behind.

Learning to demystify the past

Being unloved by a parent, or even *feeling* that you are un-loved, leaves scars. "But the wound can be healed and healthy growth can begin anew," declares Howard M. Halpern in his insightful book on coming to terms with your parents, *Cutting Loose*. First, Halpern advises, it is important for the adult to allow himself to question whether a parent who has been labeled as "unloving" really is so or whether this designation was not as true as the child had been led to believe. Halpern presents a moving example of working with an adult child of divorce toward demystifying the beliefs he held about his past. He writes:

"A young man was telling his therapist about an incident when he was two years old and his father was bathing him. His mother came in, found that the window was open and screamed at his father for not closing it. 'My mother said I almost got pneumonia from that. That's how much my father cared.'

" 'He bathed you,' the therapist said.

" 'Yes, I know, and he left the window open.'

" 'He bathed you,' the therapist repeated.

" 'Right, and he darn near killed me.'

" 'He bathed you.'

"Slowly the young man began to hear what the therapist was saying. He had before only let himself hear about the open win-dow and not the simple fact that his father, who his mother had long taught him had never loved him or done anything to care for him, had bathed him. It opened him to many early memories of his father (his parents had divorced when he was quite young) that indicated considerably more paternal caring than he had long believed was true."

And learning that you were not *at fault*

But what if there had not been paternal caring? What if the search for understanding only confirms the adult child's deep-seated belief that he (or she) did not get the loving that was really needed from a mother or father and that this has damaged his self-esteem and distorted his relationships with others? Can such destruction be repaired?

Again, Halpern is optimistic about the potential for human growth. Were this book being printed in color, his response to the above query would appear underlined and in red. It is that important and potentially liberating. "It is crucial to begin to accept that your parents' not loving you is a statement about them and not about you," the psychologist writes. "In other words, it bespeaks a defect in their ability to love rather than a defect in your lovability. [The parent's] inability to love you is a tragedy, but it is nothing personal."

By extension, Halpern also emphasizes that it is important for adult children who have lived with the belief that they are in some way at fault (either for causing the divorce or for not stopping its progress) to understand that the divorce belongs to the parents as well. "Sometimes this idea is propagated by one of the parents, sometimes it is picked up from a remark not meant that concretely, sometimes it arises out of the child's own thoughts," he writes. "There are countless such examples, and it is important to become aware whether you harbor ideas like these and now, as an adult, to challenge them with your adult knowledge *that a parent leaves a marriage because of unhappiness with a spouse, not with a child.*"

GOING BACK TO YOUR PARENTS AS AN ADULT

In therapy, the importance of re-viewing the events of the past with adult eyes and grown-up insights cannot be overstressed. The road to understanding the past in order to relinquish its hold takes different forms. It is generally accepted, however, that one of the more successful forays is for a man or woman to go back and get to know his or her parents, but now as one adult meeting another.

"You cannot cut off from your parents," says psychiatrist Murray Bowen, a pioneer in the approach that uses the family of origin as a therapeutic resource. He points out: People who cut themselves off completely from their families of origin have the greatest likelihood of repeating with their mates and children, or any intimate relationship, the irrational patterns of the past.

In his office at the Georgetown University Family Center in Washington, D.C., the white-haired psychiatrist tells me, "The important thing to realize is that parents do not set out to hurt their children. Everybody who has ever lived was doing the best they could with the situation they had to deal with at the time."

That is what Ernie Stavros discovered once he was able to see his parents as products of their own multidivorced environment. It is what Jennie Fuller learned, following the failure of her own second marriage, when she returned to Alabama to seek out the truth.

More than a score of years after the divorce of her parents, the young woman continued to feel resentment toward her mother for taking the children from their father and from Boston, a city that Jennie still regarded as the one place where she had been truly happy. On instructions from her therapist and with his guidance and support, Jennie went back to have some serious conversations, woman to woman, with her mother.

Slowly, Jennie found her resentment turning to admiration for the older woman. "For a long time I had been thinking of my mother as weak and a quitter because she had not had the fortitude to keep the family together," Jennie says. "In talking with her during the visit, I was made aware that our family had been in dire circumstances in Boston, that creditors were constantly after my parents, and that there had been *no* money coming in to pay our debts.

"As my mother and I looked together through albums of family pictures [another of the tasks assigned to Jennie by her therapist], I saw her as a young woman—someone who had been younger than I am now when she had the courage to pick up and move with three kids, taking a job for two dollars an hour so we all could survive. I don't think I would have been that brave. Therapy freed me from the resentment I had toward my mother. I learned to appreciate that she is an incredible person. There's an added bonus: being proud of my mother has made me more comfortable with being myself."

SEEING BOTH PARENTS CLEARLY

The split evaluation of one's parents by which one of them is seen as good and the other as evil is fairly typical of children who grow up in dysfunctional families. Usually, the parent who evokes the child's sympathy is the one who does not quickly enter into a new romantic relationship. More often than not, it is the left-behind parent who is favored. "My mother was left alone with four kids," says a thirty-six-year-old man whose parents divorced when he was eight, immediately after which his professor father moved into an apartment with a young woman who had been the mother's helper for the family—a woman he subsequently married *and* divorced. "My father was a bastard," says the son, describing the view he had held of the man throughout childhood and well into his growing-up years. "I spent many years in therapy until I was able to acknowledge that my mother had played some part in his walking out on us."

What the child of divorce must learn to understand is that, more often than not, both parents have human imperfections and both have worthwhile traits. As Howard Halpern writes, "It is vital to try to see each parent as a flesh-and-blood being so that you can understand what went wrong in the *mix* between the two people who, probably in hope and love, brought you into the world."

With the insights provided by his own life experience plus an unbiased reappraisal of both his parents, the professor's son was able to appreciate the circumstances that had led his father to become involved in an affair with the mother's helper. Very simply, the relationship between his mother and father had been going downhill for a long time. Where the wife had been frequently and vocally critical of her husband, the live-in helper had been adoring. And available.

As a child, the son had been made to choose between his parents. This is fairly typical, say the children of divorce, who frequently find themselves manipulated to take one parent's side against the other. For the young boy, the choice was easy. His father was a bastard! As an adult child of divorce, however, the son was better able to see his parents against the complexity of human relationships and to challenge the myth that had been handed down to him—that his mother was blameless and his father had no redeeming attributes. "I don't condone what my father did," he now says, "but I do understand it. When my mother confronted him with her discovery of the affair, she sent him packing. He went without putting up much of a struggle. He agreed with my mother, you see, that his transgression was great enough to warrant his being evicted from the family Garden of Eden. The poor guy even tried to 'do right' by the mother's helper, a nineteen-year-old whom he married although he did not love her and they had little in common. I learned to see my father as a weak man, not an evil man. And that has allowed me to move on."

In siding with her father, Jennie Fuller also allied herself with the parent whom she saw as having been left behind. Once Jennie began to see her mother in a better light, however, she found herself growing resentful toward her father. Suddenly, *he* became the one who was at fault for what happened to the family. Yes, he always spoke lovingly to his children, she acknowledged, but now Jennie was beginning to face the fact that warm sentiments weren't enough to nurture a family. She recognized that her father was a man who had failed to meet his responsibility to support his wife and children. A weak man.

At this stage in the process of making peace with the past, Jennie's earlier empathy with her father turned to anger at him for *not* being the idealized father in whom she so needed to believe. It was his fault, she now decided, that she had misunderstood and mistreated her mother, his fault also that she had experienced so much guilt, as a child, at not being able to return to Boston and rescue him from his pain and loneliness.

Jennie winced as the therapist pointed out the word she had used: "rescue." With great difficulty, Jennie faced up to a truth that she'd known for longer than she cared to acknowledge: her father was an alcoholic.

She could have wasted more time in feeling angry at her father because of his inability to conquer his addiction. Fortunately, Jennie tells me, she was guided by her therapist to look at her father and ask herself: *Why* did he drink? Engaging in the same process that helped her gain deeper knowledge of her mother, Jennie went back to try to understand her father. She was surprised that she had not earlier found it significant that he, too, was a child of divorced parents. Jennie began to look at the child in her father, began to understand that he too had been trying to live a grown-up's life without having resolved the issues between himself and his own parents. For many years of his boyhood, there had been *no* contact between him and his father. His strongest memories of his own childhood, he told his daughter when she asked what it had been like for him to grow up divorced, were of being dominated by a vengeful and abusive mother. Alcohol became a way of escaping the reality of a painful childhood. When he married, her father said, he vowed that he would never abuse his children, as he had been abused. And he never had.

What Jennie was experiencing is fairly typical of what can happen when distorted childhood fantasies of one's parents are corrected and the family's history is examined and redefined. "Usually a more sympathetic view of both parents is developed when the clients understand what their mother and father had gone through with their parents," says psychologist James L. Framo, whose work focuses on involving the family of origin in therapeutic treatment.

In an article in *Family Process*, the psychologist writes: "Coming to terms with one's inner furies and devotions, originally compounded and shaped in the relationship with the parents of childhood, and completing the mourning over losses, can free one from invisible shackles and help one to enjoy personal liberation as well as the fulfillments of deep relationship."

Here, too, Jennie's experience can serve as an example. "I realized," she says, "that in their own way each of my parents *had* loved us, that they were doing the best they knew how. That knowledge has freed me to strive to be the best person I can be. It has also enabled me, after two failed marriages to the wrong kind of partners, to make a commitment to a new and healthy relationship, one that I feel confident *will* work out."

MAKING THE CONNECTION

"The more people of the present generation can get to know their family of origin and the families from which their parents came, the more they will be rewarded in terms of their own adulthood," says psychiatrist Murray Bowen. But, he adds, "making contact with parents is more than going home for a visit. It's a complex process and not very easy."

He offers some instructions to help one begin the process. The guidelines, which follow, are useful even to those people who are not children of divorce.

Begin by talking. One of the greatest enemies to understanding one's parents is the failure to communicate.

Ask about feelings. For example: "How did it feel to be the only daughter in your family?" or "How did it feel when your parents divorced?"

Try to connect as one adult to another, not as child to parent. As one grown-up to another you might ask, "Are you happy with the way your life turned out?" In this way, you can begin to understand your parent's dreams and expectations, frustrations and disappointments.

Go home. Many people live at some distance from their extended families. It is important to go home—not just once but frequently. "If you get upset by a visit, keep going back and back again until the visits no longer cause a negative reaction in you," Dr. Bowen advises. Go home even if you have good relationships with your parents. Relationships are not static. It is necessary to go home from time to time if only to reestablish relationships and put them on a different footing, adult to adult, rather than as child to parent.

Attend weddings, reunions, any occasion that brings family members together. Family gatherings should be viewed as opportunities to learn more.

Don't lecture. Don't bring up old grievances and recriminations.

Don't judge.

Don't personalize. If your parent expresses disappointment, don't automatically interpret the statement to mean disappointment *in you.* Again, it is important to understand what your parents' hopes were—what were the unfulfilled dreams in their lives —in order to comprehend the role you were expected to fill. The problem lies, therefore, not in you, but in your parents' idealized portrait or condemnation of you. *You are not at fault.*

Don't give up on your family. Staying in touch may cause

discomfort in the short run, but it can have long-term gains for you and those who are closest to you.

Mallory Coburn is currently struggling with the process. "As I grew older, I saw a lot of my father in me," says the twenty-six-year-old woman. "I wanted him back in my life, and made a list of things to do. First thing, I wrote a letter to my stepmother, explaining my initial reaction to her and saying that I wanted to work my way back into the family. Then I began to call my father once a week, *every* week. Although there had been no contact between us while I was in college, I made sure that he took an active part in my selection of a graduate school.

"When I reestablished contact, my stepmother was suspicious. I have to work to gain her trust. I also sense that I have to walk on eggshells around my father or he'll abandon the relationship once again. It's been five years of very hard work on my part.

"Why do I do this?" Mallory asks before I am able to pose the obvious question. "I feel that the divorce still has a pull on me, that I am still controlled by it. I have to get to a point where I can bury the emotions that are holding me back. I have to be able to cut those strings so I can stand on my own two feet."

Similar feelings are expressed by Adam Norris, who has sought to make of his parents' divorce "an understood phenomenon." For Adam, the task of going back to his parents has meant reconnecting with a father whom he had neither seen nor spoken to for eighteen years. "I felt like I was dredging up my deepest, darkest secret in confronting him," says Adam, "but my own bravado got me to make the call and arrange a meeting."

Adam describes the encounter. "My father came barreling down the hall and he hugged me. He said, 'I want you to call me Dad.' I said, 'I'd just as soon call you by your first name.' I set the tone. And I was very open with him. I laid out everything. The anger I felt at him for abandoning me to the sole jurisdiction of my mother. The resentment I felt at his not offering himself as an alternative. My sexual struggles. The money that had not been forthcoming when I needed it. My stepfather, with whom I had never gotten along. And I said, 'Who are you to bring somebody into this world only to have him raised by somebody else?'

"My father allowed me to yell and to throw these things up. To get things out. How did he explain his absence from my life? 'I thought it would be better for you' . . . 'I didn't want to complicate your life' . . . 'It was your job to get in touch with me.'

"And then, in the same meeting, I brought all of my grievances up again.

"Finally, my father said to me, 'Are you going to live like this for the rest of your life—or are you going to realize that what happened *happened* and let it go?'

"I think *that* was the beginning of putting the divorce and everything that followed into context."

In speaking of how to approach one's parents, Clifford Sager advises, "Try to understand, as much as you can retrospectively and in terms of general human knowledge, *why* your parents may have divorced . . . that this was a weak man . . . this was a disturbed lady. It isn't enough to say, 'My mother and father yelled a lot.' *Why* did they yell? Understanding why parents acted as they did can bring an overwhelming resentment down to manageable size.

Over time, Adam Norris says, he *has* been able to achieve such insights, to make of his parents' divorce an understood phenomenon. "I read an article some time ago that really hit home," he explains. "In it the author spoke of people having 'irreconcilable similarities.' That was true of my parents. Both were egocentric. And I understood that my father and mother were never meant to be together.

"Their marriage was a textbook case. He was a poor boy, raised by an overbearing family, who struck out on his own and saw marriage to a classy, pretty, naive woman from a wealthy family as a shortcut to success. She was a spoiled young woman who wanted to get out of her parents' house. Theirs was a mismatch that had *nothing* to do with me."

He continues, "I am at the point now where I am *enjoying* letting go of the pain that I carried with me, enjoying letting go of all the negative aspects. I always thought that the bad times that my parents had in their marriage and divorce had to do with me. It's such a relief for me to know the truth: that my mother and father were just two people who didn't get along. It's wonderful *finally to understand* that their divorce is *not* my fault, that the ill will that continues to exist between them is not my responsibility."

The concept of going home again is not universally accepted. "There's something Pollyanna about it," says James D. Meltzer, director of psychology at New York's St. Luke's/Roosevelt Hospital Center. "I believe that there *are* people who are evil, who do harm. And I believe that some righteous indignation is a healthy response to evil that has been done to one.

"Nevertheless," Meltzer adds, "even people who have been badly harmed must reach some resolution. At some point, however it's accomplished, you have to lay the past to rest and get on with your life."

Chapter XIII

Forgiveness: Making Peace With the Past

> Children begin by loving their parents; as they grow older they judge them; sometimes they forgive them.
>
> —Oscar Wilde, *The Picture of Dorian Gray*

"How do you feel toward your mother and father now?"

I ask this question of men and women in their twenties... forties... sixties. When their parents separated and the family changed, these same adults ranged in age from toddlers to teenagers. In the intervening years, many managed to remain close to their parents (although not necessarily to both mother *and* father), continuing to find their affirmation in a loving (albeit altered) family.

Others became emotionally alienated or physically separated from their parents as a result of the divorce. Theirs was a harsher childhood, often leading to troubled periods and sometimes turbulent relationships in their grown-up lives.

The years have provided these children of divorce with ample time for judgment and, in many cases, understanding. Frequently, too, there has been forgiveness.

But not always. In the interviews, it is the children of divorce themselves who introduce the notion of forgiveness as something that is, or perhaps ought to be, part of the experience they have been describing—the experience of what it has meant to them to have grown up divorced. For example, when I ask Paul Norman the question "What are your feelings toward your parents now?" the soft-spoken fifty-one-year-old adamantly responds, "I do *not* forgive my mother or my father; I will never forgive them for shipping me around and then shipping me out." (I had not raised the notion of forgiving.) Norman remains especially embittered toward his father, who made room in his home for his son when the older man needed the then-teenager's assistance and cast the boy out once his usefulness was over.

For many years, during which time he himself was married and divorced, Paul Norman continued to hate his parents. "They abused my trust," he says. For this man who makes his living dealing with the law, that is an unpardonable sin. "The feelings that I had as a young child, of love toward my parents, are just not there," he says evenly. "My parents were *not* friends of mine. I feel horribly betrayed by both of them. They did not contribute to my life, except biologically. I am estranged from my family. When my father died, I did not attend the funeral."

Instead, as we saw in chapter nine ("Saving Graces"), Paul Norman sought and found the paternal qualities he wanted in a father substitute. It was his salvation. Psychologist Howard Halpern describes this response to an unloving father or mother as "a matter of re-parenting. Of allowing yourself to be a more loving parent to yourself than your parents were, of allowing others to love you in ways your parents could not, of allowing all the loving experiences you've ever had to make the statement about your value." It is, in a way, an experience of forgiving yourself your past, filling the voids left by unloving parents, and moving on.

Human relationships are ambivalent. Where there is intense love, as Sigmund Freud pointed out, there is also the opportunity for intense anger. In his book *Forgive and Forget,* author Lewis B. Smedes elaborates on the love/hatred theme. "We usually hate someone who is close enough to us—close enough to love," he explains. "We hate the person we once trusted, the one we expected to be loyal, to keep a promise. We do not hate strangers. We hate the people we blame for wronging us."

Paul Norman believes that he can deal with the present and face the future only by hardening his heart to the past. For other children of divorce—and here Delia Sherman serves as an example—the ability to forgive a parent remains elusive. And therefore disturbing. Like Delia, many still regard forgiveness as a resolution that is, to borrow Hamlet's phrase, devoutly to be wished.

WHY FORGIVE?

For the most part, professionals who deal with the emotional health of human beings wish this outcome for them, too. "Forgiveness is very important because when we carry hatred around it's destructive to us and to our relationships," says psychiatrist Clifford J. Sager.

"A grudge is a little like an unpaid bill: the idea of the other person owing you something keeps the relationship alive, if only in a negative way," agrees psychologist Irwin C. Rosen, who is with the Menninger Clinic in Topeka, Kansas. He adds, "You may need to write that 'bad debt' off emotionally so that you can go on with your life."

Echoes Harold Bloomfield in *Making Peace With Your Parents:* "The psychological truth is that holding on to our past resentments towards parents robs us of our current peace of mind and our ability to express satisfaction in our here-and-now relationships. . . . First and foremost, the reason to forgive is to regain your [own] emotional freedom and peace of mind."

The need to forgive is not confined to children of divorce.

Witness the case of Marie Balter, a woman who at sixteen was misdiagnosed as a schizophrenic and kept in a state mental hospital for more than fifteen years, and who has since returned to the hospital as its community affairs director. "I wouldn't have grown one bit if I didn't learn to forgive," Mrs. Balter is quoted as saying in an interview reported in *The New York Times.* "If you don't forgive your parents or your children or yourself, you don't get beyond the anger. Forgiving is a way of reaching out from a bad past and heading out to a more positive future."

The children of divorce who have been able to pardon their parents do not speak of forgiveness as a cure-all for an illness of long standing. Rather, it is a balm that soothes their wounds but does not make the scars (or even all the pain) go away. The experiences of those who *have* been able to forgive their parents round out our discussions.

FORGIVING THOSE WHO TRESPASS AGAINST US

For some children of divorce, like Jennie Fuller, their religious beliefs provide a major impetus for settling old grievances. The young woman, who went back to her parents in order to gain an understanding of their marriage and divorce, now adds a "why" to the "how" of what it was like.

"God has always been real important in my life," Jennie tells me in great earnestness. "I believe that we're infinite beings. We're here to learn and to grow. I also believe that every experience is an opportunity to know your true nature, which is an expression of God, basically. The best way to get to Him is through nonjudgment of others." Although no longer a practicing Catholic, Jennie says, "I still believe in what Christ taught: absolute forgiveness and unconditional love. I know for a fact that when I was able, at last, to make peace with my parents, forgiveness set me free."

REVERSING THE ROLES

Like Jennie Fuller, Elly Edwards speaks of the freeing effect of forgiveness. In her case, however, the catalyst for reconciliation with her mother was the fact that the older woman had grown ill and dependent. The intervention of Elly's husband, David, didn't hurt either.

When an all-powerful parent becomes ill and thereby vulnerable, it often happens that the son or daughter who has continued to feel aggrieved by that parent's behavior is able to set aside feelings of hostility in favor of charity. *And ultimately to feel better for the opportunity to place the relationship on a firmer and kinder footing.*

"Five years before she died and twenty years after there had last been contact between us, my mother telephoned me," Elly recalls. "She was failing—it turned out that she had Alzheimer's disease—and she wanted, I think, to have family around her. I must admit that I was not willing to be that family at first, but David was insistent."

"For years," says David, "I had been upset by the quality of Elly's anger toward her mother. I didn't think it was good for Elly, for our relationship, or for our children. I had a different upbringing than Elly. I was raised to believe that, no matter what, children owe some consideration to their parents. So when my mother-in-law reached out to us, I told Elly, 'She's your mother, for heaven's sake. You have to see her.' I wanted the anger to end."

And it did. "In her final years, my mother was very much a part of our lives," Elly tells me. "As she grew more childlike, there was a reversal of roles. In a way, she became my child and I became the mother. She was no longer powerful, and I was able to forgive her. I'm very glad that I got a chance to do that. It made me feel better that I wasn't so angry and wanting to get even anymore."

Naomi Brown, fifty-six, tells a similar story. Brown's parents divorced when she was three. "My mother always put her career and love life ahead of me, yet she wouldn't let me go live with my father out of spite," says the auburn-haired, youthful-looking woman, who never fails to surprise people when she proudly shows them photographs of her two grandchildren. "To say that my mother and I didn't get along is to put it mildly. At age fifteen, I left home and went clear across the country to get as far away from that woman as possible."

In time, Naomi married and had a son and daughter. Motherhood, however, did not bring Naomi closer to her own mother. The children saw their grandmother less than a dozen times in almost twice as many years. Then, three years ago, the older woman suffered a series of small strokes. Once widowed and twice divorced, she had no one at home to deliver the round-the-clock care that she now required. Naomi was her only child. Suddenly, Naomi found responsibility for her mother foisted upon her.

Feeling put upon, she nevertheless arranged to have her mother brought from California and admitted to a nursing home less than one mile from her own home in Rhode Island. Much to her surprise, Naomi has found herself dropping in on her mother almost every day. "Even more astonishing is the fact that taking care of my mother has made me feel closer to her and to appreciate certain attributes of hers that I did not see before," she says. "For one thing, she has a sense of humor. And she is always *so* happy to see me.

"There is a kind of paradox here," Naomi says. "By caring for my mother now I feel that what I'm doing is showing her, in a way, how I would like *her* to have loved me. I am able to feel compassion for her, and I can forgive her. Though I hate the illness, I am happy about what has happened because of it."

RESOLVING THE GRIEVANCES AND COMING TOGETHER

Like understanding, forgiveness is not achieved easily or immediately. The habit of feeling aggrieved or resentful—even to the point of hating one's parent—is hard to break. Author Lewis Smedes identifies four stages in the process of forgiving: hurting, hating, healing, and coming together. The hurting and hating stages are fairly self-explanatory. They deal with the pain attached to the various injustices perceived by the child of divorced parents as belonging to the divorce—from the basic fact of the end of the happy family that each child views as his or her birthright to the ways in which the divorce and its aftermath were managed.

Healing—the third stage—involves the process of letting go. "We gradually come to see the truth about those who hurt us— that they are weak, needy, fallible human beings," writes Smedes. This stage (which was treated more fully in the previous chapter) is the one in which understanding takes place. It is the precursor of forgiveness. The fourth stage, coming together, goes further in involving both the wronged and the wrongdoer in an honest attempt to reestablish their relationship on a positive basis.

John Lindstrom, forty-three, tells of being able to achieve such a "coming together" with his father. For many years, John had submerged his feelings about the divorce in a vain attempt to separate himself from it, to prove (to himself) that he didn't need anybody and could make it on his own. With one marriage down and the second in jeopardy, John had to face the fact that he was not making it, and he sought to find out why. Looking back at his past raised new resentments, provoked new pain. This time, however, John understood that the way to deal with the pain was to gain some understanding of its cause.

"Only last year," John recounts, "I finally came to the realization that my father's leaving me when I was a child had really hurt me, and I got up the courage to see him and speak to him about it. I flew to Denmark just so that we could have this meeting that I had decided was so very important. When we met, I asked my father: Why did you do it? Why didn't you stay in touch with me? Do you realize what problems I've had in my life because of the divorce and your continued absence?

"My father cried and told me he was sorry. *Sorry*. I needed to hear that apology from him. It made it possible for me to begin to forgive him, which was an enormous lifting of a burden from me." Lindstrom adds, "My mother has not yet said she's sorry, and that continues to hurt our relationship."

"Forgiveness is often the end point of a healing process that requires time, growth, and the experiencing of gratifying relationships that permit a person to transcend the hurt inflicted in the growing-up years by a parent who may have meant well but didn't act well," explains psychoanalyst Leopold Caligor. "When a person is no longer at an impasse created by a painful situation —in this case, the divorce of one's parents—he or she hopefully may be able to leave the pain of the hurt child behind."

WHO WILL CRY FOR MY FATHER?

Tobias Goodman exemplifies the kind of individual that the psychoanalyst has just been describing. Time and (even more so) the gratification found in loving relationships with his wife and children enabled Goodman, the man, to forgive the father who many years before failed to keep an appointment with a young boy who sat all day long waiting in a cafeteria for him.

"Between that day and the year I turned sixteen," Goodman recalls, "I saw my father only once. When I was sixteen, he was drafted. I wrote to him in the army, telling him how angry I was. I didn't receive an answer. When I was twenty-one, we reconnected and arranged a meeting. I knocked on the door of his house. He didn't answer. At twenty-two and in law school, I wrote him again, saying, 'You are not my father.' From that day on, he no longer called himself my father. He used his first name: Ben.

"I married and did not invite him to the wedding. He remarried and did not inform me." There is an echo. Goodman uses the same words as Paul Norman in describing the relationship between parent and son: "My father was no friend of mine."

But here the similarity ends, for Goodman goes on to say, "But, yes, I *was* able to forgive him."

He continues, "I spent my life accusing my father. Toward the end of my time in therapy, I knew that it was important to achieve some peace with the past. And so, about a year or two before he died at the age of seventy-nine, I invited my father, his wife, and their daughter to my home for dinner. My wife, Gloria, and two of our children were there.

"For reasons that I don't recall," Goodman continues, "when I walked into the living room my father was carrying on, saying negative things about my stepfather. At dinner, he started to complain that my mother couldn't wait to remarry—even though her remarriage took place five years after he had left us! So I looked at him and I said, 'What does that have to do with you and me? It was you and my mother who got a divorce. Why did you also divorce me?'

"He answered, 'Because I thought you'd be better off without me.' (I think he knew he was no good and the best thing he could do was to stay away from me.)

"Shortly thereafter"—Goodman goes on with his account—"my father's asthma became much worse and he and his family moved to Arizona. He used to send me greeting cards for the New Year. In his last year of life, he signed his card, 'If I can ever be forgiven . . . Ben.'

"At first I thought I'd write him. Then I decided that writing is a cop-out, so I phoned him and said, 'Listen, I forgave you a long time ago. I *know* that you never had a chance. It was not your fault.' I meant it. There *had* been extenuating circumstances. My father's mother died in childbirth. Life wasn't pleasant for him. He ran away from home at the age of twelve.

"I told him, 'I have spent my life trying to understand, and I forgive you.' I remember being surprised by the fact that it didn't take a great deal of effort to say that."

When Ben died, the son flew to Arizona to attend his father's funeral. "My primary reason for going," Tobias says, "is that I wanted to hear people tell me what a good person he was. One of my anxieties had always been, *Who will cry for my father?* I wanted to see people cry for him. And there were some among the mourners who did.

"I could not cry for the father who deserted me," says Goodman, at long last having outgrown the pain of his parents' divorce, "but the important thing is that I *had* been able to tell him, *It's okay. I forgive you.* And he had been alive to hear me say it. It is one thing I do not have to regret."

Afterword

Well, then, what about *the children?* This is the question I asked of myself when, some while ago, I undertook to look at the long-range effects of divorce on its children. As this work draws to an end, the conclusion seems unmistakable: Divorce is not good for children. Furthermore, its painful effects are long-lasting.

Admittedly, the matter is not as simple and clear-cut as that general response implies. I do not doubt that there are situations where the best solution to problems existing in a family is for the parents to separate and for the child to find a safe place, even if that means making one's home with only one parent or with loving grandparents. Very often the remarried household provides children with such a haven. Sometimes a foster family is needed, and can help. But the best plan for a child (if it is at all achievable) is to grow up safely in a family with both parents in residence.

It is also true, as others have remarked to me along the way, that many problems experienced by children can be laid to causes other than parental divorce. But consider the following. In the largest national study on the impact of divorce on school-children, headed by John Guidubaldi of Kent State University, children of divorced parents generally ranked lower than their classmates in academic achievement, communication and social interaction, independent learning, work effort, happiness, and health. They were also characterized as more inattentive, impulsive and intellectually dependent, less popular with their classmates, and more likely to be placed in special-education classes or referred to school psychologists.

It has been argued that these attributes might similarly be found in children who live in dysfunctional families where both parents are present. And it is also the case that, at this point, we can only ponder whether the children of divorce would be worse off if they *had* remained in such problem-ridden families. It seems far-fetched to me, however, to assert that the majority of the 50 percent of marriages that are projected to end in divorce fit this "dysfunctional" category. I think we must therefore accept the fact that many of the difficulties that children of divorce face are, in one way or another, attributable to the loss of the intact family. There is just no getting around it.

The question that others have asked me most often is this: "Is it better for the child if the parents remain in a bad marriage than if they divorce?" That question assumes that those are the only alternatives. There is another choice. I believe it is better for children to be raised by parents who are in a "good enough" marriage than to end up in a divorce situation. And I hold the opinion that such workable marriages are attainable more often than the divorce statistics would lead one to conclude.

Here's why. In my travels across the country to meet with and speak before groups of divorced and remarried families, I would frequently hear the troubled admission: "If I had realized how difficult it would be to raise a child alone, I would have thought twice about ending the marriage." A variation on that theme is provided by parents who have remarried and find their stepfamilies teetering on shaky ground. "If I had put as much effort into my first marriage as I'm investing in making this second marriage succeed," they say, "I could have made it work." I believe that husbands and wives have a responsibility to *try* to make it work, that they have an obligation to get counseling to try to resolve the issues between them and achieve a good-enough marriage. Such predivorce counseling is especially important, I believe, when there are children who will be affected by the breakup.

Another question that comes up frequently when divorce is raised as an issue is this: "What about staying together until the children are grown?" It does not seem to me that this midlife solution to a conflict-ridden or lifeless marriage is a good idea. For one thing, parents who postpone divorce but still hold it in their minds as their ultimate goal are not working toward creating a good-enough marriage. They place the family in a holding pattern in which the children do not feel safe. How could they be? They are always expecting a possible disaster.

It has become a fairly common scenario, however. Parents stay together "for the children" until the sons and daughters go off to college and are on their own. Then the parents feel it is safe to part. "Not true," says Katherine Stone Kaufmann, who wrote her doctoral thesis on the impact of this phenomenon. Parental divorce is shattering to young people who are taking their own steps toward independence, she found. It leaves the youngsters feeling abandoned, anxious, and angry.

At a recent cocktail party, I was presented with a provocative scenario for yet another possible solution to the difficulties of parental disharmony. "Well, then," asked my questioner after learning about this project, "would you agree that the European attitude toward marriage is preferable to divorce?"

"What is the European attitude toward marriage?"

"Oh, *you* know," said the gentleman in a manner which implied that *everyone* knew the answer to that. Everyone but I. He went on: "With the knowledge and consent of both partners, each is free to pursue private interests, even romantic liaisons, but the family remains intact."

Perhaps I *would* agree with that, I told him. At least the children know that both parents have reached an accord and, whatever their arrangements, their allegiance to the family and availability to the children are not in question.

IF DIVORCE IS INEVITABLE...

Suppose that attempts have been made by the parents to reconcile their differences and reinvigorate their relationship, and they fail. Then what? If the end of the marriage is inevitable, parents must try to manage the divorce so that they do as little harm as possible to the children.

There is some movement in that direction which offers hope. "More and more clients now come in for divorce counseling to find ways to uncouple without destroying their family," observes Constance Ahrons, associate director of the Marriage and Family Therapy Program at the University of Southern California and coauthor of the book *Divorced Families*.

Another heartening development has been the establishment, in a growing number of communities, of predivorce workshops for mothers and fathers. Since April 1, 1986, for example, a court order has been in effect in Sedgwick County, Kansas, requiring any couple who have filed a divorce petition and who have at least one child under the age of eighteen living at home to seek private counseling or attend a workshop that (as the brochure explains) "increases parents' awareness of their children's reactions to divorce and provides positive strategies for diffusing the impact of divorce on the family."

The counseling, which is prerequisite to being granted a divorce decree, includes coverage of the following topics: stress symptoms children experience during divorce; how divorcing couples can avoid using destructive games—keeping children out of parental conflicts; how to know when your child needs special help; and building a new relationship with a former spouse—how to continue effective parenting. Adrienne Churchill, assistant coordinator of the Children of Divorce program, says, "Many of the parents attending these sessions are themselves children of divorce. They tell us they wish this course had been available to their own parents twenty-five to thirty years earlier."

Nancy Parkhouse, who administers a similar program for the Superior Court of Cobb County, Georgia, explains that there were two primary reasons for getting it off the ground. The first: "I'd seen too many cases in juvenile court where the children were used as a battleground between their warring parents." And the second? "I'd also seen too many cases where the noncustodial parent has no contact with the child. This seminar really addresses the need children have to be in touch with both parents."

If divorce *is* the decision that couples ultimately arrive at, then *both mother and father must continue to be involved in the lives of their children.* As was demonstrated within the body of this book, co-parenting and cooperation around matters involving the children are essential if the divorce is to have a satisfactory outcome. But even where communication is hard to achieve, the noncustodial parent cannot—indeed, must not—fail to participate regularly in the lives of the children.

In the chapter on "Understanding," we focused on the fact that children cannot cut off from their parents. Even more important, in my view, is that no mother or father should be permitted to cut off from his or her children, regardless of whether such separation is voluntary or encouraged by the actions and attitudes of others.

For example, the caretaking parent must not refuse visitation to the noncustodial parent (as so often happens) in retaliation for not receiving child support in full and timely fashion. This punishes the child. Nor is any excuse acceptable for the noncustodial parent's distancing himself (or herself) from the child—either because of a belief that it will make things easier on himself or based on the supposition that taking himself out of their lives will make things better for the children. Even in those cases where children express hostility toward a noncustodial parent (as many are sure to do at one time or another), it is the grown-up's role to behave as an adult, and hang in there.

DIVORCE IS NOT A PRIVATE AFFAIR

Children of divorce are much better able to cope with the stresses and strains that divorce brings to their lives when they find kindred spirits in whom they can confide. There is a need, therefore, for more school-based support groups like the Banana Splits, a program that has been operating in the public schools in Ballston Spa, New York, an upstate community that lies between the larger cities of Albany and Syracuse. In 1978, Elizabeth McGonagle, a social worker connected with the schools, noticed two things that led her to develop the program. "In the high school," she says, "many previously good kids started to develop behavioral and academic issues that were predicated on earlier events. They were getting back at the loss of the family and the changes wrought by the parental divorce that may have happened eight years before. In high school, they had the power to act out in a way that was not available to them when they were younger and far more dependent on their parents.

"At the same time," she continues, "there were four little girls in grade school, between the ages of nine and eleven, who *asked* to meet so they could talk about problems they shared—problems having to do with being children of divorce. The support group became a safe place." Letting children know that they are not alone and that they can survive the divorce ordeal are key goals of the Banana Splits program. "If we can't change the families," says Elizabeth McGonagle, "we have to teach the kids how to cope."

Adult children of divorce *also* need to learn coping strategies.

Since they cannot change their history, they too would benefit from finding a safe place to meet and share the issues that unite them. At the close of my interview with Mallory Coburn, the young woman hands me her business card, extracting a promise from me to get in touch with her if ever I hear that there exists a support group for adult children of divorce. I have not yet been able to make that call.

Those who link their lives with adult children of divorce would similarly gain from getting together and comparing their experience with others in their situation. Having spoken with a number of spouses and ex-spouses of adult children of divorce, I have no doubt that they'd be helped by discovering that many of the characteristics they find stressful in their mates are not so much unique to their spouses as they are unique to the situation in which their partners grew up. It might have been useful, for example, for Amy Greene's former husband to understand *why* she had to surround herself with so many people, why it was hard for her to give her primary allegiance to any one person who might later disappoint her as her parents had done.

That the ghosts of the past continue to haunt the present lives of children of divorce is exemplified in the following story. It is told to me by a young man named Peter, who says that the ghosts almost destroyed his marriage (to a woman whose parents divorced when she was a girl) even before it could take place.

"Donna and I had an appointment to visit a florist to discuss the table arrangements for our wedding," he recounts. "I was to pick her up at half past two. But there was an accident on the freeway, and I didn't arrive at her home until well after four. I'd stopped at a number of phones along the way, but all of them were broken. I felt terrible knowing that Donna was likely to be worried by my lateness.

"The Donna who opened the door for me was more than concerned," Peter continues. "She was in a rage. The engagement

271

was off, she said, pulling the ring off her finger and handing it to me. She never could be married to a man who didn't keep his word! I was tired and tense from dealing with traffic . . . and resentful because Donna hadn't given me an opportunity to explain, so I said something like 'Fine' or 'That's okay with me.' And I stormed back to my car.

"Fortunately," he continues, "we both had too much good sense to leave it at that. Donna and I spoke later and decided to go for premarital counseling. It was very helpful to me in understanding the reasons behind Donna's wrath. When I failed to show up or phone her, I learned, Donna experienced a flashback to her childhood. The 'ghost' she saw was her father who had walked away from his family when Donna was seven years old. When I didn't arrive for our appointment or telephone to explain the delay, Donna had the feeling—however irrational—that she was being abandoned again. And she panicked."

Peter goes on: "Now that I understand why Donna feels as she does about promises unkept, I try to phone ahead of time about any change of plans. And when I tell her I will call I do call, because I know the importance she attaches to being able to count on me."

The last word belongs to the child of divorce. Donna, who is now Peter's wife, tells me, "And I had to learn *not* to see my father in Peter, who *is* a highly responsible person. That is one of the qualities that attracted me to Peter in the first place. . . . In counseling, I also was helped to recognize that I am my own person. I am no longer that little girl who was left behind." After a moment she adds, "While all of that makes sense to me intellectually, in my heart I am not so sure."

Bibliography

Adams, Teresa McAllister. *Living From the Inside Out.* New Orleans, Louisiana: Teresa M. Adams, 1987.

Belli, Melvin, and Mel Krantzler. *Divorcing.* New York: St. Martin's Press, 1988.

Berman, Claire. *Making It as a Stepparent.* New York: Harper & Row, 1986.

———. "Why Fathers Don't Pay," *McCall's,* May 1988.

———. "Your Parents Are People—Really," *Parents Magazine,* September 1986.

Bloomfield, Harold H., with Leonard Felder. *Making Peace With Your Parents.* New York: Ballantine Books, 1983.

Bumpass, Larry L. "Children and Marital Disruption: A Replication and Update," *Demography,* Vol. 21, No. 1, February 1984, pp. 71–81.

———. "Some Characteristics of Children's Second Families," *The American Journal of Sociology,* Vol. 90, No. 3, November 1984, pp. 608–623.

Cain, Barbara S. "Older Children and Divorce," *The New York Times Magazine,* February 18, 1990.

Cherlin, Andrew J. *Marriage, Divorce, Remarriage.* Cambridge, Massachusetts: Harvard University Press, 1981.

Clingempeel, W. Glenn, Mitch A. Shuwall, and Elizabeth Heiss. "Divorce and Remarriage: Perspectives on the Effects of Custody Arrangements on Children." In Wolchik, Sharlene A., and Paul Karoly, eds., *Children of Divorce: Empirical Perspectives on Adjustment.* New York: Gardner Press, 1988.

Duberman, Lucile. *The Reconstituted Family: A Study of Remarried Couples and Their Children.* Chicago, Illinois: Nelson-Hall, 1975.

Framo, James L. "Family of Origin as a Therapeutic Resource for Adults in Marital and Family Therapy: You Can and Should Go Home Again," *Family Process,* Vol. 15, June 1976, pp. 193–210.

Francke, Linda Bird. *Growing Up Divorced.* New York: Linden Press/ Simon and Schuster, 1983.

Friday, Nancy. *My Mother/My Self.* New York: Dell Publishing Co., 1981.

Furstenberg, Frank F., Jr. "Child Care After Divorce and Remarriage." In Hetherington, E. M., and J. D. Arasteh, eds., *Impact of Divorce, Single Parenting, and Stepparenting on Children.* Hillsdale, New Jersey: Lawrence Erlbaum Associates, 1988.

Gardner, Richard A. *The Parents Book About Divorce.* New York: Bantam Books, 1979.

———. *Understanding Children.* Cresskill, New Jersey: Creative Therapeutics, 1979.

Glick, Paul C. "Remarried Families, Stepfamilies, and Stepchildren: A Brief Demographic Profile," *Family Relations,* Vol. 38, January 1989, pp. 24–27.

———. "The Role of Divorce in the Changing Family Structure: Trends and Variations." In Wolchik, Sharlene A., and Paul Karoly, eds., *Children of Divorce: Empirical Perspectives on Adjustment.* New York: Gardner Press, 1988.

Greif, Geoffrey L. *Single Fathers.* Lexington, Massachusetts: Lexington Books, 1985.

———. *The Daddy Track and the Single Father.* Lexington, Massachusetts: Lexington Books, 1990.

Halpern, Howard M. *Cutting Loose: A Guide to Adult Relationships with Your Parents.* New York: Simon and Schuster, 1976.

Hetherington, E. Mavis. "Coping With Family Transitions: Winners, Losers and Survivors," *Child Development,* Vol. 60, 1989, pp. 1–14.

———. "Parents, Children and Siblings Six Years After Divorce." In Hinde, R., and J. Stevenson-Hinde, eds., *Relationships Within Families.* Cambridge, England: Cambridge University Press, 1988.

———, Jeffrey D. Arnett, and E. Ann Hollier. "Adjustment of Parents and Children to Remarriage." In Wolchik, Sharlene A., and Paul Karoly, eds., *Children of Divorce: Empirical Perspectives on Adjustment.* New York: Gardner Press, 1988.

———, and Josephine D. Arasteh, eds. *Impact of Divorce, Single Parenting, and Stepparenting on Children.* Hillsdale, New Jersey: Lawrence Erlbaum Associates, 1988.

———, Martha Cox, and Roger Cox. "Effects of Divorce on Parents and Children." In Lamb, M., ed., *Nontraditional Families: Parenting and*

Child Development. Hillsdale, New Jersey: Lawrence Erlbaum Associates, 1981.

———, and Margaret Stanley Hagan. "Divorced Fathers: Stress, Coping, and Adjustment." In Lamb, Michael E., ed., *The Father's Role: Applied Perspectives*. New York: John Wiley & Sons, 1986.

Ihinger-Tallman, Marilyn. "Research on Stepfamilies," *Annual Review of Sociology*, Vol. 14, 1988, pp. 25–48.

Johnson, Colleen Leahy. *Ex Familia: Grandparents, Parents, and Children Adjust to Divorce*. New Brunswick, New Jersey: Rutgers University Press, 1988.

Johnson, Nora. "Divorce Doesn't Ruin Children's Lives, But . . . ," *McCall's*, May 1981.

Kalter, Neil. *Growing Up With Divorce*. New York: The Free Press, 1990.

Kliman, Ann S. *Crisis: Psychological First Aid for Recovery and Growth*. Northvale, New Jersey: Jason Aronson, 1978.

Kulka, Richard A., and Helen Weingarten. "The Long-term Effects of Parental Divorce in Childhood on Adult Adjustment," *Journal of Social Issues*, Vol. 35, No. 4, 1979.

Kurdek, Lawrence A. "Cognitive Mediators of Children's Adjustment to Divorce." In Wolchik, Sharlene A., and Paul Karoly, eds., *Children of Divorce: Empirical Perspectives on Adjustment*. New York: Gardner Press, 1988.

———. "A 1-Year Follow-Up Study of Children's Divorce Adjustment, Custodial Mothers' Divorce Adjustment, and Postdivorce Parenting," *Journal of Applied Developmental Psychology*, Vol. 9, 1988, pp. 315–328.

Linder, Marjorie S., and Edward R. Anderson. "Resiliency and Vulnerability in Psychosocial Functioning During the Adaptation to Remarriage." Presented at the Symposium on Coping With Remarriage: The First Two Years, Conference on Human Development. Charleston, South Carolina, March 1988.

London, Kathryn A., Joan R. Kahn, and William F. Pratt. "Are Daughters of Divorced Parents More Likely to Divorce as Adults?" Paper presented at annual meeting of the Population Association of America. New Orleans, April 1988.

Meyers, Susan, and Joan Lakin. *Who Will Take the Children?* Indianapolis/New York: Bobbs-Merrill, 1983.

Papernow, Patricia. "Children in Stepfamilies: What Do We Know?", *Stepfamily Bulletin*, Vol. 9, No. 1. Baltimore, Maryland: Stepfamily Association of America, Spring 1989.

Preister, Steven, and James J. Young, eds. *Catholic Remarriage: Pastoral Issues and Preparation Models.* New York/Mahwah, New Jersey: Paulist Press, 1986.

Rhodes, Sonya, and Marlin S. Potash. *Cold Feet: Why Men Don't Commit.* New York: E. P. Dutton, 1988.

Sager, Clifford J., et al. *Treating the Remarried Family.* New York: Brunner/Mazel, 1983.

Scarf, Maggie. *Intimate Partners.* New York: Random House, 1987.

Seltzer, Judith A. "Relationships Between Fathers and Children Who Live Apart." Presented at the annual meetings of the American Association for the Advancement of Science. San Francisco, California, February 1989.

Smedes, Lewis B. *Forgive and Forget: Healing the Hurts We Don't Deserve.* San Francisco: Harper & Row, 1984.

Vanderbilt, Amy. *Amy Vanderbilt's New Complete Book of Etiquette.* Garden City, New York: Doubleday & Co., 1963.

Visher, Emily B., and John S. Visher. *Stepfamilies: Myths and Realities.* New Jersey: Citadel Press, 1980.

Wallerstein, Judith S. "The Overburdened Child: Some Long-term Consequences of Divorce," *Social Work,* March–April 1985, pp. 116–122.

———, and Sandra Blakeslee. *Second Chances: Men, Women & Children a Decade After Divorce, Who Wins, Who Loses—And Why.* New York: Ticknor & Fields, 1989.

———, and Joan Berlin Kelly. *Surviving the Breakup: How Children and Parents Cope With Divorce.* New York: Basic Books, 1980.

———, Shauna B. Corbin, and Julia M. Lewis. "Children of Divorce: A 10-Year Study." In Hetherington, E. M., and J. D. Arasteh, eds., *Impact of Divorce, Single Parenting, and Stepparenting on Children.* Hillsdale, New Jersey: Lawrence Erlbaum Associates, 1988, pp. 197–214.

Weitzman, Lenore J. *The Divorce Revolution.* New York: The Free Press, 1985.

Whiteside, Mary F. "Remarried Systems." In Combrinck-Graham, Lee, ed., *Handbook of Children in Family Therapy: The Context of Child Mental Health.* New York: Guilford, 1988.

Wolchik, Sharlene A., and Paul Karoly, eds. *Children of Divorce: Empirical Perspectives on Adjustment.* New York: Gardner Press, 1988.

Index

Claire Berman, an author and freelance journalist, has explored issues relating to psychology and the family for a variety of national publications. A popular speaker and workshop leader, Ms. Berman also served for many years as Director of Public Education at the Child Welfare League of America. She is a past president of the Stepfamily Association of America.